## Praise for *The Secret Life of the American Musical*

"Both revelatory and entertaining. Viertel combines a scholarly approach with a light touch that enables us to see anew familiar songs and musical theater moments we'd long taken for granted."
—**Robin Pogrebin,** *The New York Times Book Review*

"Viertel's knowledgeable, engaging blueprint of [the Broadway musical] framework is instructive fun for cognoscenti and general readers alike."
—**Wendy Smith,** *The Washington Post*

"A lively manual for writers and public alike on how the songs suit the story and how the story needs the songs."
—**Ethan Mordden,** *The Wall Street Journal*

"The best general-audience analysis of musical theater I have read in many years."
—**Lawrence Toppman,** *The Charlotte Observer*

"Jack Viertel changed my theatergoing life, and he might change yours . . . *The Secret Life of the American Musical: How Broadway Shows Are Built* is a delightful, accessible guide to why your favorite productions work. It's a little bit history, a little bit memoir, a little bit criticism and, for any theater fan, a whole lot of fun."
—**Michael Merschel,** *The Dallas Morning News*

"[An] engaging, insightful anatomy of a singularly American art form . . . There is much to savor."
—*More*

"Viertel articulates his rules of commercial success so lucidly that even seasoned hands will come away with a clearer understanding of why some shows work while others flop."
—**Terry Teachout,** *Commentary*

"Thoroughly interesting . . . There's just something very pleasant about reading someone intelligently and affectionately look at what makes a show tick, beat by choreographed beat."
—**Ryan Vlastelica,** *The A.V. Club*

"Viertel has written what will become a classic textbook on the architecture and construction of the American musical . . . What Harold Bloom did for Shakespearean exegesis and Peter Drucker for management, Viertel has done for theater: written a definitive work by raising the curtain and laying bare the work of playwrights, composers, librettists, choreographers, and directors."
**—Barry X. Miller, *Library Journal* (starred review)**

"Viertel is well steeped in Broadway culture, lore and productions . . . An enlightening trip for lovers of musicals." **—*Kirkus Reviews***

"A valuable addition to the theater lover's bookshelf."
**—*Publishers Weekly***

"Jack Viertel writes about the master craftsmen of the American musical, past and present, and reveals his own mastery on every page—his knowledge of the Broadway musical and of the intricate formula in the making of a show (or the breaking of it), and his passion for Broadway and the citizens who make the street come alive. I've been schooled."
**—Patti LuPone**

"In *The Secret Life of the American Musical*, Jack Viertel, a Broadway producer and dramaturgical swami, has broken down Broadway's greatest musicals into their constituent storytelling parts (a sort of anatomy of joy) and delivered a showstopper: one of the best-written, most illuminating, and most infectiously entertaining books on the genre I know. Delight and insight vie with each other on every scintillating page. 'It's boffo!' as they say on the Rialto."
**—John Lahr, author of *Tennessee Williams: Mad Pilgrimage of the Flesh***

"This is unfair: no one who knows so much should be able to write so well. And no one in the world knows as much about the shape and substance of the classic American musical as Jack Viertel. His book is a treasure."
**—Daniel Okrent, author of *Last Call: The Rise and Fall of Prohibition***

"Jack Viertel's remarkable book has the uncanny effect of making us see something we thought we knew everything about in a way that makes us feel as though we are seeing it all for the first time. He invents a way of thinking about musicals that is utterly fresh and insightful, and while doing so he makes us remember exactly why we love them so much—by somehow re-creating the overwhelming, heart-stopping feeling we had when we were likely ten years old and fell in love with them the second our first overture began. By simultaneously (and brilliantly) embracing and deconstructing a beloved American art form, he brings us back to our most innocent selves, and all we can do is be grateful to him for reminding us of who we used to be."          **—Scott Rudin**

## JACK VIERTEL

### *The Secret Life of the American Musical*

Jack Viertel is the senior vice president of Jujamcyn Theaters, which owns and operates five Broadway theaters. He has been involved in dozens of productions presented by Jujamcyn since 1987, including multiple Pulitzer Prize and Tony Award winners, from *City of Angels* to *Angels in America*. He has also helped shepherd six of August Wilson's plays to Broadway. He is the artistic director of New York City Center's acclaimed Encores! series, which presents three musical productions every season. In that capacity he has overseen fifty shows, for some of which he adapted the scripts. He conceived the long-running *Smokey Joe's Cafe* and the critically acclaimed *After Midnight* and has been a creative consultant on many shows, including *Hairspray*, *A Christmas Story*, and *Dear Evan Hansen*. He was the Mark Taper Forum's dramaturg and the drama critic and arts editor of the *Los Angeles Herald Examiner*, and he has spent a decade teaching musical theater at the Tisch School of the Arts at New York University.

# THE SECRET LIFE OF THE AMERICAN MUSICAL

THE
# SECRET LIFE
OF THE

## How Broadway Shows
## Are Built

# Jack Viertel

**SARAH CRICHTON BOOKS**  Farrar, Straus and Giroux  New York

Sarah Crichton Books
Farrar, Straus and Giroux
18 West 18th Street, New York 10011

Printed in the United States of America
Published in 2016 by Sarah Crichton Books / Farrar, Straus and Giroux
First paperback edition, 2017

The Library of Congress has cataloged the hardcover edition as follows:
Viertel, Jack.
The secret life of the American musical : how Broadway shows are built / Jack Viertel. —
First edition.
    pages   cm
Includes index.
ISBN 978-0-374-25692-0 (hardcover) — ISBN 978-0-374-71125-2 (e-book)
    1. Musicals—United States—History and criticism.   2. Musicals—United States—
Analysis, appreciation.   I. Title.

ML1711 .V37 2016
792.60973—dc23

2015023713

Paperback ISBN: 978-0-374-53689-3

Designed by Abby Kagan

www.fsgbooks.com
www.twitter.com/fsgbooks • www.facebook.com/fsgbooks

5   7   9   10   8   6

*For Daisy, Janet, and Joe,*
*who took me with them to the theater*

*And for Linda, Josh, and Anna Daisy,*
*whom I now get to take with me*

# Contents

# Tuning Up

*or, How I Came to Write This Book*

I've never been much of an international sightseer. I've never been eager to tramp around ancient ruins or bask in the architecture of the great cathedrals of Europe. I understand these activities have enormous spiritual and aesthetic value for a lot of people, who are fascinated and moved, sometimes to tears, to be in the presence of the ancients. I'm married to a woman who is rarely so content as when she has the chance to wander the corridors of history. But it's never meant that much to me. When I find myself in one of these places, more often than not I begin to think about Broadway musicals. I consider it a defect in my level of curiosity.

It's shameful, really. Musicals have provided me with the kind of nourishment that crumbling walled cities have not. I've loved them since my parents and my grandmother Daisy took me to see Mary Martin as Peter Pan just before my sixth birthday. In fact, along with nonmusical plays, they've been the source of most of my education and consumed an enormous amount of my thinking and my emotional development, which sometimes makes me feel foolish.

But I have to thank one particular set of ruins for the fact that this book got written. I was clambering around the Greek island of Delos,

Apollo's home, on a hot August afternoon when it occurred to me that I ought to teach musical theater to college students.

Why Delos? Why teach? Why that moment? Who ever knows for sure why a thought pops into your head? I could claim that it was because Apollo was the god of music and poetry, and that got me thinking, but I doubt anything that erudite was lamping around my brain. I have a feeling that the ruined columns lying in piles all around me reminded me of the poster for the Nathan Lane production of *A Funny Thing Happened on the Way to the Forum*, which probably caused me some internal embarrassment. While I was trying to turn from the mortifying to the high-minded, the idea of imparting knowledge to young people somehow slipped into my brain.

The fact is, almost everything reminds me of the theater, and certainly ancient ruins do. There are fabulous semipreserved amphitheaters all around Greece and Italy, and even ruins that never were performance spaces seem to me to be inherently dramatic—they make me think of declamatory speech and kissing in the shadows, murder in the dark, and coups d'etat. But also, to be honest, they call up Nathan Lane in a toga and distant memories of Zero Mostel, Jack Gilford, David Burns, and John Carradine singing "Everybody Ought to Have a Maid." That's always been a kind of heaven to me, and ruins are about the world of the gods.

There was another connection as well—a family connection. Shakespeare wrote about Greeks and Romans, and what little I know about them I learned from *Julius Caesar, Antony and Cleopatra*, and the others. My wife's uncle, Harry Levin, for many years head of the Comparative Literature Department at Harvard, used to spend an entire semester picking apart only four of Shakespeare's plays, holding every line up to the light and questioning why it was written the way it was written, what led to it, and what it led to. He was like a Swiss watchmaker taking apart and reassembling a perfect timepiece. It was an intense fun-house ride for Shakespeare nuts, and it was glorious. But no one had ever done that for *Gypsy* or *Guys and Dolls* or *The Book of Mormon*. Why not? Because Broadway musicals can't compare to Shakespeare? Says who? If Shakespeare is England's national theater, aren't Broadway musicals ours?*

* I acknowledge poetic realism, and the greatness of O'Neill, Wilder, Williams, Miller, Albee, Tony Kushner, and August Wilson, of course—that's our *other* national theater.

Being a man of limited imagination but a certain dull cunning, I soon thought of stealing Uncle Harry's concept lock, stock, and barrel; the only thing that would be different was the repertoire. And why should I be the one to teach it? My reasoning was simple and, I hope, not overly self-inflated. I'd been working as a dramaturgically inclined Broadway producer for two decades, developing new works and reviving old ones, and I'd been the Artistic Director of the Encores! series of concert musicals at New York City Center since 2000. I didn't, and don't, claim to have any God-given wisdom about musicals, but I'd been in the trenches for a long time, and worked on dozens.

I structured the course quickly in my head while pretending to admire all that was left of Apollo's hometown. (Was the lyric of "My Hometown" from *What Makes Sammy Run?* coursing through my brain at the time? Quite possibly.) It was Harry Levin's course, but the texts would be *Gypsy*, *Guys and Dolls*, *My Fair Lady*, and *South Pacific*. Three two-hour sessions for each show. The students would have to read them aloud to understand them. Why those four shows? A showbiz drama, a classic New York comedy, an intellectual romance, and a wartime epic. And each of them close to perfect. Why not?

New York University's Tisch School was happy to hear of my interest and assigned me a slot. The course was clean and simple, and it just kind of worked. We closely examined the four classic musicals, page by page, trying to piece out why every line of dialogue was there, what every lyric accomplished, and how music supported whatever the fundamental idea of the show was. The course assumed that every great musical has a single idea, a single stake, and that much of the writer's job is to discover what it is and then cut away the thicket of things that don't belong so that the idea can be explored and celebrated in a way that audiences take home with them. The course asked the question: How do all the diverse tools of the trade—music, rhyme, comedy, character, dance, drama, storytelling, even scenery and costumes, lights, and orchestrations—get pointed in the same direction toward the same goal? In a sense, it was an architecture class, exploring how a structure is designed and built that is strong enough to support a single vision and fulfill or confound an audience's expectations, as required in the circumstance.

The course proved popular, and it wasn't long before I added a second one, which examined what Broadway folks call a "song plot." Not to be confused with the plot of the show, a song plot is like a graph on which the songs in a musical story can be laid out. It's a surprisingly consistent diagram: an opening number, an "I Want" song for the main character or characters, a "conditional" love song ("If I Loved You," not "I Love You"), a production number, and so forth right through the finale.

The not-so-secret agenda of these courses was to point out that this kind of craftsmanship, gradually abandoned beginning in the late 1970s, has led to a much more chaotic life for the Broadway musical. It may be incredibly hip to leave basic storytelling techniques behind and light out for the Territory, as Huck Finn did on his raft with neither a map nor a rule book. But an awful lot of shows get hopelessly lost that way and disappear into the woods, never to be heard from again. And most of the works that have experienced real lasting success in the years since the Golden Age of Broadway are, when the surface is scratched, deeply traditional and craftsmanlike. I'm talking about *Sweeney Todd*, *The Producers*, *Hairspray*, *Wicked*, and *The Book of Mormon*, which, contemporary though it may be, is really just an orthodox mash-up of *The King and I*, *Guys and Dolls*, and *The Music Man* with a twenty-first-century voice and subject.

The students wanted to talk about those shows as much as the classics; this was *their* Broadway. And so *Mormon* was added to the syllabus. We examined I Want songs from *Wicked* and how a deadly serious six-character musical like *Next to Normal* copes with the need for some noisy comic relief. Everything was fair game.

I'm grateful for the opportunity to teach at Tisch and to interact with a student body that is as curious, energized, and passionate as any group of young people I've ever encountered. It's great fun for me, and for a few years I assumed that was that.

But after a while, I started to get invited to give talks outside the classroom, and that's when people started asking me when I was going to write a book about all of this. In some ways, looking at Broadway shows mapped out in the way I had mapped them seemed like a secret language that was fun to let other people in on. Frankly, I had my doubts about this book proposition, because the classes were really for young would-be professionals, not just musical theater fans. But the outside talks *were* for fans, and they seemed to be the ones urging me on. Part of the process, then, has been to take what began as an academic course and broaden it into a wider realm—the story of how musicals got made in their heyday, the much vaunted but never quite defined Golden Age, and how they get made today. Some of the songs and shows are ancient history to my students, and perhaps to the younger generation of readers as well. But I don't apologize for that. Ancient history can have its inspiring effects, as I learned, by accident, on Delos.

On the other hand, recent history can be educational in a different way, especially if you've been a part of it. When the producer Margo Lion asked me to take a look at the John Waters movie *Hairspray*, for instance, I told her I thought it was a perfectly silly idea for a musical—it felt almost like a home movie. But Lion saw in it the bones of a classic musical theater story waiting to be exposed, and she was completely correct. The show succeeds with general audiences while the original film remains only a cult classic, because the show has real architecture in addition to a real subject: it opens the door and lets *everyone* out of the closet. But it would never have worked without the first-rate craftsmanship of storytelling that took five writers and a world-class director to achieve.

I was the dramaturg, a German word that, in this case, translates as "noodge." One of the most heated arguments I lost (thank God) was with *Hairspray*'s director, Jack O'Brien, about the penultimate moment in the show. The scene is set in the local Eventorium, where the entire company is gathered for the Miss Teenage Hairspray contest of some year in the early '60s. Only two people are missing: the heroine, Tracy Turnblad, and her mother, the "ample American" Edna, played in drag by gravel-voiced Harvey Fierstein in a fat suit. But there is a surprise coming. Onstage is a gigantic can of hairspray, and someone is hiding in it. Who? It had to be Tracy, I argued: she's the heroine of the piece, she's engineered the entire event so that it will work out to a happy ending, she's the one who is going to arrive to save the day. She has to be in the can so she can arrive in the most spectacular way.

"Nonsense," said O'Brien. "Edna is in the can."

"Why?" I asked petulantly. "It makes no sense."

"Because," he said, "when the audience sees Harvey Fierstein explode out of that can in a huge red dress, they're all going to come, from sheer joy. And they won't care about anything else."

He was right, of course. Show business and dramaturgy—the happiest war ever waged. I still maintain that the end of *Hairspray* makes very little logical sense, and I'm still right. But what does it get me? Musical theater is that exact thing: the intersection of craftsmanship and the irrationally thrilling. When you know who the characters are and what they want, when you root hard for them all night, when you've been properly cared for and fussed over by artists who know how, you are set up to have the greatest creators reach right past your intellectual faculties at the last minute and press down on that joy buzzer that lurks in the back part of your brain. When they do, your spirit levitates, just like Peter Pan heading out the window to Neverland. I've seen it happen, and that's why I wrote this book.

# A Note About the Shows Discussed—
# and a Few Other Matters

The title of this book was originally "The Secret Life of the Broadway Musical," but I changed it when I realized I was going to write only about American shows. During various periods of Broadway's history, the street has been dominated by musicals from England, but I've chosen not to deal with any of them. This may reflect a personal prejudice, but I hope it has more to do with the British musical itself, which, when not imitating the American musical, has always been created around its own set of traditions and a history of entertainment—Gilbert and Sullivan, the music hall, the Christmas Pantomime, the Dickensian yarn—that are distant cousins of our own. British musicals, though they've sometimes been the economic engine of Broadway, don't actually help tell the story I wanted to tell, so I've left them out. No disrespect intended.

I've not spent a lot of time in these pages talking about dance in any formal way—I don't feel qualified to do so. Dance has been an integral part of Broadway musicals since the beginning. *The Black Crook*, arguably the very first musical, allegedly came into being in 1866 because a Parisian dance troupe was stranded when the New York theater it was supposed to appear in burned down, and the company was rescued by being shoehorned into a musical melodrama. But even so, I don't have a great deal to say on the subject of how dance has evolved in the modern musical. Dream ballets existed from the 1930s on, became standard fare in the '40s with Agnes de Mille and Jerome Robbins doing most of the innovating, and then lived on to be ridiculed by some of today's musicals. Big production numbers have usually featured dance breaks, and dance has always been a useful, sometimes blissful tool for romantic expression. As the director-choreographer Warren Carlyle said about musicals, "When you can no longer speak, you sing; when you can no longer sing, you dance." I don't think I have anything further to add.

I've also returned often in these pages to a handful of mostly classic shows, at the expense of discussing many others. *Gypsy*, *My Fair Lady*, *Fiddler on the Roof*, *Guys and Dolls*, *Little Shop of Horrors*, *Hairspray*, *The Book of Mormon*, and a few others predominate, and in some cases, their entire plots seem to emerge. The reasons for this are numerous, but the best one is simply that these are the shows that taught me the most, that I spend the most time teaching. Perhaps they're not perfect, and none of them is my absolute favorite (that would be *Follies*), but for the purposes of this book, they were the most useful to me. And that seemed reason enough. As a consequence, a number of successful and well-constructed shows—*Kiss Me, Kate* and *La Cage aux Folles* come to mind—are only occasionally mentioned. Rodgers and Hammerstein get a lot of space, but not one show in particular. There's a lot about Stephen Sondheim and not enough, perhaps, about his wonderful contemporaries, Jerry Bock and Sheldon Harnick, John Kander and Fred Ebb, Charles Strouse and Lee Adams, Jerry Herman, Bob Merrill, and the like. And there are other important musicals—*Funny Girl*, *Brigadoon*, and *Annie Get Your Gun*, to name just three—that have escaped notice altogether. A number of important creators whose work I admire—William Finn and John Weidman, to name but two—are similarly not to be found. This book isn't intended to be a survey or a complete history of Broadway musicals, and it is not even slightly democratic; it has no intention of paying tribute to all worthy competitors. Nor is it any kind of instruction manual. It's a personal way of talking about the art and craft of making musicals, very much from one man's point of view. I've tried to use what has seemed most telling to me, and

I've tended to wander off in all directions from time to time, just as I'm making the case that a well-structured musical should never do so. There are stories that I felt were worth telling, bits and pieces of trivia that I've accumulated, and somewhat off-topic observations that seemed worth a paragraph here and there. I considered cutting each one, but most have remained, for better or worse. The book is, in some senses, a ramble.

One other point is worth making. Nothing in these pages is meant to imply that the artists creating musicals knowingly follow a well-worn formula. Quite the opposite is true. While musicals tend to follow patterns, the writers and directors who create them are generally rediscovering how to make each show completely fresh and original every time out. It's only in hindsight that the patterns emerge. Not only that: there are big hit shows in which few of the patterns I describe actually appear. Take a look at *Chicago* or *1776* if you doubt it. Not every show has an I Want song. Or a conditional love song, or a main event, or even an 11 o'clock number. But most do, or a reasonable facsimile thereof, and that's what makes writing about them fun.

Still, any reader of this book who wants to point triumphantly to some show that doesn't seem to be built on the classic chassis I'm writing about will get no argument from me, just a tip of the hat. If I still wore a hat.

# THE SECRET LIFE OF THE AMERICAN MUSICAL

# 1. Overture

Is the American musical an animal or a machine? That's a peculiar question, but think about it for a moment. A machine is made from standardized, manufactured parts, assembled according to a particular logic; when switched on, it does a task, or perhaps a series of them. An animal is, in some ways, not so very different. We human animals are also standardized to a great extent. Two eyes, two lips, a nose, as Betty Comden and Adolph Green wrote, and we perform a certain set of actions, some of them repetitively. These include the mundane (brushing our teeth) and the profound (falling in love). We're like machines, but we're not machines; we're individuals with our own hearts, our own brains, our own ways of looking at the world informed by experience, temperament, taste, and desire. We're better than machines.

A lot of Broadway musicals are well-made machines, but the best ones rise above—they stand up and dance on their own, with their own unique beating hearts. This book is mostly about those very best ones, and about deconstructing the machined parts that allowed them to work.

Why? Because that other element, the lightning bolt that gives life, can be described but never entirely understood. That intangible thing that separates the special Broadway shows from the routinely competent ones—*My Fair Lady* from *Camelot*, or *Hairspray* from *Legally Blonde*—is partly a matter of craft, but who really knows what makes that final difference happen? Every now and then the divine spirit comes down for a visit, that's all. The idea behind this book, though, is that such blessed events don't have much of a chance of happening unless the machine is up and running. Without the lungs and liver, there's no way for the heart to soar or the brain to make lightning and thunder. So this book is an attempt to describe the mechanics of the great musicals—how they were planned and built, and why, so often, they get under our skin and remain a part of us for a lifetime.

The architecture of musicals dates back to Broadway's Golden Age, the dates of which can be agreed upon by no one. My opinion is that it begins on the opening night of *Oklahoma!* (March 31, 1943) and ends on the opening night of *A Chorus Line* (July 25, 1975). During those decades, musicals found a form that was so rock solid and so satisfying to audiences that the components of that form served as the road map for creators who revised and refined but never abandoned it. There were great musicals produced before and after, of course, and I do have some things to say about shows in the '20s and '30s, and about shows that Stephen Sondheim and his collaborators wrote in the post–*Chorus Line* era. And there's a lot to be written about shows like *Wicked*, *The Producers*, *The Book of Mormon*, and, of course, those produced by the Disney empire. But my Golden Age ends where it ends. By the mid-'70s, the world had changed both on- and offstage in a way that caused a flurry of experimentation, some notable disasters, and a period of wandering in the desert.

The '70s and '80s saw a scattering of attempts to exploit the fashionable on Broadway—hence musicals like *Got Tu Go Disco*, a curiosity that tried to cash in on the disco craze without a discernible plot or characters, and *Rockabye Hamlet*, a rock version of Shakespeare's classic that proved something really was rotten in the state of Denmark. There was a lot of confusion about appropriate subject matter too—was it really a strong idea to write a musical about the Shroud of Turin? *Into the Light* gave it a try, leading to one of the more memorable lead sentences ever published in a *Variety* review: "Those who never miss a musical about the Shroud of Turin will rush to *Into the Light*."

There seemed to be a lot of amateurism around, and to some extent that's still the case today. As the ideas for new musicals and the justifications for producing them got thinner and more erratic, the craftsmanship often evaporated altogether. Part of the reason for this, to be fair, was that there were suddenly some extremely compelling shows rooted in the most unlikely source material, seemingly semi-improvised: *Hair* may have started the trend, which has continued and encouraged both inspired outsiders and rank incompetents alike. Opinions may differ on shows like *Bloody Bloody Andrew Jackson* and *Passing Strange*, but their failure to find large, appreciative audiences has a lot to do with their formlessness. Audiences really do like to be told a definite story in a compelling way. It has to have captivating characters, an exciting challenge for them to solve, and a solution that's worthy of the time we've taken to watch it.

Nowhere was this clearer to me than in the long journey taken by August Wilson's play *The Piano Lesson*, which is, admittedly, not a musical (though it has a couple of amazingly powerful musical sequences in it). Set in Pittsburgh, the play revolves around an almost three-hour argument between a brother and a sister over who gets to control the piano in the parlor, a mystical heirloom onto which the family's history was carved by an ancestor who was a slave. The sister wants to save it as a testament to the family's suffering. The brother wants to sell it to a collector and buy a piece of land in Mississippi so he can start a farm and begin to help the current generation prosper. What does one do with one's legacy?

The play is also a ghost story; the spirit of the white man whose family once owned both the piano and the land in question has arrived from Mississippi and is terrifying the residents of the house, though what exactly he wants isn't stated. It is a wildly entertaining, imaginative evening. In the original script, the ghost was exorcised in the end, but the question of who winds up with the piano was left unresolved. At its world premiere at Yale Repertory Theatre, audiences appreciated the play, but they left the theater a little baffled. Through three or four out-of-town productions, I kept gently asking the playwright a simple question: After three hours of argument, who gets the piano? He purported not to be interested in the question (I actually think he just didn't know the answer). He'd given strong arguments to both combatants. With a Broadway opening staring him in the face, he finally went into retreat and came back with two new scenes, one in the middle of the second act in which the sister explains why, although she won't let go of the piano, she'll never play it again. And one at the end where, to exorcise the ghost, she changes her mind and plays it, driving away the sprits of the past. She earns the piano, and her brother gives in.

The first night the play was performed with those two new scenes, the audience whooped and cheered at the end and stood up and whistled. They had their answer. Thematically, August Wilson may have been right that it didn't matter who got the piano. The argument was more important to him than the outcome. He could have found a justification for the brother winning, and the audience would probably have been just as happy. But in a show about who will end up with a piano, the spectators want to know and won't be satisfied until they do. That's what makes a story a story, as anyone who has ever told a bedtime story to a child—or watched a baseball game—will immediately understand. Something is at stake. Someone wins the stake and someone else loses. There are mechanical niceties, and they have to be observed, "The Lady or the Tiger?" notwithstanding.

But the niceties are different for musicals than for straight plays. Unlike in any other kind of story, the characters in musicals keep interrupting themselves to burst into song. They dance, they leap, they speak one line and sing the next; they convey what's in their brains in dialogue; they turn what's in their hearts into melody and movement. And when the men and women who are creating this odd hybrid form of storytelling do it brilliantly, audiences respond in a way that is as unique as the form itself, because the storytellers are operating on different parts of the human brain simultaneously. In that sense, musicals have more latitude than plays. Audiences understand the story—the characters and what's at risk for them as they try to achieve their dreams. But sitting there in the dark, they also experience a certain kind of visceral charge that goes well beyond the logic of storytelling. Musicals tap into an emotion center that creates profound feelings of ecstasy, sadness, heroism, nobility, or simple giddiness. That's why the hair stands up on the back of your neck, that most illogical but universally recognizable sensation.

It happens right after Harold Hill says, "You'll feel something akin to the electric thrill I once enjoyed when Gilmore, Liberatti, Pat Conway, The Great Creatore, W. C. Handy and John Philip Sousa all came to town on the very same historic day," and then sings the line *"Seventy-six trombones led the big parade."* The audience falls apart right then. You can argue that familiarity is the cause, and that we're all waiting for him to sing it, and you can certainly point out that we're being manipulated and spoon-fed, but who cares? I bet it happened on opening night, before anyone had ever heard the song, and long after they could have identified "The Great Creatore."* And they've been falling apart ever since.

Certain people (I'm one of them) shed tears at the end of the first act of *Sunday in the Park with George* when the ensemble sings:

> *People strolling through the trees*
> *Of a small suburban park*
> *On an Island in the river*
> *On an ordinary Sunday*

Why? No one has died, nothing momentous has happened. But art has somehow given stature to an everyday moment—visually, musically, and narratively. The whole first act has been preparing an unsuspecting

---

* Patrick Gilmore, Alessandro Liberatti, Patrick Conway, Giuseppe Creatore, W. C. Handy, and John Philip Sousa were all popular bandleaders at the turn of the century. Liberatti and Creatore were Italian immigrants, Gilmore and Conway were Irish, Handy was African American (and unlikely to have been welcomed at such an event, had it actually taken place), and Sousa was not only an early employer of *The Music Man*'s author but was also the inventor of a marching band tuba, which is worn around the waist and, unsurprisingly, is called the sousaphone. You can see them during any worthy halftime show even today.

audience for this moment, and it's overpowering. The emotions are sudden, unexpected, apparently completely surprising and spontaneous. We weep because we've been shown something we didn't expect to see—a vision of everyday life elevated. (Sondheim has confessed that he, like many others, cries on the word "forever," which comes earlier in the song. Perhaps I'm a tougher audience.)

The strangest of these experiences for me—because it has nothing to do with anything in everyday life—occurred in the Encores! production of *Pipe Dream* by Rodgers and Hammerstein, a quite troubled show with a good score that we felt was worth exhuming for another look. But it wasn't the story that caused the magic (the story is almost impossible to explain, and, frankly, not worth the effort). Late in the first act, Leslie Uggams, who was playing the madam of the local bordello, had a number called "Sweet Thursday." It's a bouncy charm song in the manner of "Honey Bun" from the much superior *South Pacific*. But almost no one in the audience had ever heard it before, which gave it some extra charm. Halfway through it, Uggams was joined by two young sailors, each of whom took her by the arm and led her downstage toward the audience as she sang. They were shorter than she, and they flanked her with perfect visual symmetry. As she launched into the second chorus and began a gentle, three-person soft shoe, I could swear the floor fell away from me, I was suspended in midair, and I thought I felt the almost two thousand patrons of City Center having the same experience. We were floating, en masse, watching a star be a star. If I could tell you why that happened, I would.

That's why the form has endured. And that's why it's worth talking about the mechanics that help make it happen.

Most musicals are romances, and for decades the principal responsibility of the Broadway musical was to be an effective aphrodisiac. What is a night out, after all, if not an invitation to intimacy? And if the songs, heard later in a club or on a bedside radio, cause a revival of passionate feelings, so much the better. This may sound like a trivial pursuit for an art form, but it's just the opposite. The Broadway musical, in its heyday, was an integral part of human courtship for a considerable portion of the American population. It gave validity to the idea of taking sex seriously, while laughing at it, along with those of us who were perpetually trying to figure out romantic love. It showed us beautiful, sensuous, sinuous people trying to get it right, which inspired the rest of us mere mortals to redouble our efforts. It gave harmonic voice to desire and ecstasy in ways we never dared to do out loud in our own lives. And it endorsed the idea that romance—the kind that demands a bed right away—far from being destructive, was the first building block to happiness in society. That was very encouraging.

In its earliest phases of operetta and musical comedy, the American musical promoted romance in a somewhat unlikely context. The operettas of the teens and '20s were grandly ridiculous, wonderfully melodic spectaculars whose plots concerned exotic locales and remote, romantic figures: pirates, Arabian princes, Canadian Mounties, and the women who couldn't stay out of their arms. The "modern" musical comedies of Rodgers and Hart, the Gershwins, and Cole Porter used the emerging sounds of the Jazz Age to domesticate things. Suddenly couples were succumbing at Long Island garden parties and on college campuses. But with the notable exception of Kern and Hammerstein's 1927 *Show Boat*, context didn't much matter back then. Shows were a showcase for great songs, great performers, an antic spirit, and not a lot more than that. That's the real reason that the arrival of *Oklahoma!*, in 1943, was a revolutionary moment. Not only did it present songs as an integrated part of the storytelling, it also made the story itself *count*. This is more unlikely than it sounds, because *Oklahoma!*'s story really shouldn't count for much. For the first ninety minutes of it, the only real issue seems to be the burning question of who is going to get to take Laurey to the box social.

But while *Oklahoma!* did not have a plot worth talking about, it had a *subject*. It placed its rather routine romantic story against the context of impending statehood. It asked audiences to consider courtship (and marriage, and the inevitable next generation) in the light of what it meant to be an American, to *become* an American. Suddenly, sexual love was joined to responsibility to the land, to fellow feeling and patriotism, to an implied critical review of the democratic process itself. The show even ends with a murder trial, conducted by ordinary citizens who are trying to invent a system to live by. And in wartime America, it created a new landscape for the musical theater, because in some profound way it was about the birth of us—of the country we were defending.

*Oklahoma!* has gone into hiding from time to time, but it has never disappeared. Not only has it survived by itself (there have been notable productions in every decade, including one at the National Theatre of Great Britain that brought stardom to Hugh Jackman), but it has also spawned many shows that have asked the same questions about America, citizenship, and the ever-evolving habits of lovers who are bound to explore democracy in all its facets. From *Bloomer Girl* to *Hair* to *1776* to *Hairspray* to *Hamilton*, we keep wrestling with the questions raised by Rodgers and Hammerstein's first hit. Without even knowing it, today's theater makers continue to repay the debt. *Show Boat* came first, with its serious intentions and somewhat integrated score, but it straddled the worlds of operetta and the musical play—a fascinating experiment, and a great musical, but not quite modern. *Oklahoma!* joined subject to form in a genuinely new way and created the template that continued to work for generations.

That template proved a fertile one for Broadway shows that have stood the test of time. And these shows shared not only a common worldview but also a common set of rules for construction. Writers learned how to erect an opening number, introduce a hero or heroine whose burning passion would drive the plot, send in the clowns, create an uncertain romance that would blossom, founder, and, usually, recover. They learned what it meant to confront a penultimate scene in which the nub of the issue came to a head and was then concluded with a climax that would send audiences home satisfied. They weren't always able to follow these ideas to a successful outcome, but at least they knew where they were aiming, even though it was sometimes at a moving target.

Fortified with a somewhat reliable set of blueprints, the Broadway musical had found its path—romance joined to social issues, sex, love, politics, and place. It questioned American attitudes while promoting American values, and it gave us a soundtrack suitable for courtship and moral authority in equal measure. It preached tolerance, promoted dizzy passion, endorsed personal responsibility, and ultimately told us that although we might have been carefully taught to hate and fear, we still had the capacity to overcome, to love and embrace. It continued evolving along this circuitously entertaining route securely and confidently until the '60s, and somewhat less steadily until the end of the '70s. But by then the path had begun to splinter.

Changing style in America accounts for some of the evolution away from the classic Rodgers and Hammerstein model—nothing stays in fashion forever. Hammerstein died in 1960, by which time Rodgers was already at the north end of a long career. But the twin causes of the demise of the classic Golden Age Broadway musicals were—in some senses—social and racial. The grim victories of the civil rights movement, combined with the grim failures of the Vietnam War, with JFK's assassination casting a long shadow in the midst of it all, caused Americans to discard the naïve optimism that had fueled the spirit of Broadway musicals, even the most serious of them, since the triumphs of World War II. We had always been—or so we had thought—a harmonious, can-do nation. And then, one day, that conviction was gone.

There had been other dark periods in American history, of course, but by the '60s, we were able to watch it all on television as it unfolded, and that changed everything. No one enjoying *Show Boat* in the '20s at the Ziegfeld up on Sixth Avenue and Fifty-fourth Street had any real sense of what life was like for African Americans down in Mississippi, even though the show was about miscegenation on the river. But once we saw the dogs attacking black children protesting in Birmingham on the nightly news in 1963, a new America entered our consciousness.

At the same time, the record business had for several years been steadily drawing the best young writers away from Broadway, courtesy of the rock-and-roll revolution. And many young audiences went with them. There was quicker money to be made writing hit records than there was writing for Broadway. You could get your stuff heard more readily over the radio, and it didn't need to come from a show or conform to the needs of a longer narrative, so you could do the work more efficiently. Rock somehow seemed antithetical to the narrative traditions of the musical play—many of the pop hits seemed content-free—so why bother? Early rock promoted the immediacy of rhythm, not the intricacy of melody or the complexity of character. Americans were thirsty for a new music, a new means of communication, a new approach to what they were feeling as the Eisenhower years plodded onward with no end in sight. And a huge and exciting African American talent pool, which had once been segregated in a separate record chart called the "Race" or, later, the "R&B" chart, was integrated into the regular pop charts as radio stations across the country finally came to their senses. That music exploded in popularity and created a brilliant new art form that had nothing to do with Broadway. Talent, as it always has, swarmed to the place where it was most likely to be appreciated and employed. In the '40s and '50s, Broadway writers were royalty in the music world. Songwriters planned for, and expected to have, a couple of chart hits with every Broadway show they wrote. Whether it was "Some Enchanted Evening," or "On the Street Where You Live," or "Hey There," or "Small World," Broadway scores were created to sell records as well as to tell stories. Even the once ubiquitous "Mutual Admiration Society," which spent ten weeks on the pop charts in 1956, turns out to have been a show tune, from one of Ethel Merman's rare flops, *Happy Hunting*. But by the mid-'50s, theater songs were sharing space regularly with rock writers and performers. And over time, Broadway began to become something of a musical backwater. It certainly wasn't a place Lennon and McCartney, Carole King, Paul Simon, or Billy Joel thought about first, though the Beatles did record a couple of show tunes early in their career. The era's Broadway writers—Stephen Sondheim, Jerry Herman, Kander and Ebb, Strouse and Adams, Bock and Harnick—continued to do terrific work, but with few exceptions their songs didn't chart anymore. Louis Armstrong's version of "Hello, Dolly!" was virtually the end of the line until the rock anthems of *Hair* came along.

Back on Broadway, the most remarkable shift that occurred in the decade that followed was caused by a set of startlingly innovative musicals produced and directed by Harold Prince and written by Stephen Sondheim with various collaborators. After the 1970 show *Company*, the Prince-Sondheim team (with the book writer James Goldman) produced *Follies* (1971), which had the temerity to ask what happens when your dreams don't come true, when you wake up to realize that they never could have come true—that you weren't who you thought you were.

*Follies* was emblematic of the America that had been rudely awakened from the dreams fostered by *Oklahoma!* and its descendants. In addition to *Company* and *Follies*, the Prince-Sondheim team went on to create *A Little Night Music*, *Pacific Overtures*, *Sweeney Todd*, and *Merrily We Roll Along*, all in a little over ten years. Critical reaction was diverse (though ever more convinced), but it was quickly clear that these musicals had changed the form and content rules forever. Prince and Sondheim flew high above the rest of Broadway during this period, covering everything from Manhattan marriage to American imperialism in Japan to English cannibalism on Fleet Street, but they did it with the kind of daring that's earned by years of deep experience in the more traditional forms. Both had long histories of working with experienced show makers: Prince had spent decades working on, and then producing, George Abbott musicals. He had worked as a producer extensively with both Jerome Robbins and Bob Fosse. Sondheim had grown up with Oscar Hammerstein II as a mentor and had his first hits with Robbins, Leonard Bernstein, Arthur Laurents, and Jule Styne. Both men knew how to grab an audience and hold it, when to introduce a subplot, how to create a showstopper for a star. They were musical theater virtuosi before they leapt into the unknown. No matter how wild and unbridled their shows became, they were operating from a deep understanding of where the form had been and how it had succeeded. Their success set a standard, but it also hurled out a gauntlet: Could other, less grounded writers and directors take these kinds of leaps and land on their feet?

Well, not regularly. And by the mid-'80s, the American Broadway musical had lost its grip, even as some individual shows continued to succeed and break ground. To be fair, it was largely a decade of musical hits from England produced by Cameron Mackintosh, several composed by Andrew Lloyd Webber. Spectacle and big rococo melodies, once the hallmark of the early operettas of Sigmund Romberg and Rudolf Friml, returned (with the addition of some rock influences) as a principal attraction of shows like *Cats*, *Les Misérables*, and, of course, *Phantom of the Opera*. But in America, the techniques, the mechanics of show making, of musical storytelling, ceased to be passed on and built upon constructively according to tradition. The Rodgers and Hammerstein model seemed worse than dated—it seemed like a lie. Writers began trying to reinvent the wheel because they hadn't been raised in the traditions that would inspire the next steps, or because they simply felt duty-bound to reject a past they didn't believe in. Perhaps, by embracing rock, they embraced the not unreasonable half-truth that a back-beat and a narrative story are natural enemies. But in the process of revolutionizing the Broadway show, as much was lost as securely found. A few shows, notably the 1981 *Dreamgirls*, married a rock-style score to narrative strength—a memorable protagonist, the inevitable challenges of a changing era, the satisfactions of a fully told story with a moving conclusion. But for every sure-handed experiment that worked—*Sunday in the Park with George*, Tommy Tune's spectacularly imaginative production of *Nine*—there were a fistful of experiments that seemed lost in the dark—*Starmites*, *Into the Light*, and the legendary *Carrie* among them. And even a show like *Sunday* played as the experiment it was, not as a bona fide hit satisfying a general audience. That audience was still buying tickets for the deeply traditionally structured *La Cage aux Folles*, which had married a daring (for the time) story of gay romance to a formula plot that dated back to before Kaufman and Hart's *You Can't Take It with You** and a score that could have been written more than a decade earlier.

But in the '90s, as the British Invasion wound down, a kind of redemption began to be seen in American musicals—fresh ideas *and* craftsmanship. *Urinetown*, a genuine satire about a ruined world where people have to pay to pee, featured a book that actually had shape, and a smart score that took its cue from Kurt Weill's *Threepenny Opera* and updated it with a modern kick. The turn of the century brought both

---

* It seems to be a classic American theme that the zany, unconventional family is to be treasured and is inevitably under assault from the staid and the stuffy. Plots built around an impending marriage between a dull outsider and a waffling descendant of a wild and unique family include not only *You Can't Take It with You* but also *The Royal Family*, *Arsenic and Old Lace*, and others. The related but somewhat broader notion that the inmates are saner than the asylum keepers fueled both Sondheim's *Anyone Can Whistle* and the almost equally short-lived musical *King of Hearts*. In *La Cage aux Folles*, the idea was adapted for political purposes: the "unconventional" family consisted of two gay men, and the "stuffy" outsiders were bigoted homophobes. But the plot was the same.

*The Producers* and the underappreciated *The Full Monty*—beautifully shaped comic yarns with appealing scores, which took advantage of all of the traditional structural lessons of the Golden Age. *Hairspray* followed, and *The Book of Mormon*, which consciously aped and poked fun at the Golden Age classics while telling a rude yet sentimental tale in defense of faith no matter how unlikely or illogical its tenets may be. *Mormon* demonstrated that, even as America becomes more jaded, there's something inherent in an effective structure with a traditional song plot that taps into a fundamental human journey. Like *The Producers* before it, *Mormon* is a buddy story as much as a romance—a form borrowed from the movies and pretty much absent from Golden Age shows. But these shows figured out how to marry the bromance to the traditional musical theater template, and both are better for it. *Wicked*, which is a girl-girl buddy story, had a little more difficulty meeting the same challenge (though obviously, it more than succeeded in the end), but let's leave that story for another day.

The show that broke the mold again, in early 2015, was *Hamilton*, which opened off Broadway at the Public Theater, site of the birth of *A Chorus Line* forty years earlier. Written by Lin-Manuel Miranda as a hip-hop-influenced retelling of the life of Alexander Hamilton, the show demanded an immediate Broadway transfer, as had *A Chorus Line*. As unusual (possibly insane) as both the subject and the style seemed for a Broadway musical, *Hamilton* discovered an almost shocking synergy between then and now. Its Revolutionary War heroes seemed completely contemporary, reimagined as smart, angry, unpredictably high-spirited rappers, and, indeed, within moments, it was almost impossible not to begin imagining the members of Public Enemy, or Jay-Z, Nas, and Ice Cube, as the natural offspring of Alexander Hamilton, Thomas Jefferson, and George Washington, internecine feuds and all. Revolution is revolution, whenever—and messy, too.

This ricochet effect created a palpable excitement in the theater, because it implicitly raised questions about how race, immigration (Hamilton was born on the island of Nevis in the Caribbean), political cowardice, and class have been burning American issues since before the beginning of the nation and have never gone away. It also provided a fascinating discovery that should have been obvious: rap is a great way to tell a theatrical story. Unlike in classic pop-rock, where the lyrics tend to be abstractly poetic, ruminative, repetitive, or simpleminded pleas for love and/or sex, the best of rap wants urgently to communicate something bigger—a personal and political creed and a contextualized view of the world as it really is. As a key component of the hip-hop life, it is always on the attack, trying to change things and call things by their right name. In a rich and varied score full of jazz and rock influences, *Hamilton* uses rap sparingly, but when it does, the urgency is palpable.

Unlike rock, rap is a narrative form by nature, and *Hamilton* has a huge story to tell with it, as the very first iteration of the American landscape is built right before our eyes. Clearly more influenced by *Les Misérables* than by Rodgers and Hammerstein, it nonetheless follows the American rules in a number of fascinating ways, and always to its advantage.

Miranda wrote all of *Hamilton*—book, music, and lyrics—by himself, but many of the greatest classic musicals were the result of famously fractious collaborations. One might look at the master collaborators— from Kern and Berlin to Rodgers and Hart and Loesser and Jule Styne and Jerome Robbins—and come to the conclusion that the history of the Broadway musical is the history of short Jewish men yelling at each other. But to understand how these shows really came to be, it's important to know what they were yelling about: the form and function and how the pieces fit together. These are the things that Broadway writers and directors used to carry inside them. You can't turn back the clock (the world only spins forward, as Tony Kushner reminds us in *Angels in America*), but there's pleasure in understanding this unique form of American entertainment and how it worked in its heyday. In the bones of that disused machine, some writers in the twenty-first century have begun to find inspiration, although most of their shows sit side by side with others that are more inspired by theatrical rock concerts than by *Oklahoma! Hamilton* is a telling example, being a work that grows out of a tradition and grows radically away from it at the same time.

Within the story of how a Broadway show is built is an actual story as well—about several eras on Broadway, the characters who populated the street, the things they learned from each other, and the rivalries, partnerships, competitions, and collaborations that made the creative process as intriguing as the results are enduring; but also about the inexorable move forward, as each generation carried some of the past on its back while blazing trails into the future.

In form, this book somewhat resembles the "song plot" course that I teach at NYU. I'm going to examine the musical as it moves forward from opening number to first-act climax to finale, drawing examples from many shows that remain with us, and a few that have been lost over time. I've pulled examples from all directions, and left out a lot that could probably have served exactly as well as what I've chosen. You have to draw the line somewhere. I hope that by the time I get to the curtain call, readers will have a sense of how this work got done by the people who did it best, at a time when aspiring to do it well was the highest goal an American songwriter or librettist could set.

# 2. Curtain Up, Light the Lights

*Opening Numbers*

**W**hen the curtain goes up," the director Michael Blakemore once said, "the audience is in trouble."

Blakemore, the much decorated director of classics and new plays, didn't try his hand at a Broadway musical until he was in his sixties, and the show he picked, *City of Angels*, was enough to get anyone into trouble—especially audiences. Its dizzying plot involved a '50s pulp novelist adapting his work for Hollywood, and the action swung between the novelist's travails and those of his fictional detective hero, whose world was depicted in black and white. The detective tried to solve a murder while the novelist tried to prevent the studio from murdering his script. Keeping audiences engaged, laughing, and dazzled by all the complexity, rather than confused and defeated, was the task at hand. The book writer Larry Gelbart's masterful ability to organize and control the material led the way, and Cy Coleman and David Zippel's jazzy midcentury score pumped a heartbeat into the show. But despite the A-list team, Blakemore knew he had to be as sure-handed as possible: confusion was his enemy. Using his great skill, experience, and intelligence to lead the audience swiftly through the action, he demanded absolute clarity above all things. The meticulous attention to detail worked, and *City of Angels* was a surprise hit. But many less complex and less challenging shows have foundered at the very moment Blakemore pinpointed: they get in trouble as soon as the curtain goes up. That's when confusion reigns—who is everybody onstage, how do we tell them apart, and what does each one want? Which characters are important and which ones are little more than window dressing? Where are we supposed to look?

"My job," Blakemore explained, "is to get the audience out of trouble."

How do you begin a show? How does a musical greet its audience at the door? How do creative artists introduce the characters, set the tone, communicate a point of view, create a sense of style, a milieu? Do you begin with the story, the subject, the community in which the story is set, the main characters? How much can audiences handle, and how quickly? Do you invite them to dip a toe in to test the water, or do you plunge them in up to their necks before they know what's happening? There are no hard-and-fast answers to this litany of questions, and, frequently, even the experts don't know the answers until the whole show is almost complete. That's why opening numbers are often written last.

One thing is certain, however: opening numbers can make or break a show. They have turned flops into hits (*A Funny Thing Happened on the Way to the Forum*), and their conception can be a cause for completely rethinking and reworking everything that comes after them (*Fiddler on the Roof*). They can be fabulously elaborate (*A Chorus Line*, *Ragtime*) or breathtakingly simple (*Oklahoma!*), but whatever they are, they launch the enterprise. If they do what they're supposed to, they hand Mr. Blakemore—or any capable director—the tools to do his job.

Overtures help, of course. They've become something of a rarity today, but they can be one of the real pleasures of a Broadway musical, and they should set the tone for what's to come. Some are written and fussed over by the composer, or by the composer in collaboration with an orchestrator, while others have been left to the arrangers and orchestrators alone. In some cases they are thrown together from "utilities"—all-purpose orchestrations of songs from the show that are created to be used as scene-change music and as underscoring, and for any other need that arises while a show is working its way through a tryout. In this last situation, the lack of a well-thought-out overture is usually the result of a show going through so many changes in such a state of chaos that the overture gets continually pushed to the bottom of the work list and never gets properly dealt with. That situation is even more normal for entr'actes, those short musical interludes that precede the beginning of the second act. They're often perfunctory, on the theory that they're mostly used to cover the sound of audiences settling back down in their seats. Though on a couple of occasions I've heard masterful ones.

Overtures vary in quality, of course, but a good one—*South Pacific*'s or *Gypsy*'s or *Forum*'s—leaves no doubt as to what the tone of the evening will be, whether epic drama, period showbiz, or farce. It helps to have great tunes, since almost all overtures are medleys, but even some B-level shows—*Wildcat* and *Goldilocks*, for instance—have overtures that are such masterful demonstrations of the orchestrator's art that they are worth hearing repeatedly. But good, bad, or indifferent, at the (usually) thunderous conclusion of the overture, the play begins, and that's when the choices become critical.

There's a lot to think about when creating an opening, but the first question is: What kind of show is it? A dark romantic fable, obviously, will want to begin differently from a knockabout farce. After paying top dollar for a ticket, most audience members will assume they're in capable hands. Quite quickly, they'll expect to earn their money back in entertainment value. And so it's crucial to let every audience member in on what has been planned, somehow or other. This doesn't mean that opening numbers have to attend to a laundry list of requirements. But it does suggest that we should live by one of the principles of the Hippocratic oath: first do no harm.

*Forum*, famously, was saved by the replacement of its opening number. The show was an unusual one for 1962, written by brilliant young collaborators who were not particularly interested in following rules. Burt Shevelove had the idea to take three ancient Roman comedies by Plautus and cook up a vaudeville-style evening out of them. Inevitably, the writers were making a point about the ageless verities of comedy. Plautus lived in about 200 B.C.; vaudeville was in its heyday in the 1920s; and the show was being written in the 1960s, by which time comedy had moved on to the era of political satire and improv in the style of Mort Sahl and the Second City.

But Gelbart, Shevelove's co-librettist on this one, was fond of quoting a twenty-five-hundred-year-old joke from Plautus that demonstrated the immutability of comic subject matter:

FIRST CITIZEN

How's your wife?

SECOND CITIZEN
*(with a heavy sigh)*

Immortal.

Luckily, there were still a bunch of vaudeville and borscht belt clowns milling around Broadway looking for work, and *Forum* managed to snare a handful of really good ones. Gelbart and Shevelove's script was truly funny and extraordinarily inventive in the way it threaded the Plautus plots through one another to create a giant pileup of crises before the final resolution. Stephen Sondheim's score—his first as lyricist and composer—was similarly unusual and innovative. Even the orchestrations were anomalous—full of offbeat percussive effects and lacking violins altogether. So *Forum* faced a challenge no one knew it faced: it wanted to earn deeply traditional waves of laughter, but it was actually much brainier and more sophisticated in its construction than it pretended to be. Its authors were not only smart, they were also smart-asses.

The show begins with a charming number called "Love Is in the Air"—a sweet little soft shoe about how romance tends to drive people nuts. It's a honey of a number. But it tells us nothing about where *Forum* is headed—its style, its knockabout point of view, its plot, or its characters. It tells us to prepare for charm, the one characteristic that this singularly bountiful musical doesn't have much time for.

The show opened disastrously in New Haven: bad reviews and empty houses. In other hands, it would have shuttered right then and there, or limped into town and disappeared into the vortex of misbegotten Broadway dreams. But the producer, Hal Prince, and the director, George Abbott, had almost seventy years of experience in the business between them. Sondheim was coming off two straight hits—*West Side Story* and *Gypsy*—as a lyricist and was also very well connected on the street. So they called Jerome Robbins to come take a look. Stubbornly, they believed in this strangely intractable comedy that they'd created, and they were too far inside it to divine why it wasn't working.

Robbins, who had once had an interest in directing *Forum*, spotted the problem at once. It was the opening. In that moment when the curtain went up and the audience was in trouble, *Forum* promised charm and delivered mayhem instead. It betrayed the audience's trust. In the face of the light and adorable "Love Is in the Air," the show itself seemed vulgar and coarse, not funny. Robbins laid out his analysis. Sondheim protested that he'd already written a number that did exactly what Robbins felt needed to be done, but Abbott had rejected it because he couldn't hum it.

"Write him a number he can hum," Robbins told him. "He's the director."

Robbins agreed to stage the new opening and advised Sondheim to write something "neutral" so that he—Robbins—could create a lot of vaudeville-style schtick while it was going on. "Don't tell jokes," Robbins said. "Just write a baggy-pants number and let me stage it." He didn't want anything brainy or wisecracking, but he did want to tell the audience exactly what it was in for: lowbrow slapstick carried out by iconic character types like the randy old man, the idiot lovers, the battle-axe mother, the wily slave, and assorted other familiar folks. Sondheim wrote "Comedy Tonight," a neutral, bouncy tune that anyone, even Abbott, could hum. It allowed space not only for Robbins's staging but also for sections of narration in which the world of the piece, the major characters, and the overall style could be shown to the audience. This included, among other things, an opportunity for Zero

Mostel, who was playing the leading role, to address the audience directly and explain things, in dialogue that didn't include jokes but promised funny and potentially overripe comic situations. One thing Sondheim was unable to be neutral about was his natural genius with a comic rhyme when, at the conclusion of the number, he described the elements of the upcoming evening as

> *Pantaloons and tunics,*
> *Courtesans and eunuchs,*
> *Funerals and chases,*
> *Baritones and basses,*
> *Panderers,*
> *Philanderers,*
> *Cupidity,*
> *Timidity,*
> *Mistakes,*
> *Fakes,*
> *Rhymes,*
> *Crimes,*
> *Tumblers,*
> *Grumblers,*
> *Bumblers,*
> *Fumblers*

He erased all doubt as to what kinds of things were going to happen next. The audience was securely in the show's pocket. His skill extended to beginning with lines of six syllables and working his way down to four-, three-, two-, and one-syllable lines before putting a cap on the whole stack with "Tumblers, grumblers, bumblers, fumblers." This created a sense of acceleration and excitement in the song without actually having to speed up the tempo. It also meant that every member of the company could have a line or a word to sing before the song's conclusion. The audience met everybody and knew everything, except for the plot, which was satisfyingly worked out later. The number went in at the beginning of previews in New York, and the show was a smash. In its final form, *Forum* is among the most happily launched of all Broadway musicals.

Years later, when it was being revived in a production directed by Jerry Zaks starring Nathan Lane, a question was raised about who owned "Comedy Tonight." Clearly the authors owned the song and the book material that was written down on paper. But did Jerome Robbins own some undefined bit of intellectual property? And what about the staging? The most famous bit in the number involved the show's "proteans," three comic male chorus dancers who played all the nonprincipal roles. In "Comedy Tonight," they performed a dance behind a piece of drapery that covered their midsections, and it quickly became apparent that the three of them shared seven legs instead of six. A remarkable amount of comedy was wrung out of this seven-legged dance before Zero Mostel simply grabbed the extra leg and hurled it offstage, which got an even bigger laugh than the dance itself.

Robbins was represented by a Broadway legend, the attorney Floria Lasky, who was by this point toward the end of a legendary career. She was tough, caustic, and gravel throated. She argued that Robbins should be compensated for the use of the opening number. Zaks promised that he would completely restage it so that any implied rights that Robbins might have had would not be violated. There would be none of Robbins's work visible in the number. The producers went over to negotiate with Lasky. Hearing this pledge, she glared at the men over her desk for a long time. Finally she said, "Okay. But if there's a wooden leg in it, Robbins gets a royalty."

The negotiations for the *Forum* revival also involved Sondheim's agent, Flora Roberts. Flora and Floria were the Gold Dust Twins, aging old pros, impossible to intimidate. They didn't shout, but they could stare you under the table in a heartbeat. Both were fiercely protective of their clients, and both, while enormous negotiating challenges for producers, were almost universally beloved. In a meeting between Roberts and the *Forum* revival producers, Roberts was bemoaning the loss of Burt Shevelove, one of *Forum*'s two book writers, who'd died too young. The other writer, Larry Gelbart, had gone on to create the TV show *M\*A\*S\*H* and write screenplays like *Tootsie*. The book writers, living and dead, were asking for a lot of money. And Roberts was laying it on thick.

"Burt," she intoned grandly, "is in heaven. But Larry called just this morning to remind me that he's very big in Hollywood."

Scott Rudin, who was one of the revival's producers and a hugely powerful movie mogul, shot back, "Actually Burt's bigger in heaven than Larry is in Hollywood."

The show was always funny.

"We learn more from the flops than we do from the hits," a wise producer once said. Actually, every producer says it every time he mounts a flop. But the point is well taken. Some shows, like *Forum*, were unlikely to be hits but pulled the rabbit out of the hat. Others, like *Mack and Mabel*, seemed destined for easy success but somehow could never find the hat, much less the rabbit.

*Mack and Mabel* had everything going for it: a swell Jerry Herman score, the visionary director Gower Champion (Robbins's only real rival for dominance in the late '50s and the '60s), and two big and wonderful stars in Robert Preston and Bernadette Peters playing the silent film magnate Mack Sennett and his great love and most famous female star, Mabel Normand. And it had a delightfully nostalgic, colorful milieu: the silent movie era in Hollywood. What in the world went wrong? Unsurprisingly, it starts on page one of the script and continues through the entire opening number, which, ironically, is a terrific song.

*Mack and Mabel* is a love story narrated by Mack Sennett at the end of his career. The curtain goes up on his old, bankrupt movie studio, abandoned except for a night watchman. Mack, still virile and full of fight, comes back for one last look at where it all began, and then he starts to talk. This is our first shot at what the evening is going to be, and here's a little of what he says:

MACK

Aw, what do those jerks know about making movies, anyway? . . .

I'm Mack Sennett, I know the difference. Oh, you'll make money with the crap you grind out . . .

Go on, try all the tricks you can think of but it's still not gonna be worth one reel of *Birth of a Nation*, not one frame of Chaplin, not one eighth of a quarter of an inch of my Mabel . . .

So what have we learned? Mack Sennett is angry, tough, bitter, unsentimental, down on his luck, and living in the past but with a big heart for film, *The Birth of a Nation*, and Charlie Chaplin. He *believes* in them, and he's angry because that era of pure, silent cinema is being replaced by newfangled garbage. Art is being supplanted by garbage. That's our first clue as to who he is. He may not be much fun to spend time with (always risky in a musical), but he has passion for something of value (always a good idea in a musical). Then he begins to sing, and here's what he sings:

> Swanson and Keaton and Dressler and William S. Hart
> No one pretended that what we were doing was art
> We had some guts and some luck
> But we were just makin' a buck

By now we're on page three, and the game is already over. Why? Because after telling us in dialogue that his anger and bitterness are caused by art being supplanted by garbage, he's just turned 180 degrees and sung to us that his career was not about making art after all, but about having the guts to make money instead. In the lyric, he describes himself as being the very thing he was attacking in the dialogue.

So which is it? What's going on? Our narrator, upon whom we're forced to rely, is unreliable. He can't keep his own point of view straight; he's suffering from multiple personality disorder, and so is *Mack and Mabel*. The problem may seem like a technical glitch, easily correctable, but it's actually huge and insurmountable, because it leaves the audience in trouble—puzzled and fearful that they'll never figure this one out. And they won't, because the authors can't decide for themselves. Is the show going to be about how wonderful the silent movies were, or about how venal and commercial? Is it nostalgic or angry? If the former, why the bilious and combative narrator? If the latter, why the misty-eyed tribute to Chaplin and D. W. Griffith? What's the tone supposed to be? Is the point of view fundamentally dark or light? Bitter or celebratory? And will we ever be able to take anything Mack says at face value? Words are coming out of his mouth, but they don't add up.

This is not to say that you can't write a show about someone with personality disorders, as the surprise success of *Next to Normal* proved a few decades later. And, in fact, one can argue that silent movies were fantastically artful *and* the product of venal commercial interests. And you'd be right. But you can't introduce the argument right at the start in a musical. The book and the song are taking opposite points of view. When you talk out of both sides of your mouth, it's just too damn confusing. In fact, the hallmark of *Mack and Mabel* is that, for all its many assets, it remains stubbornly schizophrenic throughout—it never arrives at a clear view of what kind of experience it is supposed to be. This is partly the result of the limitations of the source material, the real Mack being something of a cold megalomaniac, and the real Mabel being something of a self-destructive drug addict. But it's also important to understand that the show was created in the mid-'70s by artists who had done their best work in the mid-'60s, when musicals were still largely projecting blue skies and optimism. By 1976 there was a darker vision of America on display on Broadway. *Mack and Mabel* wants to have it both ways—it's the awkward love child of *Hello, Dolly!* and *Follies*. The score, which contains a couple of terrific ballads, largely consists of upbeat, classic Jerry Herman tunes, while the book keeps getting darker and darker and darker until the lights just go out. But this bifurcated point of view is on display right from the moment the curtain goes up, and the audience never could find its way out of trouble.

*Forum* and *Mack and Mabel*, notwithstanding their varying degrees of success, illustrate the two most common forms of opening number. In the former, we get to meet and hear from everyone. In the latter, we are left in the hands of one protagonist, who sets the scene with no help from the rest of the cast. The first—the all-hands-on-deck number—has been serving musicals since their inception, although its function and style keep evolving. The second was more or less invented by Richard Rodgers and Oscar Hammerstein, with "Oh, What a Beautiful Mornin'," back in the '40s.

The invention was inspired, but also pragmatic. Both men had been writing shows (although not with each other) for a long time, and both knew the value of startling an audience. You could startle it with content, but you could also, if you had a good enough idea, do it with form. It was easy to startle with more noise but more interesting to do it with less.

Long before Hammerstein had begun writing operettas in the early '20s, musicals usually began with lots of people onstage singing, often rows and rows of chorus girls. Ziegfeld's *Follies* were famous for their parades of American beauties right at the opening curtain. The hall-of-fame set designer John Lee Beatty once said, with characteristic dryness, that an opening number was just an opportunity for the audience to take a good look at the company and decide whom they most wanted to sleep with. Once that problem had been gotten out of the way, the play could begin. He was only half kidding.

Having agreed to adapt a play set on an Oklahoma farm at the end of the nineteenth century, Rodgers and Hammerstein were left wondering what would happen if decades of theatrical tradition were given the heave-ho, and a Broadway musical began with a middle-aged woman churning butter in a barnyard while a handsome cowhand wandered on and sang a solo. It was a question born out of practicality—choruses of girls were hard to justify on an Oklahoma farm. It's hard to have merry villagers when there's no village. It's also the way the play they were adapting, *Green Grow the Lilacs*, begins. So they took a chance, then took many more, and then revolutionized the form in the process.

They were mature writers as well as experienced showmen. Hammerstein wrote a lyric for the cowhand that, in only a couple of dozen lines, did a lot of the work that "Comedy Tonight" had in seven minutes. The song is short, but it's long enough. Hammerstein knew he had to set the scene, create the language of the piece, get us to like this cowhand, create a point of view for the show (earnest, not satiric, romantic but of the earth, not fussy), and create a stake. By the end of this little number, we had to believe that the place the cowhand described was so splendid in its simple beauty and virtue that it was worth defending, with a gun if necessary: it was America. And in 1943, America was at war in Europe and the Pacific, protecting the values of democracy and liberty against the deadly incursions of tyranny and bigotry. The show was set at the turn of the century, but like all shows, it had to speak to the audiences of its own time.

This sounds like a tall order, and it required a mature artist to tackle it. But Hammerstein was a practical artist, too, and the first thing he did was to purloin the ideas of the opening stage direction of Lynne Riggs's original play. The stage direction, in part, reads:

> It is a radiant summer morning several years ago, the kind of morning which, enveloping the shapes of earth—men, cattle in a meadow, blades of the young corn, streams—makes them seem to exist now for the first time, their images giving off a visible golden emanation . . .

From that bit of purplish prose, the lyricist fashioned this much more singable vision:

> There's a bright, golden haze on the meadow,
> There's a bright, golden haze on the meadow,
> The corn is as high as a elephant's eye
> An' it looks like it's climbin' clear up to the sky.
>
> Oh, what a beautiful mornin',
> Oh, what a beautiful day.
> I got a beautiful feelin',
> Ev'rythin's goin' my way.
>
> All the cattle are standin' like statues,
> All the cattle are standin' like statues,
> They don't turn their heads as they see me ride by,
> But a little brown mav'rick is winkin' her eye.

He dealt with flora first, then fauna. (Hammerstein dealt with a lot of fauna in his career. In a wonderful if slightly mad essay by the statistician Eric Thompson, 491 creatures are accounted for in Hammerstein's lyrics—"75 sea creatures, 240 creatures of the land and 176 birds.")

For two stanzas, the verses are purely descriptive, though it tells us a lot that the cowhand singing them is so vividly observant, and his passion for his surroundings begins to show in each chorus. But in the third stanza, the cowhand loosens up and tells us what he thinks about all of this:

> *All the sounds of the earth are like music—*
> *All the sounds of the earth are like music*
> *The breeze is so busy it don't miss a tree*
> *And a ol' weepin' willer is laughin' at me.*

> *Oh, what a beautiful mornin',*
> *Oh, what a beautiful day.*
> *I got a beautiful feelin',*
> *Ev'rythin's goin' my way . . .*
> *Oh, what a beautiful day.*

We have moved from appreciative description to a more personal statement, and suddenly we're in the hands of a cowhand who's a self-deprecating poet and who loves his surroundings with a kind of plainly expressed passion that is as romantic as it is proud. He's ardent but masculine. He speaks for all of us who love our country, and he speaks in a bit of a strange patois, which is American but remote from New York and Broadway. The simplicity is deceptive, and the song is so well known that it's hard for us to hear it afresh. But it's worth noting that it is structured like a folk song, with its repeating chorus, not like a standard thirty-two-bar theater song. And Hammerstein's notion of repeating the first line of every verse twice is borrowed from the rural blues songs that grew out of field hollers at the turn of the century. In those ways, it's nothing like a Broadway song. But it contains all the hallmarks of a great opening number, distilled down to their essence and appropriately formed for a rural "folk" setting. Hammerstein changed the form without ducking his responsibility to the content.

Rodgers's melody respects the simplicity of the ideas in the verse and celebrates the ardor that's implicit in the chorus. So it isn't just the *idea* of a solo that's revolutionary—it's the confident invention and expertise of its execution. (It's also worth noting that this opening number, Rodgers and Hammerstein's first, is so clearly echoed in their *last* opening number, in which a rebellious nun named Maria points out that *"the hills are alive with the sound of music."* Whenever Hammerstein went outdoors, the earth seemed to sing to him.)

Since that time, most Broadway musicals have begun one way or the other—a blowout for the entire company or a solo for the protagonist. But in their second collaboration, R&H tried something that was also new: an opening ballet. "The Carousel Waltz" replaced the more traditional overture in *Carousel*. In the course of this instrumental prelude, dancers and actors took the audience through the world of a traveling New England carnival somewhere on the coast of Maine. Taking his cue from the sound of a carousel's calliope, Rodgers wrote a richly textured piece of music, and the choreographer Agnes de Mille, working from Hammerstein's scenario, painted the landscape of a working seaside town, with its factory girls and fishermen squeezing a night's entertainment on the midway out of a few nickels.

It was tremendously effective, but it's only occasionally been imitated, most notably—in an entirely different tone—by *Guys and Dolls* in "Runyonland." This opening presents a more familiar landscape— Broadway itself—and a wise-guy tone that is as far from *Carousel* as one could hope to stray. *West Side Story* adapted the idea of an opening ballet to yet another New York location but stitched dance to a classic ensemble-type number—the "Jet Song." Each in its own way lays out the territory of the show it introduces with astonishing clarity, imagination, and confidence.

But opening ballets are the exception—wordlessness always runs the risk of further confusing an already wary audience at the opening curtain. Solo opening numbers are somewhat more common. Hammerstein used another in *The King and I*, a few years after creating the tiny little opening duet in *South Pacific*, in which two Eurasian children sing a bit of doggerel in French, "Dites-Moi," which nonetheless underlies the largest themes and dilemmas in that epic show. *"Tell me why,"* they sing, *"life is beautiful and happy? Is it because you love me?"* The show then spends three hours trying to arrive at a place where life is beautiful and happy, and the hero and heroine finally allow themselves to love each other. The journey encompasses war, racial prejudice, sexual obsession, pandering, terrible economic disparity, and human disaster. It's a monumental show, slyly begun by a pair of tots whose racial makeup and parentage turn out to be at the center of the argument. They ask a simple question in rhyme (in French, yet), but, for anyone listening, it's the right question, and it allows the audience to slip comfortably into the evening in a beautifully exotic setting. Once seduced into this pleasant place, theatergoers belong to the writers, who are then free to put them through glorious hell.

There's probably no such thing as a perfect musical, but when fanatics gather to compare notes, the most frequently mentioned candidate is undoubtedly *Gypsy*. Written with dispatch by Arthur Laurents (book), Stephen Sondheim (lyrics), and Jule Styne (music), this examination of a show business family certainly comes as close as you can get. And in Madame Rose, the authors created the greatest show business monster-mother of all time.

*Gypsy*, first produced in 1959, is based on Gypsy Rose Lee's memoir of the same name. It's the somewhat reinvented, or at least laundered, tale of Ms. Lee (née Rose Louise Hovick) growing up as a kid in vaudeville and her emergence as the famous stripper. Many of the eccentric details in the musical are drawn directly from the memoir, which gives the show a lot of texture and a remarkable feel for time and place. But the actual subject—the crushing damage that a parent can inflict on her children and the myriad consequences—is entirely the invention of the musical's authors. It's also one of the key reasons *Gypsy* has stood the test of time: this is a subject that never gets old. How we love, ignore, or smother our children, how we project our own dreams onto their unwitting psyches, how we may drive them away while living in terror of their abandoning us—these are profound concerns, and *Gypsy* takes them seriously. Yet for a musical that has a lot on its mind, it begins with a kind of charming innocuousness, and it plays like a house on fire. Two children sing an apparently trivial song, rather like in *South Pacific*. But while Rodgers and Hammerstein were digging into History with a capital "H," Laurents, Sondheim, and Styne were writing a personal drama more indebted to Freud than to Herodotus. Still, the show is a musical, and it begins by behaving like a musical comedy.

The curtain goes up on the rehearsal for a kiddie-show amateur night in Seattle in the 1920s. This is made clear by a heroic feat of expositional writing by Arthur Laurents (the entire opening scene, including the song, takes up only four pages of the script). We're introduced to Uncle Jocko, the seedy host of the contest, who, in the course of a very few lines, lets us know that the contest is fixed, that his biggest problem is not the kids who want to be in show business but the mothers who push them into it, and that the talent-free kids themselves are so bad that they will soon "kill vaudeville." These are all important points: *Gypsy* concerns itself with a monstrously powerful mother figure who is absolutely determined that her children will be stars in vaudeville. The problems she faces are conjoined: the kids aren't talented, and the business is going out of business. She's in a race against time and doesn't know it. By the time her children are grown, the form will have all but disappeared, a fact that audiences in 1959 were well aware of. Her challenge is insurmountable, but her will is indomitable.

This makes it interesting. Every good show, in some sense, is about a mountain that's hard to scale. The bigger and more unpredictable the mountain, and the more determined the climber, the more engaged we're likely to be. In this regard, *Gypsy* may be the all-time champion musical-as-athletic-contest.

We meet the kids before the mother. Uncle Jocko, after suffering through sixteen bars of "Arnold and His Accordion," turns the stage over to "Baby June and Company"—"Company," in this case, being the shy, thumb-sucking Louise, age eight. The two girls launch into a somewhat pathetic little number called "May We Entertain You." This is *Gypsy*'s opening number, and it appears to be about nothing. But it tells us almost everything. The kids are lousy: June is overzealous and annoying, and Louise is lost. And as soon as we learn this much, their mother, Rose, bursts upon the scene midsong, making a great star entrance down the aisle of the theater, to try to fix the number, which is impossible to do. Jocko tries to get rid of her, the stage manager tries to get rid of her, even her own children tacitly wish her somewhere else, but she cannot be dispatched. She cajoles, she threatens, she extols her kids' virtues and denigrates everyone else.

Here's what she says, with ineffectual interruptions by Uncle Jocko, who is quickly losing control of his own domain:

ROSE

Louise, dear, if you don't count—

JOCKO

Madam, do you realize you are absolutely—

ROSE

I do, Uncle Jocko, but I want to save your very valuable time for you.

JOCKO

In that case—

ROSE

When I saw your sensitive face at the Odd Fellows Hall—my first husband was an Odd Fellow—

JOCKO

I am not an Odd Fellow!

ROSE

I meant a Knight of Pythias. My second husband was—

JOCKO

I'm not a Knight of Pythias!

ROSE

Then where *did* you catch our act?

JOCKO

At the Elks.


ROSE

My father is an Elk! I have his tooth here someplace. *(She dumps the dog into Jocko's arms as she rummages in her handbag)* If you'll just hold Chowsie for me—that's short for chow mein. *(Baby talk)* Mommy just loves chow mein, doesn't she, Chowsie Wowsie? Stop sucking your thumb, Louise. *(To the conductor)* Professor, I just marvel how you can make a performer into an artist.


JOCKO
*(Following her as she gads about)*
What is going on here??


ROSE

Now if you could help my little girls by giving them a good loud la da *da* de da da *da*—(*To Jocko, whom she delicately shoves back as he moves to intervene)* God helps him who helps himself. *(To the drummer)* Mr. Zipser—when the girls do their specialty would you please ad lick it? Show him, girls.


JOCKO

Is this really happening?!


ROSE

Oh, Gus? Gus, would you please slap Baby June with something pink? She's the star. Smile, Baby dear!


JOCKO

I have seen all kinds of mothers—


ROSE

Do you know of a really good agent—don't hang on the baby, Louise, you're rumpling her dress—who could book a professional act like ours?

We may be horrified by her performance, but unlike Mack Sennett at the top of *Mack and Mabel*, we do sort of want to spend the rest of the evening with her. For one thing, she's fixing things rather than complaining about them. She lacks any trace of self-consciousness or self-pity. And despite all her frightening gall, she's knowledgeable, resourceful, funny, and shocking, and in some demented way, she even seems to love her kids—though she's continually demeaning one and protecting the other. She's instantaneously memorable, which is always a good idea in a musical. Musicals—the great ones—are rarely about ordinary life plodding by. They're about the outsize romance that can't be controlled, the special world we'd love to live in for a while, the faraway time and place we're waiting to be seduced by, the larger-than-life force of nature we so rarely encounter in real life. That's Madame Rose.

She's the most powerful person onstage as *Gypsy* begins, and it's made blindingly clear that the least powerful is not Uncle Jocko, whom she berates, but poor, pathetic Louise, so paralyzed by fear that she can barely move to hide behind her sister. The trajectory of *Gypsy* is such that by the evening's end, the two characters will have exactly switched places. Louise will be in charge of everything, and her mother will be reduced to wearing a borrowed fur over her frumpy dress while begging to come to a showbiz party in Louise's honor. Precisely how this dramatically perfect power exchange happens is the challenge the authors handed themselves. *Gypsy* has clarity of purpose. It also has an announced stake.

"Don't you laugh!" Rose barks at Uncle Jocko. "*Don't you dare laugh!* . . . That child is going to be a star!"

From that moment on, the word "star" peppers the text of *Gypsy* with increasing frequency, to the point where it seems peculiar that no one ever notices how many times it's spoken. Stardom is the stake in *Gypsy*, and stake is a great and powerful way to organize the story: Rose is determined to make her daughter a star, and the world is conspiring to make sure it never happens. Everything is about this stake. It's like the flag in a game of capture the flag—it may not be interesting on its own, but every show should have one, and only one. It's the thing everyone fights over, and wants, and most often it's a physical thing or a person: Sweeney's daughter, Johanna, in *Sweeney Todd*; the verdict in *Chicago*. Anything that's not related to it in some way can probably be written out. And probably should be. Sometimes the stake is puzzlingly irrelevant to what's good about a show: the stake in *Guys and Dolls* is the Save-a-Soul Mission itself. It's not a humorous or flavorful place or a location that anyone who sees the show really even talks about. But the fact that it is threatened with being shut down is the gas that powers the engine that drives the joy machine. Great shows have clear stakes.

With the stake established quickly and with utter clarity, *Gypsy* confronted an unusual structural challenge. Most shows unfold over a few weeks or months. *Gypsy* covers more than a decade. Holding it together, keeping it, and the audience, focused, is hard work. But the show takes an innovative route to meeting that challenge, and it involves the opening number.

First, it uses the opening to set up the typical old-time vaudeville show as a storytelling device. Every scene thereafter resembles, in some ways, an act in a vaudeville show. And each is announced by a title card propped on an easel on either side of the stage, just as would have been the case in a real vaudeville house. So there's a concept that justifies the episodic structure and helps set the style of the evening. Second, the authors use the opening melody as one of a series of musical and lyric motifs that evolve but always remain recognizable. They recur just often enough to keep us in thrall to the story. Without realizing it, we come to depend upon them to reinforce time, place, and emotion. These include a powerfully dark, driving piece of music that is accompanied by Rose's assertion, "*I had a dream*," the self-motivating, self-deluding reminder that she must, at all costs, stay in pursuit. It also includes the terrible corny vaudeville act that Madame Rose keeps trying to redress and reinvent without ever really changing it significantly—a mishmash of patriotism, sentimentality, and showbiz. At the center of that number is the piece of music that serves as *Gypsy*'s opening, "May We Entertain You," which later becomes "Let Me Entertain You." Its simplicity is deceptive; the phrase "Let me entertain you" holds no special cleverness on its own but means one thing when sung by an overeager child of seven and something else entirely when worked over by a dazzling stripper in her twenties. The show is now so famous that it's hard to appreciate the shock that must have rippled through the audience late in the second act when Louise, now Gypsy Rose Lee, cannibalizes her baby sister's idiotic theme song and turns it into an irresistible siren's call of sex and sin.

As opening numbers go, *Gypsy*'s does the most with the least. The song, fully integrated into the scene that surrounds it, sets up a vanished world, introduces us to the key relationships in the piece, sets up a stake, hints at the themes of neurotic family ties and their consequences, makes clear the storytelling concept of a vaudeville show, and brings onstage a hugely larger-than-life character whose possibly insane ambitions will power the evening. Five minutes into it, we're dying to know everything that will happen next. And, indeed, what happens next is demonstrated by the song itself, which keeps morphing into something stranger and more powerful as the evening works its way home.

Sondheim and Laurents had their first hit with *West Side Story*, which opened in 1957. *Gypsy* followed in 1959. Meredith Willson's *The Music Man* opened right after the former, and it was still running when the latter closed. *West Side* and *Gypsy* made people think and empathize. *The Music Man* just made them feel good; quite naturally, it ran longer than the two Laurents-Sondheim shows combined. But let's not be smug about its popularity. It's a terrific piece of work and has a brilliant, unique opening number.

Most every musical theater fan thinks this opening number, named "Rock Island" for the railroad on which it takes place, is about a train. And in one way, it is. Meredith Willson, who had been a piccolo player in John Philip Sousa's famous marching band, wanted to write a knowing but nostalgic love letter to the lost world of his youth in small-town Iowa. As befits a former marching band musician, his writing gifts had a lot to do with rhythm. His music starts with percussion, and his show starts with a percussive idea: the curtain goes up on a railroad car sitting on the tracks one stop away from River City, as a conductor announces its imminent departure. There is no music, just the accelerating rhythm of the passengers' voices jabbering as the train lurches forward from a stop and gradually reaches cruising speed, powered by the chuffing steam locomotive. Right away we are located, happy to be in the presence of this postcard world, and delighted by a conversation that sounds perilously close to nonsensical. The word "cash" serves all the necessary purposes of sounding like a train, with its *click-clack* beginning and *sh* at the end that gives us the steam escaping.

The car is populated by salesmen whom we'll never see again, and the conceit of the number is that simply by eavesdropping on their gossip—small-minded, self-interested bickering—we will learn everything we need to know about what this show is going to be. In some senses, the number is just an exercise in onomatopoeia. The opening lines go like this:

> *Cash for the merchandise, cash for the button hooks*
> *Cash for the cotton goods, cash for the hard goods*

This gets the train going, and then it speeds up to the rattling tempo of a skeptical salesman asking

> *Look, whatayatalk. Whatayatalk, whatayatalk, whatayatalk,*
> *whatayatalk?*

But the salesmen in question aren't just rhythm; they're philosophy and politics in motion. As the number progresses, quickening in tempo and delighting in its own ability to make meaning out of sound, we learn a lot. These men are frightened: frightened of change and frightened of time passing them by. We're in a world that is lurching scarily toward modernity, away from safe, old-fashioned values into a new America of mass production and homogeneity. Like *Gypsy*, *The Music Man* is about a world in transition and the instability that ensues.

> *Why it's the Model T Ford made the trouble,*
> *Made the people wanna go, wanna get, wanna get up and go . . .*

*Who's gonna patronize a little bitty two by four kinda store
anymore?*

The salesmen are virtually in mourning for the passing of their own time and place:

*Gone with the hogshead cask and demijohn, gone with the sugar
barrel, pickle barrel, milk pan, gone with the tub and the pail
and the tierce*

By this time we're getting quite a picture. The early twentieth-century imagery of Norman Rockwell's America is everywhere. (Even in 1957, when the show opened, it's doubtful that anyone on Broadway could have told you what a tierce was—it's a wine cask holding forty-two gallons.) But audiences, most of whom had never seen a Model T or a cracker barrel in their lives, were feeling quite stricken by the loss, and quite charmed. This was going to be a wonderful evening. The world of the show was as attractive as an old magazine cover, at least from a distance; its rhythmic technique was irresistible. Best of all, modern theatergoers didn't really share the salesmen's concerns. The automobile, not to mention the Uneeda Biscuit, which also comes in for a skeptical going-over in the number, were by now fixtures of our daily existence; they made things better, not worse. It just gave us pleasure to visit a place where old-fashioned people found such everyday things threatening to their very way of life. And it told us, without saying so explicitly, that *The Music Man* was going to be about conservative small-town life challenged by newer, less reliable values. We didn't know exactly how that was going to happen, but we sensed it, and the number was only 70 percent done. In the last 30 percent, Willson takes care of the rest of the job:

**2ND SALESMAN**

*Ever meet a fellow by the name of Hill?*

**1ST SALESMAN**

*Hill?*

The name is unfamiliar to all of them, which, of course, makes it stand out for us. Not only have none of them heard of Professor Harold Hill, but they have the deepest contempt for his chosen line of goods once they hear that he's a "music man."

### 1ST SALESMAN

*Well, I don't know much about bands but I do know you can't make a living selling big trombones, no sir. Mandolin picks, perhaps and here and there a Jew's harp . . .*

### 2ND SALESMAN

*No, the fellow sells bands, boys' bands. I don't know how he does it but he lives like a king . . .*

By this point the train has slowed (the repeated "yessir, yessir" imitating the sound of air brakes), and it comes to a halt just in time for the one salesman who has been sitting silently with his back to us since the curtain went up to rise and jump off in River City, letting the audience see the legend emblazoned on his sample case: Professor Harold Hill.

So: in an unstable, changing America, a charismatic charlatan salesman has hopped off a train in a hidebound Iowa town hoping to fleece the locals by selling band instruments. Do we need to know anything more? Certainly not, and the miracle is, we don't even know how we learned it. We thought we were listening to a train.

Peter Stone, the Tony-winning book writer of *1776* and *The Will Rogers Follies*, once said, "If you want the audience to really hear something, don't put it in a lyric." He was, in some sense, protecting his turf as a book writer, but it's not generally bad advice. The word "song" derives from the French *chanson*, which shares a root with "enchantment." Melodies put our brains in a different place, where we are likely to be emotionally engaged and logically distracted. But "Rock Island" has no melody, so we're better able to focus on the words. Willson's lyric repeats Harold Hill's last name nine times in a row, as if anticipating Stone's advice. We pay attention. Somehow, in the course of this wonderful bit of doggerel, we hear just what we need to.

André Bishop, Lincoln Center Theater's artistic director, began his career running Playwrights Horizons, which was dedicated to discovering and producing important new writers. Bishop said in an interview that every young playwright has a play in him that could be called *The House I Grew Up In*. In this sense, *The Music Man*, which could have been called *The Town I Grew Up In*, is a close cousin of works as diverse as *The Glass Menagerie* and *Ah, Wilderness!* Bishop went on to point out that a successful treatment of this subject didn't necessarily mean that the writer in question had a great career ahead of him. That point would be proved—or not—only by the plays that followed, when the autobiographical traumas of childhood had already been harvested. In Meredith Willson's case, his success with *The Music Man* was never to be repeated, or even approached. He was one of the infrequent one-hit wonders of the Broadway musical.

In contrast, Jerry Bock, Sheldon Harnick, and Joseph Stein were well beyond *The House I Grew Up In* when they turned their attention to the Sholem Aleichem short stories that became *Fiddler on the Roof*. They'd matched inspiration to craftsmanship a number of times and were at the top of their games. *Fiddler* was more or less *The Village Our Grandparents Grew Up In*, and it was, like *The Music Man*, a labor of love about yet another world in transition. But it didn't come together until a new opening number called "Tradition" gave it stature and made sense of the initial impulse to begin writing it in the first place.

Sheldon Harnick, who wrote the lyrics, tells of the frustration of early meetings with Jerome Robbins, who was slated to direct and choreograph.

"Jerry kept saying to us, 'What's it about? What's it about?' And Joe Stein would try to patiently explain that it was about a milkman with five daughters who needed to get married, and Jerry would stop us and say, 'No! I mean what's it *about*?'"

Robbins was talking about the show's subject, and Stein was describing its plot, which was, at bottom, a domestic story about family life. They are entirely different things, though the latter must serve the former. Finally, as they worked through the possible reasons that the show should exist at all, they hit upon the underlying idea. *Fiddler* is about the destruction of a culture and its hoped-for transmutation to a new place. The "little village" of Anatevka is one of many shtetls, tiny, poor, but self-sufficient Jewish communities within the larger, largely hostile country Russia. And what happens in the course of the show is that Anatevka is dismantled piece by piece, despite the best efforts of its citizens to hold it together. Once again, the world is in transition, and our little corner of it is threatened with oblivion (although Anatevka and River City, Iowa, are about as different as two little self-sufficient worlds could be). But this was a favorite theme of Robbins's—most of his serious shows in some way confront the clash of cultures and the cost of the outcome. *West Side Story* deals with the arrival of Puerto Rican immigrants on American soil and how the world shifts. *Gypsy* is concerned with the death of vaudeville as show business marches on. Even *The King and I*, which Robbins choreographed but didn't direct, reaches the height of its powers when dealing with what it means that the British have arrived in Siam, bringing a threatening modern world to a settled ancient one.

*Fiddler on the Roof*, which was to be Robbins's last Broadway show, takes the theme to its logical conclusion. Anatevka is destroyed and the diaspora moves on, to Chicago, New York, and the beginnings of Israel, where the culture will flower in different ways, carrying its ideas on its back along with its conflicts and its traditions.

"Finally," the show's producer, Hal Prince, recalled, "when Jerry Robbins asked, 'What's it about?' for the hundredth time, Sheldon snapped back, 'It's about tradition! What else can it be about?' And Jerry said, 'Okay—write a song called "Tradition."'"

Tradition, in the end, was the best way that the authors could think of to express what kept the people of Anatevka secure enough to stay alive and define themselves for as long as they did. In the course of their show, traditions crumble from within, as Tevye's daughters take marital decisions into their own hands. The first marries for love, rejecting the tradition of arranged matches. The second binds herself to political radicalism, leaving the village behind to be with her imprisoned husband and betraying the tradition of the nuclear family. The third falls in love with a non-Jew, tearing asunder the last bit of the fabric of homogeneity left in the community. And just as the internal traditions are breaking down, the larger world is moving in to wipe this little village off the map. The Russians begin systematically expelling the Jews, so that by the final curtain, the stage will be devoid of virtually everything. Where once there was a thriving community held together by the integrity of a carefully defined way of life, now there is only empty space.

This idea is so clear and so moving that it left the authors with a great challenge: how to give stature at the opening moment to a story that had once been a domestic comedy/drama but that had somehow morphed into a grand landscape of humanity confronting the end of an era. The answer came in two pieces. First, someone recalled Marc Chagall's 1913 painting *The Fiddler*, which depicts a Jewish peasant with a violin perched insecurely on a rooftop. This seemed like a more than apt metaphor. The show's long-debated title became *Fiddler on the Roof*. Second, Bock and Harnick distilled all the discussions that had brought them this far into the number Robbins asked for—"Tradition." It is, in some ways, not so very different from "Comedy Tonight," in that our leading player (again Zero Mostel) steps out onto an empty stage and tells us what kind of an evening it's going to be. Then he sings. Then he introduces the various factions of this little society—papas, mamas, sons, daughters—and *they* sing. In a stroke of great theatricality, each has a different melody to sing, but all four melodies fit together so that they can be sung at once, which makes the music itself a metaphor: the strength to survive derives from the weave; all together, these simple strands make a beautiful, complex, and enduring sound, far stronger than any one of them might create alone. In its finished form, "Tradition" gives voice to virtually everyone in Anatevka: the beggar, the rabbi, the matchmaker, the businessman—it's a community portrait. It describes good times and bad, harmony and dispute, but, like "Comedy Tonight," it leaves the plot for later. It parts company with "Comedy Tonight" in one important way, however: Prologus, the narrator in *Forum*, tells us what to expect, and then the show delivers exactly as promised. Tevye explains the world of Anatevka and tells us what to expect, but he hasn't the foresight to see the oncoming end of things. He is brought up short by it just as we are. At the beginning, he knows some things about fragility, but hardly everything. *Fiddler* has more up its sleeve than "Tradition" can describe, and the ensuing action plays *against* what the number tells us. Tradition is everything, it says. Then the show demonstrates that it's not enough. But the number sets up such a clear and profound idea in such an exciting way that what was once domestic never seems less than epic. And Tevye, the beleaguered milkman with the nagging wife, becomes an iconic figure, who, like Chagall's fiddler, will live forever.

The number also made it necessary for the rest of *Fiddler* to respect the size of the idea. It became of central importance to demonstrate and celebrate the traditions in question: the Friday-night Sabbath prayer, the bottle dance at the wedding ceremony, each an explicit expression of implicit strength and faith. The authors made sure that throughout the evening, even the most domestic events carried larger implications and fit within the weave. The opening number forced their hand.

Anatevka wasn't the only world in transition on Broadway in 1964. The street itself was beginning to crack open as a new generation of theater-makers took matters into their own hands, responding to the end of postwar self-satisfaction and the beginning of a new age of anxiety—the '60s.

Hal Prince, who produced *Fiddler*, had turned to directing, and after a few faltering steps, he helmed the innovatively experimental hit *Cabaret* in 1966. "Willkommen," its iconic opening, owed a lot, structurally, at least, to "Tradition" and to "Comedy Tonight," but the show—an exploration of Weimar Germany—had a kind of presentational, neo-Brechtian quality that made it an effective transition from the well-established musical play to a newer kind of concept musical. It was presented as a series of seedy cabaret acts, a more stark, sexualized, and theatrical version of what *Gypsy* had done with its vaudeville sketches.

Prince learned from the masters whose work he had previously produced, chiefly from Abbott and Robbins. Then he and Stephen Sondheim began turning out consistently fascinating, highly conceptualized collaborations, beginning with 1970's *Company*. There's plenty more to be said about these shows, which, more than any others since *Oklahoma*, revolutionized the form. But it's worth a word or two here on *Company*'s opening, which combines both genres—giving voice to the full ensemble of the show as well as to its leading character as a soloist. The time is the present (that would be 1970); the place is New York, whose heartbeat, one character says, is "a busy signal"—this was before call-waiting was invented. And, indeed, the opening number pulses like a busy signal. We meet a series of married couples spouting social niceties like *"Bobby, come on over for dinner!"* and we come to quickly understand that all these couples are, for some reason, obsessively interested in the life of someone named Bobby, whom we haven't met yet. When he bursts onto the scene, singing, *"Phone rings, door chimes, in comes company!"* we may be puzzled—he seems like an ordinary fellow, maybe an adman or a business executive, but that's about it. And what he's telling us is a big distance from "there's a bright golden haze on the meadow," though, interestingly enough, it's just as redolent of his time and place. And that's the point. He's nobody special. He's the focus of a lot of needy people who project their hopes, dreams, fears, and anxieties on a blank slate of a man who, whatever else he does, appreciates the attention.

The number is so propulsive, and it attacks the audience with so much nervous energy, that we also come to understand that this is a show about a Manhattan gripped by its careening—if sometimes pointless—pace. There's no time to stop and think; there's no time for anything except "come on over for dinner." The show was audacious in many ways: it was virtually plotless, organized around an idea instead of a story, written so that the songs commented on the action but were not exactly a part of it. But its greatest contribution to the development of musical theater in America may simply have been that it was gimlet-eyed: it didn't promise a happy ending. It had propulsive energy but no simple joys. It used musical theater conventions for ironic commentary, not simply to gin up the audience. It cast a jaundiced eye on urban Americans and found them wanting. There was no propaganda about our can-do, communitarian population. In many ways, it signaled the end of the Rodgers and Hammerstein ethos, though it was shot through with the kind of craftsmanship R&H most admired. And the opening number laid all this out by giving us the familiar huge buildup to the protagonist, but lacing it with irony and an energy that was more neurotic than positive. Then it dared to introduce its hero and hand him the floor, just for him to reveal that he was only Bobby, with nothing much to say. By the end of the evening, the hollow man found desire, and the audience found itself in shock, in a wonderful and new way.

The Sondheim-Prince musicals drove the decade artistically but not commercially. That was left to others with less upsetting ideas about life but just as much theatrical savvy. In 1975, the era turned, with the arrival of *A Chorus Line*, conceived and directed by Michael Bennett, who, as a choreographer, had been Prince and Sondheim's junior partner on *Company* and served as codirector of *Follies*. *A Chorus Line* presented a fascinating challenge: a twenty-five-headed protagonist. The hero of this story of a Broadway audition is everyone who came to try out.

Given the impossibility of individually introducing each of the eager young applicants for a job in a Broadway chorus, Bennett chose to go in the opposite direction. He exploited the disorientation. The curtain went up on all of them, mid-audition, fighting to learn a dance combination as quickly as it was hurled at them by a taskmaster choreographer. The performers and the audience were in the same boat, trying to process information at a pace beyond the normal capabilities of the human brain. It was audacious. Bennett had everyone in trouble—on purpose. He seemed to have complete faith that kinetic energy alone, expertly deployed, would grip the attention of an audience even if no one could figure out exactly what was going on. On this occasion, he was right.

His impulse reflected more than just a theatrical notion; Bennett was young, and he understood that the human brain seemed to be evolving. Experimental recreational drugs, loud rock, quick cuts in the movies, and the scattershot delivery of bits of information on children's shows like *Sesame Street* had produced a cumulative effect—people were receiving information in a different way than they had a generation before. Fragmentary storytelling was not only acceptable, it was a preferred method of communication. Hence, "I Hope I Get It," the galvanizing opening number of *A Chorus Line*.

The number is both simple and complicated. It begins with only a piano as twenty-four dancers are drilled in the dance combo; the music is a driving vamp, more redolent of rock than of Broadway (the music is by Marvin Hamlisch). The dancers struggle, pull themselves together, and meet the challenge as the choreographer shouts out information about the next steps and then asks them to take it from the top with the ubiquitous cry "5-6-7-8." The orchestra blares its entrance, the lights bump up, and we're in the middle of what many theatergoers consider one of the most glamorous settings there is—a dingy rehearsal hall filled with writhing bodies in tights and T-shirts. The excitement is palpable, and the information is, amazingly enough, clear. We're at a competitive audition for a Broadway musical with a bunch of performers who are wonderful to watch, whose grace and energy light up the room.

We want to watch every single one, but almost immediately, we're told that they're not all created equal:

> *God I hope I get it.*
> *I hope I get it.*
> *How many people does he need? . . .*
> *I really need this job.*
> *Please, God, I need this job.*
> *I've got to get this job.*

Not everyone will be chosen, and all of them desperately need a job. The evening is already clear. What needs amplifying is not the circumstance—we already know what the show is going to be about—but the emotional landscape. Who are these people? What drives them? What world do they live in? Why should we care? Bennett gets right to work.

The choreographer teaches a ballet combination to a bit of waltz music (the introduction of new music continues to vary the information that is coming at the audience), and the dancers try to execute it. Then they react to their own work:

> *God, I really blew it!*
> *I really blew it!*

*How could I do a thing like that?*
*Now I'll never make it!*
*He doesn't like the way I look.*
*He doesn't like the way I dance.*
*He doesn't like the way I . . .*

Not surprisingly, we're in the hands of some insecure people—this is the theater, after all. The question we're being asked is: Do we see them as individuals or, as the title suggests, as a chorus line? And that's the question the show keeps trying to dig deeper into—that's the subject. The stake is the job. The plot, such as it is, is about whether one of the older auditionees can get back into the chorus after having briefly been a headliner. It's the weakest element of the evening, especially tied, as it is, to her former relationship with the dictatorial director. And, as is typical, it isn't hinted at in the opening. Instead, Bennett keeps after the general sense of ego, anxiety, and economic precariousness of the whole line. After a third combination, the dancers have changed their minds about their performances:

*God, I think I've got it.*
*I think I've got it.*
*I knew he liked me all the time . . .*
*I've got to get this job!*

In other words, we're listening to a stream-of-consciousness internal monologue, musicalized—people berating themselves, then pumping themselves up, internal vulnerability masked by external self-confidence. And, of course, that's what makes them irresistible characters, even if we don't know much about them individually. Bennett drives the number to a fever pitch in a way that suggests a huge climax, but then, as the audience is cheering, he pulls the rug out from under it in a wonderful way. To a series of repeating stings, each dancer places an eight-by-ten glossy in front of his or her face. Now we're looking at the sales tool, not the person. And then, one performer slowly pulls it away, shows his face, and, as the music turns soft and slow for the first time, asks:

*Who am I anyway?*
*Am I my résumé?*
*That is a picture*
*Of a person I don't know . . .*
*Oh, God, I need this show.*

And, suddenly, we know we're going to get to know them.

Because the number is flashy and comes at the audience in a torrent of sound and fury, the ideas in it need to be simple, clear, and telling. And they are. A group of hungry young dancers has shown up to audition for a musical, and they won't all be hired. We in the audience have never stopped to consider who they might be, how hard they must work, how insecure their lives are both economically and emotionally, and tonight we are going to be shown what they pay for our pleasure. So do we want to stay and learn? You bet we do.

The number is in four sections, each with only a single purpose: the work, the need for the job, the brave insecurity of showing oneself to the world, and the introspective question: Who am I, and what should I try to be? It's almost impossible not to be touched by Bennett's larger question, because he himself had been an individual dancer in the line, giving up his individuality to a choreographer's vision. Only after that did he graduate to being the man who shapes the line, who expresses his vision by removing the individuality of others.

It's striking that in discussing *A Chorus Line*, virtually everyone describes it as Michael Bennett's show. There was, after all, a composer, a lyricist, and a book writer: Marvin Hamlisch, Edward Kleban, and James Kirkwood. And all of them did capable jobs. But this show, more than any other, ratified a fact of life on Broadway: the creative control center had moved from the authors to the directors. And in some ways the center has never really moved back (although one could argue that it should). Robbins and Abbott and Gower Champion undoubtedly influenced the shows they worked on as much as any directors ever have. But by the mid-'70s, even Broadway was being infected by the auteur theory, and directors—Bennett, Hal Prince, and Tommy Tune—became very glamorous. Only Stephen Sondheim matched their allure, until the 1980s, that is, when the composer Andrew Lloyd Webber, the director Trevor Nunn, and the producer Cameron Mackintosh collaborated on a series of British megamusicals and each of their names became its own brand.

*A Chorus Line* marked the passage of time in another way that suggests Bennett uniquely understood audiences' minds in the mid-'70s. Traditionally, shows began with opening numbers, after which they introduced the principal desire of the hero in something industry people call the "I Want" song—a solo number in which the protagonist tells the audience what's driving her or him. That spot, usually the second song in the show, is the subject of the next chapter of this book. But *A Chorus Line* couldn't wait. Its opening number *is* its I Want song. And it also announces the plot. It triples the usual pace of things and gets us right to the point: these are the heroes and heroines of our evening. They're at an audition. They want—nay, must—have this job. Ready, set, go.

The movement-driven concept musical had replaced the musical play, and the song plot of a typical Broadway show had begun to telescope inward as the audience—nourished on a new kind of music, armed with new high-speed receptors, and living in a brave new world—demanded unabated acceleration. Speed, pulse, action, and texture were all layered together, testing the limits of sensory overload. It was a new kind of opening number, and musicals will always need to begin somewhere. But just like that, with one supercharged musical smash, the Golden Age of classic Broadway had vanished into the mist, like Brigadoon itself.

# 3. The Wizard and I

*The "I Want" Song*

**A**ll I want," explains the wet, bedraggled, all but homeless Cockney flower girl Eliza Doolittle, "*is a room somewhere, far away from the cold night air.*"

It's a simple enough desire, touching in its clarity and modesty, but apparently unachievable. And to whom does Eliza turn for these simple creature comforts? To a bilious, obnoxiously witty upper-class bachelor who has his own desires—such powerful ones that they have left him permanently on edge.

"Why can't the English teach their children how to speak?!" he bellows after hearing her mewling on the curb. Eliza, of course, can't speak proper English, and Henry Higgins isn't likely to provide for her simple creature comforts until she learns, and maybe not even then. Her "want" seems warm, human, and tender. His seems arbitrary, snobbish, and intolerant. But, of course, it's not that simple. Higgins, the linguist, disdains the lower-class butchers of language as barbarians. In his own semi-blind, hopelessly elitist way, he is seeking a civilized, respectful society. Eliza wants a couple of chocolates before a good night's sleep in a warm bed. In some ways that's also the mark of a civilized, respectful society, but expressed from such an opposite point of view that there seems no real likelihood that the two of them will ever see things the same way—a way that might lead to, say, kissing. How they manage to get together, then, is likely to be a pretty good story. Why? Not simply because their desires are the same while appearing to be opposite, but because they are so clearly expressed. Considering its deliberate pace and elegant, stately approach, *My Fair Lady* has a surprising amount of energy, because both of its protagonists are driven by a wild passion to get something they don't have, something that seems perpetually out of reach.

There are no inviolable rules for the creation of enduring, popular musicals, possibly except this one. The hero has to want something that's hard to get, and go after it come what may. The sooner the audience understands this, the better. The I Want song is the mark of an active hero. It may seem obvious, and it may actually be obvious. A lot of these songs come right out and say it: "I want to be a producer," "All I need is one good break," "I'm the greatest star, but no one knows it," "On the other side of the tracks, that's where I'm longing to be." Subtlety has never been a hallmark of the American musical. And, to be fair, in some exceptional cases it's not a song at all but a dialogue scene. Still, the I Want song is a convention. In the case of *My Fair Lady*, Eliza's "want" is obvious, and Higgins's, for all his bluster, is subtler; he never actually says, "This is what I want," he merely complains that he doesn't have it, while making us laugh at his furious, blind belief in its value. But his meaning is clear, and that's half the battle. The other half is this: for a show to be worth our time and money, we probably have to hope our heroes get what they want, and it has to be damned hard to get. Is the goal something we care about? Or is it too trivial, selfish, or muddled for us to get involved? Is the protagonist up to the task? Is it too easily achieved? If the hero doesn't have to work very hard, we won't care very much. In the case of *My Fair Lady*, Alan Jay Lerner and Frederick Loewe had the assistance of George Bernard Shaw, who, in the original play, *Pygmalion*, draws the characters and the conflict with brilliant clarity. But Lerner and Loewe managed to crystallize the play musically and transform it from a comedy of ideas with a bit of an implied romance into a glamorous romance with a number of provocative ideas. It was a titanic hit.

Four years later, they tried again with *Camelot*, and, despite the pedigree of the source material (T. H. White's novel *The Once and Future King*) and virtually the same creative team, they stumbled badly. *Camelot* managed to become a hit in its day despite itself, in part through its identification with the idealism of the all-too-brief JFK era, but it isn't well remembered. One of the principal reasons is that it gets off on the wrong two feet. Its matched pair of I Want songs is even cleverer in some ways than the pair in *My Fair Lady*. They're well written, witty, even memorable. But together, they work principally to alienate the audience from the people singing them.

When the curtain goes up on King Arthur, he is a young, callow man waiting for his bride to arrive in Camelot, a bride he's never met and doesn't want to. While he waits, he frets. In "I Wonder What the King Is Doing Tonight," he lets us know what he wants—to be left alone. To not get married. To avoid facing the inevitability of kingship, or even responsible adulthood. It's kind of charming in a way that a king is so terrified, and the lyric is clever and funny. But do we really find this man worth our time? While we're wondering, who should appear but the prospective bride, the elegant, overbred, and deeply entitled Guinevere. *"Where are the simple joys of maidenhood?"* she wonders, as she's about to be married off. She doesn't want to get married any more than Arthur. She wants to be admired and pampered, and she wants men to fall not simply at her feet but also into their graves, on her behalf. It's not that "The Simple Joys of Maidenhood" is a bad song, exactly. It's just a song that reveals a character we don't want to spend time with. If the future queen Guinevere's greatest desire in life is expressed when she asks, petulantly, *"Shall kith not kill their kin for me? Oh where are the simple joys of maidenhood?"* we're pretty much distanced from her point of view. The song is clever but ultimately poisonous. Unlike with Eliza and Higgins, we don't care if these people get what they want. They want to be left alone, and our instinct is to oblige them and go get a drink. We're worried they're going to bore us with their clever narcissism, and on that point they deliver.

The impulse behind these songs was undoubtedly a good one: take two immature young people with too much power and too little knowledge of the world, satirize their shallowness, and then, in the play itself, chronicle their coming of age, their understanding of the world as they inexorably experience it. As they acquire the scars of living, and strive—once again, as in *My Fair Lady*—to civilize the world, we'll come to appreciate how far they've traveled, how noble their ultimate desires really are. *Camelot* has a great subject. It chronicles the mythical attempt by a young royal family to create a civil society in a world that has so far been dominated by killing, conquest, lust, and greed. It's no wonder that the young President Kennedy and his spectacular first lady were enchanted by it. It spoke to everything in the president's program that was directed at humanizing American society, from the civil rights movement at home to the quest for democracy abroad. It was easy to fall in love with the show's ideas but harder to like the show itself. To make it work, the audience had to get attached at the beginning. You have to get on the ride when the ride starts. In the case of *Camelot*, Lerner and Loewe depended on cleverness, not on our actual sympathy. The audience almost reattaches when Arthur sings to Guinevere of Camelot itself, in the charming second number of the show— the title song. But in some sense, it's already too late. And that is *Camelot*'s curse—it keeps wobbling back and forth between sin and redemption. Audiences admired its brains and ambition, and the loftiness of its goals, but it made them irritable, impressed, and drowsy by turns.

Why do we need these I Want songs at all? Not all forms of storytelling require this early expression of passionate desire. Lots of successful movies and novels concern themselves with protagonists who think they're perfectly happy the way they are. It may take them a very long time to comprehend their discontent. *Clueless*, the blockbuster 1995 movie based on Jane Austen's 1815 novel *Emma*, underwent a number of attempts to convert it into a musical. To one producer after another, it seemed like a natural. But every incarnation was ultimately doomed by this problem: the heroine starts out happy. Her ignorance of the world is so comically complete that she's utterly content in her upper-class Beverly Hills world. This wasn't a problem for the film, which had energetic fun satirizing the morals and mores of overprivileged teens living in an ultracomfortable, technologically miraculous, but emotionally empty bubble. And the novel has stood the test of time, heaven knows. But the musical simply couldn't be brought to life.

Self-satisfied protagonists aren't the only challenge. There is a whole other class of stories that stubbornly resist adaptation. These concern the Everyman thrust into a situation he's not equipped to handle—a nice enough fellow who makes an inadvertent wrong turn into adventureland. I struggled mightily and futilely for ten years on one of these—Jack Finney's wonderful time-travel novel *Time and Again*. In it, a vaguely discontented but unmotivated adman is thrust back into the nineteenth century, where he finally engages with the world in an era a hundred years before his own. The novel is a fascinating mystery-romance full of period detail and surprising plot developments. The front end of it is kept alive by the common device of having the protagonist, Simon Morley, narrating it and continually promising magical events to come. His constant unpreparedness for what is about to happen to him is entertainment enough, because he's the one describing it to us. But without his narrative voice, we were sunk. No matter what my collaborators and I did (I was the book writer), and despite a wonderful, sophisticated score, we couldn't interest anyone in the first half hour, and by then it was much too late. Watching an average Joe wander around New York worrying vaguely about whether he's wasting his life designing soap ads just doesn't motivate an audience on Broadway, and why should it?

In the first volume of his complete lyrics, Stephen Sondheim suggests a reason for this peculiar structural requirement that seems to drive—and be a necessity of—successful shows. "Farces are express trains," he writes. "Musicals are locals." They keep stopping for songs, dances, and set changes. If they're not powered energetically right from the start, the distractions take over completely, and the story gets lost, along with the audience. Novels can often survive on the strength of the author's voice alone, if it's strong enough. And we can read at whatever pace we choose, savoring the poetic, breezing through the expositional, taking control of the prose. In the theater, however, the show comes at the audience at the pace of the spoken (or sung) word. Someone has to be gathering up the audience to take them on the journey, right from the start. Hence, the I Want.

Of course, anything that comes this close to being a basic minimum requirement runs the risk of also becoming a cliché, and audiences are inevitably bored if they think they've heard it all before. What keeps these songs fresh? Unique characters, striking situations, and vividly drawn worlds.

Madame Rose in *Gypsy* wants to get her two little girls out of Seattle and into the big time—onto the Orpheum vaudeville circuit. Her father wants her to settle down and find a (fourth) husband. Rose isn't having any of that. In *Gypsy*'s second scene, she lets him have it:

> *Some people can be content,*
> *Playing bingo and paying rent—*
> *That's peachy for some people,*
> *For some*
> *Hum—*
> *Drum*
> *People to be,*
> *But some people ain't me!*
>
> *I had a dream,*
> *A wonderful dream, Poppa,*
> *All about June and the Orpheum Circuit—*
> *Gimme a chance and I know I can*
> *Work it.*
>
> *I had a dream,*
> *Just as real as can be, Poppa.*
> *There I was in Mr. Orpheum's office,*
> *And he was saying to me:*
> *"Rose!*
> *Get yourself some new orchestrations,*
> *New routines and red velvet curtains,*

*Get a feathered hat for the baby,*
*Photographs in front of the theatre,*
*Get an agent—and in jig time*
*You'll be being booked in the big time!"*

There's nothing generic about Rose. Her specific description of vaudeville defines her and teaches us some things we might not know. You can hear this woman's passion, her strange combination of savvy and naïveté about show business (she really believes there is a "Mr. Orpheum"), her thirst for life, and her contempt for everyday drudgery. You can also, subtly, hear the era in which she lives—feathered hats, bingo, words like "peachy" and "jig time."

Rose is impossible to miss, and that's part of the point of an I Want song. The stage may be full of people singing and dancing, but the I Want song tells the audience, *"Watch this one. This* is the important one. This is the one with the superhuman passion." We want our heroes to be somehow heroic.

At the beginning of *West Side Story*, we're introduced to two street gangs of young men—bristling with anger, hostility, clan loyalty, and the danger that goes with those things. They're the world of the play— an unending gang war for turf that has no real value—and we spend enough time with them to see how that world, defined by poverty, racism, and a grim lack of opportunity, is likely to crush their unbridled energy. They are youth, testosterone, and possibility, but with no outlet for it all, it's a toxic cocktail.

Then we travel to Doc's neighborhood drugstore, where we meet young Tony, who is patiently painting a sign for Doc. He's an artist of a sort—or at least a young man with artistic impulses—and his latest move has been to resign from his gang, the Jets. Why? "Something's Coming," he sings. He doesn't know what, but it's out there—something better. This is a hard kind of I Want song to write, because Tony doesn't actually know what he wants—he just knows that it's going to be superior to what he has, more valuable, more human, more poetic, some kind of trajectory away from hopelessness and toward a meaningful life. He has an inchoate desire, yet Leonard Bernstein's music and Stephen Sondheim's lyric make it feel specific and hugely important. Musically, the song pulses with possibility and trails off into dreams. Tony has a different rhythm than his erstwhile cohorts—more introspective, more complicated. The lyric matches this tone, as Tony sings of miracles that are right around the corner—or "cannonballing down through the sky." Tony believes in it, because he *has* to have it. And among the rabble that surrounds him onstage, with all their desires to crush each other, we know that this is the man we're supposed to watch. He's of more moment—he's better than his surroundings, though what's valuable about him is also what's vulnerable. He's the reason there's going to be a story: his escape—if any—will be difficult and by no means certain. But it will be worth watching the attempt.

Valuable and vulnerable also describes Lin-Manuel Miranda's Alexander Hamilton, who, almost half a century after Tony stepped away from his gang, also defined himself as an individual outside of his surroundings. But Hamilton is no Tony—he's the immigrant, the Shark, so to speak; he's arrogant, self-assured, and charismatic, which also makes him a natural target in the emerging world of American politics. Hamilton's I Want rap (it's not a conventional song) is called "My Shot," and it's a distant but recognizable descendant of "Something's Coming." Hamilton is trying to *join* a gang, not escape from one, but it's a gang of aspirants, revolutionaries with a new idea about a new country. They're going to fight a war to get it, and Hamilton is eager to fight a war. But unlike the rest of them, he lacks breeding, finesse, a common background. He's an outsider, and he's the one worth watching. Of course, each time he declares

> Hey, yo, I'm just like my country
> I'm young, scrappy and hungry
> And I'm not throwing away my shot . . .

we wince a bit, because in the end, what Hamilton does is throw away his shot, first figuratively, then literally, while Aaron Burr takes deadly aim and wipes out one of the great characters and intellects of early American history. "My Shot" happens in a context that we barely recognize as American musical theater—the actors are dressed in costumes that might have been preserved from a production of *1776*, but from the neck up they look like a motley gang of street-corner revolutionaries in the Bronx in 2015. And they sound like that too. Yet *Hamilton* presents an opening number that sets the style, the tone (unique as it is), and the point of view of the show perfectly (complete with the information that the hero will be dead at the final blackout) and then proceeds to "My Shot," secure that its insurgent style will only be helped by adhering to the classic niceties of getting a show off the ground.

If Tony is a descendant of *Carousel*'s Billy Bigelow—an earlier man with poetry locked away inside him and violence in his future—and Hamilton is his offspring many generations down the line, Seymour Krelborn, the meta-schlep at the center of *Little Shop of Horrors*, stands between them as the nephew or uncle they would probably both want to forget. *West Side*, *Little Shop*, and *Hamilton* all deal with a dangerous underbelly of the American landscape, in three wildly divergent tones. In *Little Shop*, Seymour lives in a cartoon version of *West Side Story*'s mean streets. Like the denizens of *West Side Story*, the characters in *Little Shop* occupy the slums—skid row, to be specific. And for the most part, they're acclimated to it. Racial disharmony and general dissatisfaction make up the daily diet, just as they do in *Hamilton*. In the show's weirdly cheerful-sounding opening number (irony and camp are hallmarks of the whole event), they describe their surroundings—the grime, the bums, the minimum-wage jobs, the overwhelming sense of hopelessness—until a spotlight picks up young Seymour, a clerk in an all but bankrupt flower shop. He sings of his orphanhood, his dependence on the misanthropic, intolerant owner of the shop, and his existential nightmare:

> *Poor!*
> *All my life I've always been poor.*
> *I keep asking God what I'm for*
> *And he tells me, "Gee, I'm not sure,*
> *Sweep that floor, kid!"*

The tone is as far from "Something's Coming" as one could get, but the problem is the same. Seymour doesn't have Tony's gift of poetry—in fact, he seems short on gifts altogether. But he's lovably direct, as a cartoon character should be. After making sure that we understand his circumstances, he turns directly to us, stops whining, and starts venting his passionate desire:

> Someone show me a way to get outta here
> 'Cause I constantly pray I'll get outta here
> Please won't somebody say I'll get outta here?
> Someone gimme my shot, or I'll rot here!

The tone is knowingly dopey, but the passion and the desire could not be clearer—or more real. It's the rock-and-roll version of "Something's Coming" minus the big dreams, and Seymour is begging, not promising. Little does he know what's about to come cannonballing down through the sky. And, of course, when his shot comes, he doesn't throw it away—with catastrophic consequences. Howard Ashman, who wrote the lyric for the composer Alan Menken's music, was a young man at the time—but one with an almost encyclopedic knowledge of musical comedy mechanics. He combined the opening number and I Want into one song, but his interlude for Seymour appropriately trumps the rest of the number and sets up the character and the arc of the show: Seymour's journey out of skid row and what he'll pay to escape.

The source material, Roger Corman's grade-Z horror film *Little Shop of Horrors*, is a mad rewrite of the Faust legend, in which Seymour sells his soul to the devil (in this case a giant man-eating Venus flytrap from outer space) to achieve his escape from the living hell of skid row. The original was a low-budget bit of cheesy nonsense, but that's part of what made it so ripe for musical adaptation: it had a unique bargain-basement tone, its own voice, and a cast-iron set of bones: Faust. Ashman and Menken used the fact that the film dated from the early '60s to inform the score, which became a series of early rock-and-roll pastiches. The show opened off Broadway in 1982 and set the world on fire in a small way.

Seymour's beloved, Audrey, also has a sensational I Want, and in some senses it's also a lift—in this case from Eliza Doolittle, who seems a remote musical theater cousin. Audrey, as poor, chilly, and hungry as Eliza, is under the thumb of a sadistic dentist whom she's dating, while Seymour loves her from afar—or at least from across the flower shop. Ashman and Menken update "Wouldn't It Be Loverly" by changing almost everything about it—the tone, the locale, the era—but leaving the desire the same. It's the early '60s in America, so Audrey expresses her pathetic I Want in a cockeyed paean to the lower-middle-class American dream in a song called "Somewhere That's Green." Eliza craves a room somewhere far away from the cold night air. So does Audrey—in Levittown:

> A matchbox of our own
> A fence of real chain link,
> A grill out on the patio
> Disposal in the sink
> A washer and a dryer and an ironing machine
> In a tract house that we share
> Somewhere that's green.

She's swallowed what she's read in magazines and seen on TV. She's Eliza in '60s cartoon drag, and like Eliza, she's turned to an unlikely hero—Seymour. There's not much chance he'll ever provide any of this. And then the plant intervenes, and off we go.

Other than Stephen Sondheim, Ashman was probably the greatest potential link between the Golden Age and the New Age, but where Sondheim's career took him to an expansion of the serious musical plays of Rodgers and Hammerstein, Ashman's impulses emulated the lighter, musical comedy men who provided merriment and disposable entertainment in the R&H era. He was a pop culture type. If Sondheim seems to be a descendant of *Carousel*, Ashman comes from the line of *Kiss Me, Kate* and *The Pajama Game*. After the off-Broadway triumph of *Little Shop* and a failed attempt to convert the film *Smile* into a musical (composed by Marvin Hamlisch), Ashman and Menken decamped for Hollywood and Disney Studios. Once there, they performed the great service of resurrecting the animated features unit, by writing the film that brought greatness back to G-rated Disney cartoons—*The Little Mermaid*.

Disney had not turned out a distinguished full-length animated feature in decades, and hadn't done a fairy tale in thirty years. Ashman and Menken applied the principles of the classic musical theater piece— complete with a typical I Want called "Part of Your World," the requisite comic production number ("Under the Sea"), a romantic ballad ("Kiss the Girl"), and the rest. The film was a classic '50s Broadway show reconceived in '80s animation. They next turned to *Beauty and the Beast*, which also followed a classic model, and was also a smash. But in the midst of transmuting Broadway's Golden Age to Disney animation, Howard Ashman died—one of the thousands of artists lost to the AIDS epidemic. He was forty.

Disney completed the film he was working on at the time of his death, the charming *Aladdin*. And Alan Menken remained the studio's most successful composer, writing several fine scores with other collaborators. But the Ashman-Menken touch really existed for only two and a half movies. With the exception of *The Lion King*, about which more later, and *Frozen*, currently on its way to Broadway, the studio hasn't reached those artistic heights in animation again.

A direct line can be drawn between *Little Shop* in 1982 and *Hairspray*, which opened almost exactly twenty years later, in 2002. They share a tone and a point of view, they're both based on camp cult movies, and they both have a lot more on their minds than their loopy styles would suggest. They also use their opening numbers in almost identical ways, and like a number of classic shows, they use their I Want (which is incorporated into the opening number) to do something diabolically subversive. Unlike the simpler if no less passionate desires that inform shows like *A Chorus Line* and *Gypsy*, the desire that drives these shows seems sufficient at the time but leads to a surprise. There is a deeper, greater desire hidden behind the first one, which allows the show's real subject to expand exponentially at the halfway mark without interrupting the antic spirit that grabs the audience in the first place. If you consider the initial desire as a hill to be climbed, the experience of these shows is like discovering that there's a hill behind the hill—and a more interesting hike in store than you might have imagined.

Tracy Turnblad, the heroine of *Hairspray*, has a simple desire, but one that's difficult for her to achieve: she wants to dance on the local Baltimore equivalent of *American Bandstand*, the ubiquitous TV show that featured "regular" teenagers dancing to the latest hit-parade rock-and-roll records in the late '50s and early '60s. Tracy has a problem, though: she's fat. The term "regular," in that day (and this), didn't include the latitude of having a fat girl on TV, especially not on a dance show. So Tracy has to fight for what she wants, and even though it seems like a trivial desire in one sense, in another, it's a fight for equality, for acceptance, for recognition that we may be created equal, but we may not look that way.

In *Hairspray*'s I Want moment, Tracy pleads for a chance to dance and makes it clear that her identity is defined—for her—by the fact that in those moments when she's moving to the beat, she's "a movie star." Of course, no one will let her onto *The Corny Collins Show*, *Hairspray*'s version of *American Bandstand*. Yet, halfway through the show's first act, she accomplishes her desire—she wins a place on the TV show. And *Hairspray* should be over right then. This is where the "hill behind the hill" starts to function. For in joining the cast of *The Corny Collins Show*, Tracy discovers that she's not the only one with a history of oppression. Once a month, the show features "Negro Day," when the black kids get to dance. But never with white kids, and only on that one day. Struck by the idea that this injustice has no appropriate place in American life, Tracy is transformed from a girl with a problem to a crusader for everyone's problems, and her need to dance is replaced by her much greater need to integrate television—and the world.

There's something thrilling about seeing a cloistered young person's consciousness raised in a way that redefines her life and her mission, and, even within the somewhat goofy confines of a show like *Hairspray* or *Little Shop*, it's moving—it turns a protagonist into a hero. It's what *Camelot* was trying to do, in fact. Seymour makes his bargain with the plant and then has to figure out what to do when the bill comes due. Tracy has to risk losing her parents, her new boyfriend, and maybe even her liberty to fulfill the dream she didn't even know she had when the curtain first went up.

The granddaddy of this structural form (in musicals) may be *My Fair Lady* itself. Shaw's irresistible combatants, Eliza and Henry Higgins, make a bargain with, apparently, no strings attached: he will teach her proper English, she will do her best to learn it, and if she succeeds, Higgins will win a bet. That's it. What neither can see is that this feat, if achieved, will inevitably transform them, and leave them on a ledge. Once Higgins has reinvented Eliza as a new person, what is he to do with her? Once she has entered his world on her own terms, how is she to return to the one she escaped? The original I Wants are suddenly forgotten and irrelevant. The problem is much bigger than anyone imagined. The second hill is spectacularly more interesting than the first, but the first was interesting enough to start us eagerly climbing.

The same thing happens in *The Producers*, in which the down-and-out Broadway producer Max Bialystock and his little mouse of an accountant, Leo Bloom, each sing a confident I Want song that defines the first hill: Max wants, needs, and must have a hit show—his reputation is in ruins. Leo wants simply to be a producer—of anything. His life as an unhappy cog in a CPA's office is killing his soul. What neither of them knows is that their monumental scheme—to produce the biggest flop in Broadway history and run off with the unspent money—will bring them what they are truly seeking: a friendship, the companionship of another human being. It's something neither has ever known. The original film of *The Producers*, like both *Little Shop* and *Hairspray*, was a cult favorite—a scattershot bit of craziness with a voice (Mel Brooks's borscht belt caterwaul, in this case) but very little structure and a chaotic third act that rides off the rails. The musical, on the other hand, was a huge popular success, in part because, while the film's voice was retained, its structure was retooled to chronicle Max and Leo's dawning realization that they need and love each other.

A more typical romance is introduced, as Max lusts for, but Leo falls in love with, the ridiculously overendowed Swedish bombshell they hire as a secretary. But the enduring relationship is between the two men, and the result is infinitely more satisfying than the film because it tells a human story all the way to the end. The first hill is about something concrete; the second is about something humane. And that trajectory makes sense. Even people who seem to care only about Broadway understand that human contact is more rewarding than a hit show. Or some of them do.

It's no coincidence that one of the collaborators on the book of both *The Producers* and *Hairspray* was Thomas Meehan, who had written the book for *Annie* back in the '70s and had an innate sense of musical theater storytelling. His view was that no matter how well disguised, musicals are usually far-flung rewrites of classic tales, one way or the other. After looking at an early draft of *Hairspray* to see if he'd be interested in joining the team, he said, "It's Cinderella. She wants to go to the ball but no one will invite her. And her family tries to stop her. She gets there anyway, meets the prince, but runs away from him. In the end, he catches her, and the worlds of the common people and royalty are joined together. It's worked before, God knows."

Of course, he was completely right, and though he was not responsible for a lot of the jokes in *Hairspray*, or the thematic idea of equality for all, he distilled the structure and drew a map.

*Annie*, it should be noted, is faultlessly built and also owes its structural impulses to a sturdy source, *Little Lord Fauntleroy*, from which it is lifted, at least in part. This isn't to take anything away from Tom Meehan—it's a most admirable theft, in fact, reconstituting a very Victorian tale into a uniquely American one. In an earlier era it would probably have been greeted with uncomplicated joy by critics and audiences alike. But it opened almost two years after *A Chorus Line* had redrawn the playing field, and insiders, especially, were reluctant to offer a full embrace, even while audiences were falling all over themselves.

"You may love *Annie*," one theater wag commented, "but you'll hate yourself in the morning."

The smart set couldn't stop it, however. Time has been good to the show, because structurally and emotionally it delivers. It's not just the famous little redhead and her scruffy dog, Sandy, that have kept the show in constant circulation. It's the power of myth and the skill of the telling.

*Annie* also features one of the most perfect I Want songs ever written—little orphan Annie's plea to her unknown parents, "Maybe." Who, in almost any audience, can resist a little mop-headed girl in a filthy orphanage in the depths of the Depression fantasizing about a real home life (somewhere that's green) with real parents?

> *Bet you he reads*
> *Bet you she sews*
> *Maybe she's made me a closet of clothes*
> *Maybe they're strict*
> *As straight as a line . . .*
> *Don't really care as long as they're mine!*
>
> *So maybe now this prayer's*
> *The last one of its kind . . .*
> *Won't you please come get your Baby . . .*
> *Maybe*

The song manages to capture not only her indomitable desire but also her ambivalence about whether she's ever going to be able to achieve it. She's strong and vulnerable at the same time (that's what that last "maybe" is doing there). So, of course, we start rooting hard—on page three. "Tomorrow" may be *Annie*'s immortal standard, but "Maybe" is its secret weapon. Charles Strouse's music and Martin Charnin's lyric both make a virtue of unsophisticated simplicity, appropriate to a little girl with no real education. The song makes no great claims as a work of art—it's only trying to be a foundation for the story. That it succeeds so completely is what elevates it to the realm of art, in spite of itself.

As the plot plays out, it takes the combined efforts of the richest man in the world and the president of the United States to help her solve her problem, but Annie remains determined, and she leads them, not the other way around. She's a model of the active hero, or in this case heroinette. Surely it is among the greatest American myths that in our country, even the busiest and the most powerful will stop what they're doing and help a poor orphan find her parents. In today's world, it's a lot more fairy tale than myth, alas, but it's one we're all too happy to be told, even now.

The theater critic Martin Gottfried once wrote, "Any show the audience likes is a good show."

This may seem an obvious tautology to everyday theatergoers, but it's heresy to a lot of critics and theater professionals. The theater page of *The New York Times* has waged many a campaign against shows it couldn't shut down. Having rendered a negative verdict, most critics find it unpleasant to see their opinions cheerfully disregarded by paying customers. It's a condemnation, they feel, of the taste of the theatergoing public, which should pay at least as much attention to the critic as to the play itself. There's nothing new about this—when Robert Benchley was covering Broadway for *Life* magazine back in the '20s, he ran a weekly blurb for the infuriatingly long-running comedy *Abie's Irish Rose* that read, "People laugh at this every night, which is why democracy can never work." Benchley was poking fun at himself, but generally critics really don't like audiences to disagree with them. It's embittering. Yet sometimes, and ever more frequently, it happens.

Before the Internet, demand pricing, social networks, and the many other sophisticated marketing plans that are now deployed to sell tickets to Broadway shows, the best sales tool producers had was a fistful of rave reviews. Generally, if the notices were bad, the show closed. But that's no longer true. Audiences aren't local anymore—at least not after the first couple of months of a run; most of them enter the theater never having seen the *Times* review or any of the others. They don't care what they're supposed to think, and this can be seen only as a good thing for both business and democracy, Benchley be damned. From a loftier perch, one might argue that discernment in most aesthetic matters is on the wane in the twenty-first century, but Broadway surely doesn't care about that—it's a business. And, as Tim Zagat said about eating out, "Most customers like most restaurants better than most critics do." The same is obviously true of the theater.

The year I started teaching at NYU, *Wicked* had just opened to largely negative and dismissive reviews, and my students didn't care for it any more than the critics did. But as time went by and the show established itself, first as a hit, then as a smash hit, then as an international phenomenon, each successive class's opinion rose accordingly. By now, twelve years into the run, the show has become a bona fide masterwork—and much admired by NYU students. And it's exactly the same show the critics and that first class slammed around back in 2003. I don't think it's because *Wicked* was ahead of its time.

*Wicked*, in any formal analysis, has structural issues. It struggles with the problem of compacting a long, sprawling novel into a form—musical theater—that is often at its best when it is tidy. Long novels are hard to adapt for the musical stage. The successful ones are rare, beginning with *Show Boat* back in 1927 and including *Oliver*, the megahit *Les Misérables*, and, in their day, *Camelot* and *Man of La Mancha*. More common are the novelistic adaptations that have been crushed under their own weight, from *Saratoga* to *Here's Where I Belong* to *Shōgun*. Succeed or fail, all these shows do their best to contain multitudes and travel through too much time. They tend to be long (the original production of *Les Miz* clocked in at well over three hours, as did *Show Boat*) and yet feel somehow incomplete and sketched in in certain places—as if a lot has been left out or quickly approximated, because it has. Big novels tend to tell their stories in incremental ways through dozens of characters and hundreds of incidents, and don't yield up their bounty easily in a form that typically depends on a few big, broad-stroke plot developments. *Wicked* is no exception. It opened out of town to bad reviews and was continually retooled on its way to New York, where the critics again dismissed it as murky and discursive, dark and overplotted. Yet over time, all of that has become legitimately irrelevant. Why?

It's easy to see why critical opinion was so cranky. In its prologue, the show tries to get off the ground beginning with a flashback from the Wicked Witch Elphaba's death to the day when she is conceived, and thence to the day when she arrives in prep school. The show isn't ten minutes old yet, and we've already been in three different decades and three different locations; we hardly have any idea why. Or where. Or when. The design is abstract enough to keep us guessing, and not necessarily in a good way. The story is told by the good witch, Glinda, but by the time we hit the midpoint of the act we've also had to keep track of a goat who is being hounded out of his teaching profession by anti-animal fascists, Elphaba's handicapped sister and her growing crush, a blooming friendship between Elphaba and Glinda, an increasing rivalry between them over an apparently worthless rich boy named Fiyero, and the motives of the headmistress of the school they attend, who is tutoring Elphaba in sorcery. And yet, despite all this plot material (endemic to big-novel adaptations) and *Wicked*'s occasional forays into explaining the sources of *The Wizard of Oz* (it is, after all, a prequel), audiences remain enchanted much of the time and happy to be tolerant of the rest. Part of the reason, I believe, is that it has an I Want moment that is so big and powerful, and a want that is so universal and recognizable, that audiences are willing, even eager, to struggle with a lot. And any show the audience likes is a good show.

What might it be, this universal desire, this thing that we'll latch on to fiercely because we all feel it? It is expressed by a green-skinned girl with some kind of undefined telekinetic powers. She's not much like us on the surface. But the surface is a metaphor. She's exactly like us on the inside—desperately afraid of the spectacle she's making of herself, convinced that she will be friendless and powerless for her whole life, bewildered by the casual cruelty of her peers, and always alone. She is, in some instinctively understandable way, the sum of all the insecurities felt by young people, perhaps especially when they first arrive at school, and perhaps especially girls. When the headmistress, noticing her apparent natural gift for sorcery, offers to take Elphaba under her wing and introduce her to the great Wizard of Oz, the dam breaks. Elphaba sings "The Wizard and I," about what glories might await her if the most powerful figure in Oz were to notice her. The song builds in intensity and performance opportunity well beyond the normal I Want, practically to the point of an "Everything's Coming Up Roses," which brings down the first-act curtain of *Gypsy*. The actress playing Elphaba (the role was originated by Idina Menzel, who won the Tony for it) can't help but pull out all the stops vocally and leave nothing unexpressed. It's a chance not simply to explain but also to dazzle. Elphaba's dream of being a person who matters, whose gifts are recognized, who has a place in the world, overwhelms everything around it. It's long, and loud, and, as my former boss Rocco Landesman once said in another context, "You can't get out of its way." Giving this much space and theatricality to an I Want song may seem unwise, because Elphaba appears to be shooting the works vocally at an awfully early point in the evening. But the first-act curtain will ice the cake by having her wailing an even bigger song while flying on a broomstick above the crowd. *Wicked* takes no chances, luckily for its audiences. And the composer-lyricist Stephen Schwartz is a past master at creating big power ballads that stay just on the right side of the barrier between theater and pop songs, which gives the songs a broad appeal to audiences and affords critics the opportunity to turn up their noses.

As befits *Wicked*'s overall style, "The Wizard and I" is discursive. It allows Elphaba to imagine the next stages of her life in some detail, including the ways she'll unshackle herself from all the pain that she's suffered as the ultimate outsider; shed her ugly-duckling exterior; and become a woman of substance. And millions of theatergoers want to make that journey.

Admittedly, we are now much more used to putting up with the cacophony of incidents that are featured in *Wicked* than we were back in the days of *My Fair Lady*. Our brains are much better at putting half-sorted events on hold and coming back to them later. We process information differently than our parents did. And our children are vastly ahead of us in this progression. What older audience members and many critics found wanting in *Wicked*'s structure, its storytelling, and its driving but sometimes melody-challenged score were not a problem for younger theatergoers. But *Wicked* has two other assets worth noting. It's a spectacular, and the special effects, the flying, and the quirky but grandly imaginative design scheme all serve to take the audience on a trip it won't soon forget. And it has a subject that is worth the trouble. Elphaba's lonely journey begins as a struggle for respect, set against a darkening world in which Oz is threatened by fascism. Her friend and ultimate rival Glinda is the ultimate in-crowd girl, blond, pretty, entitled, and thoughtless. The ways they struggle to come to terms with what the world has given them and what they must take from it by force may not be as clearly articulated as they could be, but simply wrestling with them at all is enough to engage us. It's no coincidence that the show's book was written by Winnie Holzman, creator of the iconic TV series *My So-Called Life*, in which a teenage Claire Danes struggled to figure out the world. *Wicked* has a grip on the most confusing parts of the passage from girl to woman, and it feels no need to deploy its points with the kind of great clarity that is admired by grown-ups. In some sense, confusion is its best friend. It's like a *Camelot*, but for teens and those of us who vividly remember the pain of adolescence. Like *Camelot*, it deals with big questions about what is civilizing and what it means to become a citizen of the world, but it looks at these questions through the lens of youth just beginning to grow up. And when Elphaba ultimately succumbs to wickedness, we're to understand that it was her inevitable fate, given the cruel vicissitudes of the world and the particular set of cards she was dealt at birth. It's the struggle that counts, says *Wicked*. "No One Mourns the Wicked" is the show's opening number, but by the end that's exactly what we do—mourn for Elphaba and the valiant battle she ultimately loses. It doesn't hurt that audiences enter with a fixed point of view about the Wicked Witch of the West and are then forced to question every assumption they've carried with them since their first encounter with the movie of *The Wizard of Oz*. That idea gets them in the door. But they stay because, in this spectacular, confounding, and sometimes wandering show, the I Want grabs them at the start and won't let them go.

# 4. If I Loved You

*Conditional Love Songs*

Back in the 1970s, when I was a struggling screenwriter (a struggle no more successful than Elphaba's, by the way, and a lot less interesting), a collaborator and I got hired to write a werewolf movie. It was to be directed (though it never got made) by the great cinematographer Michael Chapman, and, like most werewolf movies, it featured a love story at the center. When we turned in our first draft, Chapman came at us with a barrage of notes, one of which was about the first meeting between the young woman and the older man who would, in the course of the story, fall in love.

"This is awful," he said, though he may have used a stronger word. "If you want to understand how to write the first encounter between two future mates, there's a book that will tell you everything you need to know."

This was intriguing. These scenes are damned hard to write. What was this secret book, the key that would unlock one of the mysteries of screenwriting?

"It's called *The Courtship Habits of the Great Crested Grebe*," he said. We were, unsurprisingly, deflated. A dryly written ornithological monograph was hardly what we had hoped for. But it was only eighty pages long, so we read it. It told us everything we needed to know.

The great crested grebe is a lake bird, and all I really remember about the book today is that it detailed, painstakingly, the odd ritual of courtship that the male and female go through, which is baffling to the human eye but hard not to watch if you are lucky enough to get the chance—ungainly birds approaching each other on water, flapping their wings aggressively, retreating from each other, pecking at each other's necks, retreating again, shaking their bodies in something that looks a little like a dance and a little like a fit, and then, for no discernible reason, building a nest together.

No one knows why they do it that way, but as a metaphor, it's a study in fear and desire, and humans do it just like the grebe—awkwardly, with a lot of insecure, wasted motion, overaggression followed by apology, sufficient preening, and sufficient modesty. Bravery and cowardice, hope and hurt feelings play out a tug-of-war, with a big dose of uncertainty about the outcome. It's the inevitable upshot of seeing someone we want; it will change two lives forever. And it's almost always compelling to watch. As the Stage Manager in *Our Town* says, right before he serves strawberry ice-cream sodas to the teenagers Emily and George, "I'm awfully interested in how big things like that begin."

In a musical, after the protagonist has told us of his or her hopes and dreams and the accompanying determination to achieve them, in the I Want moment, there's usually an encounter with a love interest. And there's usually a song, which is called, generically, a "conditional" love song. It's called that because of Rodgers and Hammerstein's "If I Loved You," which is embedded in what people in the business refer to as the "bench scene"—Act 1, Scene 2, of *Carousel*. It's arguably the most perfect scene ever written in a musical, in part because it beautifully imitates, unwittingly I'm sure, the courtship habits of the great crested grebe.

*Carousel* goes in and out of favor as its sexual politics are continually put on trial by audiences and critics—it's about a man who loves his wife and strikes her, and a wife who doesn't want to and won't leave. But the magnitude of its achievement tends to overwhelm the objections. Based on the play *Liliom* by Ferenc Molnár, it treats the fatality of love, as two quietly desperate people choose the freedom of romantic passion over the prison of everyday drudgery, and pay an awful price. Julie

Jordan, its heroine, is a naïve millworker, destined to live out her life at the weaving loom in a bleak and gloomy factory, surviving on a menial's wages. Billy Bigelow is a young tough making his scant living as a carousel barker at a traveling carnival. Neither has much of a future, unless they take it into their own hands.

As previously noted, *Carousel* begins with a dance prelude (Scene 1) that reveals both the straitened circumstances and the petty pleasures of a life defined by rural poverty and routine. There's nothing romantic, or even hopeful, about Julie's existence. The carnival is the best she can expect, and it's a tawdry thing. "Carousel Waltz" is a beautiful piece of music, and the ballet that accompanies it can be dazzlingly good theater—but the world it depicts is a sad one, bereft of real hope. The magnificence of the wooden horses on Billy's carousel promises something noble, romantic, and grand, but it seems impossibly far off from the daily life of this hidebound Maine fishing village.

After the waltz, Julie and her friend Carrie are discovered running from the woman who owns the carousel through a corner of the local park, which contains nothing but a bench. The scene begins in action and peril, and the stakes just keep going up. To be fair, considerable credit is due to Molnár, whose play, ironically, is said to have been translated into English by Lorenz Hart, Richard Rodgers's first lyric-writing partner. (Hart was an employee of Benjamin Glazer, who got credit for the translation, according to Hart's biographer Gary Marmorstein.)

Hammerstein shortened the scene by almost half, and while the structure remains the same, the intensity is expertly ratcheted up. From the very first line, there is an argument going on, and the scene is a series of engaging, quickly shifting, and escalating disputes, which result in two lives being changed forever. It begins with the carousel's owner, Mrs. Mullen, hurling accusations at Julie about her behavior on the carousel. Julie, whom we don't really know much about, has been "taking liberties" with Mrs. Mullen's barker, according to Mrs. Mullen. This Julie hotly denies, in a manner that suggests she's not easily cowed. Soon Billy arrives, and it develops that Mrs. Mullen may only be suffering from a bad case of jealousy. But she may not be entirely wrong, either. Julie has seen something she wants, and she's not about to back away—from Mrs. Mullen or anything else that might stand in her way. She doesn't completely understand her own behavior, but something is driving her. She fights off the accusations, and she fights off Mrs. Mullen, and while we're not sure what it is that she's after, we do know, in that classic musical theater sense, that she's the one to watch. She's *"quieter and deeper than a well,"* her friend Carrie sings, but not at the moment. In some way she's unknowable, and unrevealing, but there's something inside her struggling to get out. She's the one who is battling the hand she's been dealt, not wisely, perhaps, but with an unquenchable thirst and the determination that goes with it.

Once Mrs. Mullen has been dispatched by Billy (she fires him in the process), Billy goes to get his gear from the carousel, and Julie and Carrie are left alone. Carrie confesses that she's found the man of her dreams—an industrious herring fisherman named Mr. Snow—and wants to know whether Julie feels similarly about Billy. Julie can't say. She just doesn't know what's happening to her, as a young but strong-willed mill girl might very well not. But we do. And when Billy returns and Carrie goes off, leaving the two of them alone, we see it start to unfold, as Hammerstein wrote in an earlier lyric, like "passion's flower unfurled."

Billy is a risk, but Julie appears to have little to lose. Yet the risk keeps getting bigger and worse. In the course of a few moments, we learn that Julie will lose her job if she stays another minute with Billy. She'll be locked out. She's even offered a lifeline: a ride back to her mill dormitory by the mill's owner, who appears serendipitously, but she turns it down and—like Billy—is fired. Now she has nothing. She learns from a passing policeman that Billy has a reputation for betraying young girls, that he's up from Coney Island, in the reckless precincts of New York. She doesn't care. Billy can't rob her—she has no money. Each black mark against Billy seems to cause her to get closer to him, not further away. As the stakes for her future go up, she becomes more and more determined to ignore them. She wants to stay—that's all. And once alone with Billy, she can't really say why.

Hammerstein's dialogue proceeds in a grebe-like fashion. Billy and Julie work their way toward the subjects of love and marriage through contradiction and defiance. Neither of them knows anything about either subject—but they can't stop talking about them. Finally Julie explains, "Y'see, I'm never goin' to marry," which turns out to be a challenge to Billy that he wasn't expecting.

"Suppose I was to say to you that I'd marry you . . . ," he says, not knowing where the thought has come from. "But you wouldn't marry anyone like me, would you?"

At this point, the die is cast, but neither of them can even begin to admit it. Instead, they sing, and their song is woven through dialogue—a musical scene, really, more than a conventional duet. They leave their fantasies of life with the other in the conditional tense. But nature is working against them. The lyric of "If I Loved You" is almost entirely about fear—fear of confusion, of an inability to communicate love, of a tragic ending. All these fears will be justified by the events to follow, yet something about the scene suggests, counterintuitively, that it will all be worth it anyhow.

Why? Because the blossoms of the trees are beginning to cascade down on them. "The wind brings them down," Julie says distractedly. But Billy points out that there isn't really any wind. And suddenly we've slipped into a dreamlike space, supported by Rodgers's stately but trance-inducing music, which perhaps justifies Billy's next lyric, an unexpectedly philosophical and poetic one, especially coming from the mouth of an uneducated carny. "Ain't much wind tonight. Hardly any," he begins, speaking, and then sings:

> *You can't hear a sound, not the turn of a leaf*
> *Nor the fall of a wave, hittin' the sand.*
> *The tide's creepin' up on the beach like a thief*
> *Afraid to be caught stealin' the land.*
> *On a night like this I start to wonder what life*
> *Is all about.*

Julie does her best to bring the conversation back to the normal realm of things, but Billy has a point to make, and he makes it:

> *There's a helluva lot o' stars in the sky*
> *And the sky's so big the sea looks small*
> *And two little people—*

*You and I—*
*We don't count at all.*

By this point he, and the magic of the evening, have somehow won Julie over, and she contributes two simple lines—she's moving toward what she always wanted anyhow, but it's still a leap. If she's going to contribute to Billy's melody and his philosophy, the mating dance is nearly done:

*There's a feathry little cloud floatin' by*
*Like a lonely leaf on a big blue stream*

Billy answers her:

*And two little people—you and I—*
*Who cares what we dream?*

These aren't the famous lyrics in "If I Loved You"—popular versions of the song eliminate this slightly supernatural interlude—but they are, in some ways, the most important ones: they carry the "two little people" beneath a sky that's bigger than a sea into the realm of myth and fate, and bond them.

The well-known lines of the lyric are all about how they would want to treat each other *if* they were in love—with tenderness and reassurance. But they wouldn't be able to do it. They'd let all their "golden chances" get away. And in fact, by grand design of the authors, that's what happens. It takes the whole course of the play for either of them to be able to say the words "I love you" to the other. By the time Julie says it, Billy is dead. By the time Billy says it, fifteen years have gone by and he's a ghost. They have, indeed, let their golden chances pass them by, and by that time there's no turning back. But here, in their initial meeting, they can't stop the primal pull, no matter how much they intuit their future failures. The interlude confronts the fact that they can't stop themselves—they're going to be together anyhow because they are a part of something bigger: the magnetic force that pulls people together. As a result, at least there will be a moment of passion in what are otherwise empty lives without prospects. What will happen to them now is not really in their own hands anymore; a scene that started out with a noisy but petty squabble has become somehow an examination of the universal state of falling in love. And Billy has joined the little army of American leading men who are frustratingly inarticulate in the cold light of day but who have poetry locked in them, which, in rare and unexpected moments, finds its voice under the stars.

It's a poetry that cannot be allowed to flower for long, however, or Billy would risk no longer being masculine under the definition by which he lives.

"I'm not a feller to marry anybody," he reassures Julie after singing about the likely unhappy ending of any such adventure. She pulls back with him, almost to a comfort zone.

"Don't worry about it, Billy," she says. But she's used his name—for the first time.

And just as they seem perhaps to have reached dry land, nature intervenes, in the form of those persistent blossoms, which once again begin to flutter to the ground all around them.

"You're right about there bein' no wind," Julie says. "The blossoms are just comin' down by theirselves. Jest their time to, I reckon."

And with that, the conspiracy is complete. Julie and Billy kiss, as we now know they were always destined to do, the music swells, and the next time we see them, they'll be married.


Hammerstein (sourcing Molnár and improving the source) has held off the kiss for about twelve minutes. The scene has a slow natural tempo, but it is pulled as tight as a high-tension wire. What the writing achieves is a sense that this romance isn't domestic, isn't upper or lower class, isn't constrained in any way at all. It's bigger than all of that. Billy's claim that their lives don't matter at all is both the ultimate truth and the ultimate fiction. Their courtship is the essence of human need— it's what drives the whole species. It gives *Carousel* size and stature.

This is part of why musicals endure. Their mythmaking continues to speak to us. And for that to happen, they have to communicate human experience in some way that tells. The bench scene is justly celebrated along Broadway because it does that—and no single scene has ever done it better.


Hammerstein wasn't the first person ever to write a conditional love song, of course—they exist in American operettas and in European operas that were written before there was any American musical theater. And no doubt they cross cultures because, as Cole Porter pointed out in one of the most primal and least weighty of them, "Birds, do it, bees do it" . . . and all the rest of us, too. But it was Hammerstein who became a master of these initial moments of human anxiety and desire, who took them seriously and transformed them from light entertainment into something deeper and better, beginning with the somewhat primitive "Make Believe" from *Show Boat*, and including "People Will Say We're in Love" from *Oklahoma!*, "If I Loved You" and its bench scene, and the "Twin Soliloquies" from *South Pacific*, an innovation driven by, of all things, performance anxiety.

Sometimes the contract is the mother of invention. In the case of *South Pacific*, Mary Martin, playing the army nurse Nellie Forbush, was cast opposite the famed opera basso Ezio Pinza, as a European planter named Emile de Becque, who lives on an island, literally and figuratively. Martin could put across a Broadway song as well as or better than anyone, but she knew that she couldn't outsing Pinza. She had it written into her contract that she and Pinza would never be asked to sing simultaneously, which created an interesting challenge for R&H as they approached the conditional love song moment. They solved it inventively with the "Twin Soliloquies," a matched pair of musical moments in which Martin and Pinza sing privately of their desire for the other, of how life might change for the better if they were together, and how unlikely it is that it will come to pass. Each has a few lines of hope, a few lines of crippling self-doubt, and a cautious prayer for a chance to make it work—but they never actually communicate, except with the audience. Then, as their uncertain first date reaches an impasse, de Becque sings "Some Enchanted Evening," which gives Nellie an awful lot to think about. It's a conditional love song as solo.

Conditional love songs, like opening numbers, come chiefly in two varieties. There are the ones like "If I Loved You," full of uncertainty but powered by desire and hope. And there are the others, expressions of pure hostility but powered by desire and hope. If Hammerstein was the master of the first variety, no one ever did the second better than Frank Loesser, in "I'll Know" from *Guys and Dolls*.

*Carousel* is a dark-hued musical drama in which reluctant lovers trust themselves to fate. *Guys and Dolls*, on the other hand, is a brightly painted war-between-the-sexes comedy. The milieus could not be more different, although both shows begin with ballets. *Carousel* transports playgoers to a rugged rural seaside village, while *Guys and Dolls* leaves them right where they got their tickets torn—in Times Square. But it shows them the underbelly of the theater district they might never have imagined—cockeyed, unpredictably comic, and charmingly disreputable. Based on a handful of Damon Runyon's popular short stories of the '30s and '40s, the show focuses on two couples seen through the prism of Runyon's gaudy take on the horseplayers, gamblers, chorus cuties, and tough guys who populated Broadway (I mean the street itself) back in its heyday. In some ways, it's a tossed salad of sketches, specialty material, ballads, and production numbers—a throwback to the Gershwin and Rodgers and Hart musicals of the '30s. Yet despite this, and unlike any of those early shows, it is also a perfectly structured tale in which every action by one character or couple triggers a reaction from the other—and the plot can't be worked out until the consequences are totaled up and paid for.

The book was written by Abe Burrows (and cocredited to Jo Swerling, who wrote a first draft that was replaced). But some considerable credit is undoubtedly due to the director, George S. Kaufman, the master structuralist of American comedy. The plot shuttlecocks back and forth between two couples, Nathan Detroit and his fiancée of fourteen years, Miss Adelaide, and Sky Masterson and the Salvation Army lass he falls in love with, Sister Sarah Brown. The device that hinges this quartet together is a simple stroke of genius—a bet.

Nathan needs $1,000 to pay off a local garage owner so that he can hold his floating crap game in the garage. To get it, he bets Sky—who is addicted to crazy propositions—that Sky can't take the religious crusader Sarah to Havana for dinner. If Sky loses, Nathan wins, of course. But it's better than that. All Adelaide wants is to get married and Nathan to stop running the crap game. So if Nathan wins, Adelaide loses. And Sarah is just trying to keep the Save-a-Soul Mission and her reputation intact, so if Sky wins, she loses, and Adelaide wins. How, in this tipsy equation, can everyone ultimately come out on top? That's the fun of *Guys and Dolls*. Structurally, the show kicks back and forth between the couples scene by scene, as each of their plots thickens the other, and ricochets closer to chaos. The stakes keep going up, as do the odds against the inevitable happy ending.

Sky and Nathan—in basic conflict, but not unfriendly—are each on a mission that drives the story forward. Adelaide and Sarah, who don't meet each other until late in the first act, are left to figure out how to wrangle the two men they've wound up with. Good women, bad choices. It's a traditional kind of comedy that asks an age-old comedy question: How much trouble can you get into in two and a half hours? And since it is written by men of the postwar era, you know that the women will ultimately get the upper hand. That's the romantic joke of the '50s: the men have all the power, but the women always win—they have all the brains. Shot through all this well-wrought anarchy is a tale of the inexorable pull of love. It turns out there is something bigger and better than a bet, even in Runyon's world. Like *A Midsummer Night's Dream*, *Guys and Dolls* is a puzzle box that reveals one delight after another and is always heading toward multiple weddings.

The composer-lyricist Frank Loesser, a recent arrival from Hollywood, wrote the score, and no one has ever captured the voice of his source material better. Loesser's lyrics are continually smart and colloquial without seeming educated, and funny without a trace of self-conscious wit. And his music sounds the way a good corned beef sandwich tastes. It's irresistible, surprisingly complex, tangy, sweet, a little peppery, and whatever other adjectives you want to associate with corned beef, brown mustard, and seeded rye.

Nathan and Adelaide have been together for years, but Sky and Sarah meet for the first time in Act 1, Scene 2 (naturally), and, ill matched as they are, they're going to sing about it.

She's in a foul mood, having scoured Broadway for sinners willing to convert—and come up empty. He's surprisingly upbeat. He has to enter a place he normally wouldn't be caught dead in and convince a chilly religious volunteer he's never met to get in an airplane and go to Cuba with him, and there's a part of him that enjoys the challenge. He dives in, pretending to be a sinner who has seen the light. She sees through this pose in about a minute, of course, and tries to kick him out. He's not going anywhere, though, not when $1,000 and his pride are at stake. And a pure stroke of luck—an inaccurately attributed quote from the Bible that is hanging on the wall—saves his bacon. Strangely, for a self-described gambler and sinner, Sky knows his religious verses. And Sarah is just the tiniest bit intrigued.

"There's two things been in every hotel room in the country," he explains. "Sky Masterson and the Gideon Bible. I must have read the Good Book ten or twelve times. I once won 5 G's on a triple parlay—Shadrach, Meschach and Abednego."

This is not what Sarah is used to hearing, and it buys him another couple of minutes, but things deteriorate quickly. He offers to guarantee her a dozen sinners at her midnight prayer meeting, which will prove to be an important part of the plot later on, but she turns him down flat. He accuses her of hating men; she denies it vigorously. He alters the accusation: maybe she just hates him. She won't even agree to that. But the man who might appeal to her, she admits, will never, ever, be a gambler.

This piece of information is like a trip wire and does to Sky what his correction of the Bible verse did to Sarah. He's suddenly challenged and awake to the woman in the room.

"I am not interested in what he will not be," he says. "I am interested in what he *will* be."

And Sarah, who, if she genuinely didn't care, would just tell him it's none of his business, instead takes the time to paint a portrait—of the anti-Sky:

> *I've imagined every bit of him*
> *From his strong moral fiber*
> *To the wisdom in his head*
> *To the homey aroma of his pipe.*

Sky's having none of it:

> *You have wished yourself a*
> *Scarsdale Galahad,*
> *The breakfast-eating,*
> *Brooks Brothers type.*

She doesn't even hear the sarcasm. "*I'll know,*" she sings, "*when my love comes along.*"

The irony, of course, is that he's just walked in the door. And she doesn't know. But she keeps singing, and so does Sky, even though she asks him not to. "*Mine, I'll leave to chance and chemistry,*" he asserts. She's baffled by his use of the word "chemistry," but he stands by it. Sex plays a big part, he implies, and in this song it does. It's all about chemistry—it certainly has nothing to do with what they're saying to each other.

The form of these conditional love songs is fairly consistent, and it plays on the subconscious of the audience in a way that is structural and subtextual. First one sings and then the other sings a rebuttal, but both assertion and response have the same melody. So there's something that tells us, subliminally, that these two have more in common than they think they do—they have the same music. At the end, for a moment, at least, the two actually sing together, in simple harmony. And when a couple sings in harmony, the groundwork for eventual emotional harmony is laid, so to speak. In the case of "I'll Know," Sky and Sarah sing one line together, "*I'll know when my love comes along,*" but it sounds so right that at the end of it, he kisses her. She kind of kisses back. Then she slaps him. The acting challenge of the song is to transcend the words, which are an argument, and somehow move inexorably toward the kiss, and the slap, which land things in an emotional mess—just the kind we like in these stories.

After the slap, he exits, leaving her to contemplate what has just happened.

"*I won't take a chance,*" she sings, insisting on her original vision. But we all know what's going on when people start talking to themselves about not taking chances. Round one has been a technical draw, but Sarah's bewilderment gives the advantage to Sky. And from the dramatist's point of view, an awful lot has been accomplished in one conditional love song.

Mike Ockrent, director of *Crazy for You* and *Me and My Girl*, among others, developed a number of shows and always insisted that the key to romance in a musical is the inappropriateness of the couple. "If you believe they belong together because they have the same background, the same ideas about life, the same tastes, what's the point of the show?" he asked. "If you think they have no real chance of getting together, that they're entirely mismatched, then there's something to watch. Of course, you know they'll end up together—it's a musical—but the question is, how will the story accomplish it? If it's easy and obvious at the beginning, the audience won't be there at the end."

For Sky and Sarah, the likelihood of a united outcome seems remote, especially because one of them would have to give up everything—a way of life that is complete, ingrained, and seemingly unshakable. Which is pretty much what happens. Like Higgins and Eliza, or, for that matter, Tracy Turnblad and Link Larkin, an ocean of difference has to be crossed before the lovers can become lovers. That's a journey we believe in—at least for other people—and we want to watch it.

Frank Loesser was a restless writer who never repeated himself. Having done the essential mug show in *Guys and Dolls*, he turned his attention to a pastoral operatic romance, *The Most Happy Fella*. After stumbling with the folktale *Greenwillow*, he returned with an urban satire of American enterprise, *How to Succeed in Business Without Really Trying*, for which he won a Pulitzer. Each of these shows contains an original conditional love song idea, and two more of them (let's leave *Greenwillow*'s grave undisturbed) are worth at least a brief look.

In *Happy Fella*, Tony, an aging immigrant Napa Valley grape grower, tricks a young San Francisco waitress into becoming his mail-order bride by sending her a picture of his handsome, rugged ranch hand, Joe. On the night of her arrival in Napa, an anxious Tony gets drunk and gets in a near-fatal car accident. Not surprisingly, Rosabella, as Tony calls her, ends up in the arms of Joe. That's Act 1, so the conditional love song between Tony and Rosabella doesn't occur until Act 2, by which time Tony is in a wheelchair and Rosabella is pregnant by Joe, though married to Tony. It's going to be a bumpy ride, and the two of them barely know each other.

Loesser constructs an ingenious musical scene for them in three little acts, in which Rosabella tries to improve Tony's English. "Happy to Make Your Acquaintance" begins as a simple obligation—Rosabella is nursing the husband she wishes she hadn't agreed to marry. But before the song is done, Tony has proved his humanity; he's brought Rosabella's best friend from San Francisco up to Napa to stave off his young wife's loneliness, and this gesture, unasked for and unexpected (the friend arrives in the middle of the song), completely changes the temperature. By the time the number has concluded, we've gone from feeling that the relationship is hopeless to feeling that it's somehow fated. Tony's English hasn't gotten any better, and it never will. But the two of them have somehow preserved at least the possibility of a happy ending for themselves and the audience.

The song features something that gives these moments a chance to be fresh: a subject other than love. Rosabella is giving an English lesson. That's the raw material that makes the emotional connection possible. Other songs in other shows have been written about everything from disputes over horoscopes to baptism rites—as long as the combatants have differing attitudes toward the subject, it hardly matters what the subject actually is. There's something to talk about.

In *How to Succeed*, Loesser again tried something new: he turned the conditional love song into a trio. Observing the grebe-like natural shyness of first approaches, he positioned his young would-be lovers in the elevator of a tall office building and gave them a kind of fairy godmother—the boss's secretary—who introduces their romantic intentions to the audience as they try to find ways to flirt, while remaining virtually tongue-tied. The song is called "Been a Long Day," and that cliché serves as its chorus, while the verses are full of the usual comic stumbling and fumbling that presages nest building. In the course of one elevator ride, the deed gets done, though without the narrator, we would have no idea what just happened. It's a small invention, but it gives great pleasure.

Invention is key to keeping these songs, and the moment they dramatize, fresh. Since it's a well-worn situation in life as well as in the theater, it's likely to seem overfamiliar, and freshening it with wit and a different point of view tests a songwriter's mettle. Stephen Sondheim wrote a terrific conditional love song using a different kind of invention from Loesser: "Your Eyes Are Blue," which was cut from *A Funny Thing Happened on the Way to the Forum*. In this case, it's not just a matter of shyness or communication skills—the lovers themselves have extraordinarily limited brain power. They are, in fact, archetypes from Roman comedy, innocent kids with hormones raging and IQs lagging far behind. Hero, the boy, tries to make Philia, the girl, understand what's going on between them, but he's bashful. So he makes up a story. To disguise the identity of his beloved and himself, he puts them in the third person—or tries to—and charmingly fails.

He sings:

> Once upon a time,
> It happened
> It happened there lived a boy
> Who loved a girl . . .
> Your eyes are blue . . .
>
> And every single night
> He'd see her across the way.
> I'd want to say—
> He'd want to say,

*"Your eyes are blue*
*And I love you!"*
*But never had they spoken,*
*Never had he dared.*
*Beautiful as she was,*
*I was—he was—*
*Scared.*

Hero's inability to keep himself out of the story is matched by Philia's difficulties in keeping the story straight at all. She can't even remember what color the girl's eyes are—and she's the girl. In the end, as in *Guys and Dolls*, but with sweetness instead of tart hostility, the two sing a line together and kiss. But Sondheim constructed the kiss as a missing line in the lyric:

**PHILIA**

*When suddenly one day*
*She met him.*
*He looked so tall.*

**HERO**

*He felt so small.*

**PHILIA**

*What did he do*
*To break the wall?*

**BOTH**

*What could he do*
*To break the wall?*

*(They kiss.)*

*And that was all.*

The number was replaced by "Lovely," an almost equally charming if less clever song, largely because it made a hilarious second-act reprise when sung by Zero Mostel and Jack Gilford, the latter clad in a diaphanous white gown and pretending to be dead (don't ask). But "Your Eyes Are Blue" is as admirable as it is rarely heard. It's a textbook example of the kind of thing that Hammerstein crystallized in the bench scene but, at the same time, a complete original.

There is a subset of the conditional love song, which might be called an "aftermath song." In shows where, for one reason or another, the couple in question never get their crested grebe moment, or don't have it onstage, we may catch up with them after the first date, or the first encounter, or whatever it is that's drawn them together. One of them, left alone to contemplate what's just happened, has our full attention, and an unquiet mind to explore. What happened? What is this I'm feeling? What's going on in this brain and body that I've trusted for so long?

Because of its multiple plots (four of Grimm's fairy tales and an invented fifth one all woven together by James Lapine and Stephen Sondheim), *Into the Woods* leapfrogs through much of what we think of as traditional structure, seeking inventive solutions, and getting in and out of trouble. Its audacity more than makes up for its occasional murkiness, however, and it is never less than clear thematically. It deals principally with parents and children and the gulf that accompanies the love between them.

There is, however, time for romantic love as well. Cinderella, returning from her first encounter with the Prince in *Into the Woods*, comes to a dead halt somewhere on the path back home to ponder her fate. She's been to the ball, but we haven't, so she needs to tell us what happened—or at least what's happening to her.

Has she lost her shoe, or left it behind on purpose? And if the latter, why? Well, the Prince is from another world, and Cinderella doesn't think she could ever be a part of that world. But maybe she could. Certainly he could never join hers. So now what? The ambivalence in the song is very much cut from the cloth of conditional love songs—the hope, the anxiety, and the self-doubt are all there, but the form is different. It's just her and us. And she begins to explain:

*You think, what do you want?*
*You think, make a decision.*
*Why not stay and be caught?*
*You think, well, it's a thought,*
*What would be his response?*
*But then what if he knew*
*Who you were when you know*
*That you're not what he thinks*
*That he wants?*

Cinderella's mind is racing, but in circles, which is usually what happens when one is smitten. And it's all happening too fast. Nothing can really be figured out under these conditions. Unlike Julie Jordan and Billy Bigelow, who succumb to nature in the moment, Cinderella has dodged that bullet, only to wonder whether she regrets giving the Prince the slip. She's more like Nellie Forbush, keeping her defenses up until she knows a little more. But she doesn't know how she'll learn it. Or what she'll do when she learns it. So she settles on what seems like the best course of action, which is, of all things, inaction.

*Then from out of the blue,*
*And without any guide,*
*You know what your decision is,*
*Which is not to decide.*

But justifying indecision requires some significant explanation to oneself, making sure not to leave room for self-doubt through reflection or second-guessing. Cinderella has to project certainty and wisdom in a situation where she may actually possess neither. And Sondheim accomplishes this through a dizzying set of rhymes that make her sound emphatic. And what a set of rhymes!

*You'll just leave him a clue:*
*For example, a shoe.*
*And then see what he'll do.*
*Now it's he and not you*

*Who is stuck with a shoe,*
*In a stew, in the goo,*
*And you've learned something, too,*
*Something you never knew,*
*On the steps of the palace.*

As a character, Cinderella shares a lot with Eliza Doolittle. They're a pair of waifs, each trying to improve her lot and escape her destiny and her family. They're both headed to a ball, and they find unlikely matches in an upper-class prig and an upper-class prince. But Eliza's first taste of romantic possibility (it's barely that) leads not to ambivalence but to uncontrolled—if unrequited—ecstasy. She falls, and hard. "I Could Have Danced All Night" can hardly be justified as a conditional love song, but it's a not-so-distant cousin.

Eliza, you may recall, has endured a spirit-crushing tutorial: Henry Higgins's "instruction" in proper English speech. She's not the only one to suffer. In one of the most accomplished of all sequences in a musical, Higgins has explored all the various ways he can think of to get her to use "h" and "ai" in their proper pronunciations. He's had her blowing "h" words at a Bunsen burner, and he's stuffed her mouth with stones. He's harangued her; deprived her of sleep, food, and drink; and generally insulted and tortured her for days. His staff is ready to quit, and his friend Colonel Pickering is about to end the friendship. Then, in a final, exhausted attempt, at three in the morning, he switches gears and transforms himself, just for a moment, from brutal tyrant to tender poet-confessor.

"Think of what you are trying to accomplish," he says. "The majesty and grandeur of the English language. It's the greatest possession we have. That's what you've set yourself to conquer."

He gives her credit. He makes what she's doing important to her, instead of simply a means to a better job in a flower shop. He elevates her instead of trying to crush her.

Like Sarah Brown's declaration that her lover will never be a gambler, Henry Higgins's one moment of noble tenderness is a trip wire. For no other apparent reason, the words suddenly come out of Eliza's mouth as directed, as if she'd been holding out on him all along, waiting to see his heart instead of his lash: "The rain in Spain falls mainly in the plain," she says. And a reckless celebration explodes on the stage. It's one of those moments of letting go that audiences remember for decades. The buildup has been meticulous and excruciating, and the release is orgiastic. Higgins, in the midst of it, takes Eliza in his arms and does a bit of a gavotte—nothing more than that. But the die is cast. Left alone at the end of the scene, she can't sit still, can't calm down, can't let go of the memory of it. It's almost four in the morning. She's supposed to go to bed, and she might be eager to; but not to sleep.

"*I could have danced all night*," she sings blissfully, "*and still have begged for more.*" The word "begged" is perhaps innocently chosen by Alan Jay Lerner, but it reminds us that there is something intriguingly sadomasochistic about the relationship between Eliza and Higgins. They don't ever, in the course of *My Fair Lady*, seem to have an actual sex life, but the give-and-take, the power exchanges that fuel the relationship, the fantasies of beheadings, firing squads, starvation, and beatings that pepper their conversation and their lyrics create something more dangerous that replaces a vanilla romance. They're suited to each other in a way that neither expected, and they continue to discover and savor it, even at their most antagonistic. In the world of well-mannered Mayfair, there's something unsettlingly erotic going on between them that never quite gets stated. And looked at through that lens, the final, thrilling high G that concludes "I Could Have Danced All Night" serves as an unforgettable autoerotic orgasm in song. There's rarely been a sexual moment in a musical that is as simultaneously raw and decorous. It's not for nothing that the show never becomes irrelevant.

*My Fair Lady*, in 1956, may have been speaking in code. But as the Golden Age faded and the sexual revolution took hold, the conditional love song's traditional sense of public decency began to collapse. All that fancy dancing gets less credible in a world where people are having sex first and asking questions in the morning. And musical theater had to learn how to cope, which it started to do when, in 1970's *Com-*

*pany*, the hero Bobby wakes up to discover the flight attendant he's spent the night with is already up and dressing. *"Where you going?"* he sings plaintively.

"*Barcelona*," she replies.

He tries to dissuade her but doesn't have much ammunition:

BOBBY

*Look, you're a very special girl,*
*Not just overnight.*
*No, you're a very special girl,*
*And not because you're bright—*
*Not just because you're bright.*
*You're just a very special girl, June*

APRIL

*April . . .*

Oh, well. One thing they didn't do was dance all night.

In some cases, innuendo replaced the confusions of first encounters. Sex, rather than the possibility of lifelong romance, was the first subject to come up. In *City of Angels*, the detective Stone is retained by a beautiful but mysterious woman named Alaura and finds himself trying to resist her charms, but not really. Students of detective fiction, particularly Raymond Chandler's *The Big Sleep*, will recognize the situation immediately: Alaura, glamorous and apparently helpless, is up to no good, and Stone will be cautious before taking her into his arms—but not cautious enough.

In the classic Warner Bros. film of *The Big Sleep*, Humphrey Bogart played the detective opposite Lauren Bacall's glamorous heiress. After a tepid sneak preview (this was back in 1946), the director, Howard Hawks, was prevailed upon to go back and shoot more scenes with Bogart and Bacall, who sizzled together and would go on doing so personally and professionally for years. One of the new scenes was an encounter in a restaurant, where the two of them spar ostensibly over the subject of horse racing, while the actual subject hardly stays beneath the surface.

"Speaking of horses, I like to play them myself," Bacall says. "But I like to see them work out a little first. See if they're front runners or come from behind."

After assuring Bogie that she sees him as quick out of the gate, it's his turn to rate her.

"You've got a touch of class," he says, "but I don't know how far you can go."

"A lot depends on who's in the saddle," she shoots back.

The lyricist of *City of Angels*, David Zippel, who knew a good thing when he heard one, took his inspiration where he found it, changed the subject from thoroughbreds to tennis, and created "The Tennis Song," a similar match for his detective and client.

STONE

*You seem at home on the court*

ALAURA

*Let's say that I've played around . . .*

And then . . .

STONE

*I'll bet you're a real good sport*

ALAURA

*Shall we say the ball is in your court?*

STONE

*I'll bet you like to play rough*

ALAURA

*I like to work up a sweat*

STONE

*And you just can't get enough*


ALAURA

*I'm good for more than one set . . .*


And so it goes. *City of Angels* was set in the '40s but written in the '80s, and the language of "The Tennis Song" was unexpected for Broadway. The innuendo is fun but unmistakably remote from "If I Loved You," and, like the show, it's a hard-edged kind of comedy, well beyond the bounds of what we might call "romance." Hammerstein would have blushed, and even Frank Loesser might have mentioned matters of taste. But Zippel was bold and memorable. And modern. The audience, for better and worse, had left behind the old ways, and the theater, as it always does, was seeking the theatergoers of its own time.


Even more modern was a moment from the failed musical *The Wedding Singer*, from 2006. Based on a popular 1998 film of the same name, *The Wedding Singer*, charming in its way, was doomed as a musical by its most basic premise: it's about a wedding singer who just wants to be a wedding singer. No great goals, no active hero, no mountain to climb. But a lot of incidental fun. Robbie, the hero, is abandoned by his bride at the altar—a particular irony since he spends his life doing weddings for other people. In a plot development that none of the classic writers of musicals could have imagined, he disgraces himself onstage at someone else's wedding, causes a brawl that nearly destroys the New Jersey catering hall, and, overcome with shame and alcohol, hurls himself in despair into the dumpster in the alley. He wants to die, or at least be left in isolated misery in the garbage.

Yet one of the catering hall waitresses, Julia, sees something in Robbie she likes. And she thinks maybe it will make him feel better if he knows he's needed, though what she needs him for is to play at *her* wedding to an obnoxious young Wall Streeter. There isn't any reason for her to deal with this right now, but of course we in the audience understand that there's something else going on. Julia's attraction to

Robbie isn't just that of a prospective employer. She won't admit it, even to herself—she's engaged, after all—but she doesn't have to. The lovely young waitress is not going to end up with the greedy, faithless stockbroker in this story, but the story has to get started. Tentatively, Julia approaches the dumpster, suspecting that Robbie's in there, and sings:

JULIA

*So tonight you made some mistakes*
*I admit it, you hit a few bumps*
*But I hate to see you like this*
*Down on your luck, down in the dumps . . .*

*So come out of the dumpster*
*Don't leave me standing here*
*Come out of the dumpster*
*It's ok; the coast is clear*

*The cop cars are leaving*
*Channel 5 packed up its crew*
*So come out of the dumpster*
*I'll be right here waiting for you*

The song, with a lyric by Chad Beguelin and music by Matt Sklar, plays innocence and delicacy against the grotesque. A drunken young man is coaxed out of a heap of rotting rubbish in the sweetest possible way, and we find Julia's appeal actually touching, not just amusing. These characters are, in a sense, contemporary equivalents of Julie Jordan and Billy Bigelow—stuck in a low-paying, no-expectations world, but in 1980s New Jersey instead of 1880s Maine.

Location, of course, is far from the only—or the significant—difference between *Carousel* and *The Wedding Singer*. The former places its romance against a backdrop of fate and myth—don't forget those blossoms descending.

"You're right about there bein' no wind," Julie Jordan says to Billy Bigelow. "The blossoms are just comin' down by theirselves. Jest their time to, I reckon."

This kind of exchange, even if you could figure out how to update the language, could never find its way into *The Wedding Singer*, yet it's one of the key reasons *Carousel* has endured. It treats the fate of a lower-class couple in love as an essential examination of human nature, and makes bold to say so—it strives, not always gracefully, for stature. *The Wedding Singer*, on the other hand, remains determinedly domestic. It is also about working-class stiffs, and it seems to believe that nothing more ambitious than sitcom-world thinking is available to them, that any other claims to a real subject would inevitably be pretentious, given the often silly and trivial events of the story itself. And that's probably true, and probably another good reason it wasn't appropriate underlying material for musical adaptation. It can amuse an audience, but never soar.

"Musical successes," according to the producer Kevin McCollum, "have to ascend to heaven in the end." It may not be a clear dictate, but it's not wrong.

And yet, "Come Out of the Dumpster" remains a lovely, unique conditional love song—a link in the chain that stretches back to "Make Believe" in 1927 and marks how social interaction—and style—have evolved while human need remains immutable.

As the Golden Age slips further into the past, the American musical has refocused its search for underlying material on almost a single source: the movies. This trend has been decried in various quarters, and there are certainly a few bad things to say about it. It's a trend born partially out of fear of the unknown; producers like a nice famous title to depend upon for advance sales and a structure already worked out by some high-priced screenwriters before they begin the adaptation process. Neither is a really honorable desire from the point of view of trying to make art. But the truth is that most modern musicals have been adapted from some kind of underlying work—all of Rodgers and Hammerstein's hits were based on books or plays, as were all of Loesser's, most of Lerner and Loewe, and even Jerry Herman and a lot of Sondheim. Add a single ballet (*Fancy Free*) and you can throw in Leonard Bernstein.

But that's the point. Producers and artists used to have lots of variety when they went looking for source material. Light novels like *The*

*Year the Yankees Lost the Pennant* (which became *Damn Yankees*) and popular stage comedies like *My Sister Eileen* (which became *Wonderful Town*) were there to be harvested. All those genres have grown scarcer over time. Neil Simon, the last of our great "light" playwrights, had his last hit more than two decades ago. What's left to adapt? Movies and TV. Completely original Broadway hits were scarce in the Golden Age—actually, there are probably more of them now, beginning with *A Chorus Line* and including *Avenue Q* and *Next to Normal*.

Why should this be so? First of all, Broadway musicals have always been a business, and most businesses look for safety. Only the rare product generators actually prefer to innovate. But beyond that, the great original storytellers, the creators of striking and memorable characters, the writers with prodigious imaginations, are unlikely to decide that the best use of their talents is writing the librettos for musicals. They tend to write novels or plays or screenplays or, these days, TV. They're not so interested in having the emotional high points of their work cannibalized by songwriters who get all the credit. For the most part, good book writers are craftsmen. They're dramaturgical cabinetmakers, and it's a great skill. But it's not the same as having a completely original turn of mind and the particular talent to express it. So musicals tend to lean on story material that comes from somewhere else—that already works and has stood the test of time. These days, that often means successful films.

This has led to at least one interesting challenge: the conditional love song in the age of the buddy story, or, in that awful Hollywood term, the bromance.

*The Producers* was among the earliest of these—the story of two men who need each other to make their dreams come true but are ill matched in every other way. All they have in common is a goal—to produce the biggest Broadway flop in history. But in the number where they express this desire, "We Can Do It," something slightly larger is going on—they're forming a bond, one that will eventually lead to the discovery that the musical they produce, *Springtime for Hitler*, has been nothing more than the means to a much greater end—true friendship, albeit behind bars. (*The Producers*, as previously noted, is a classic hill-beyond-the-hill story.)

*Wicked*, which, refreshingly enough, is actually based on a novel, meets the challenge in the same way, in a number called "What Is This Feeling?" It's a song of mutual loathing that—like "I'll Know" in *Guys and Dolls*—joins the characters in a common emotion that is, presumably, the opposite of attraction. But of course we know better. In this case, it's a womance, and, as in *The Producers* and *The Book of Mormon*, which I'll get to presently, there is an actual opposite-sex romance to follow. But first there are the two buddies / best girlfriends / rivals, who use the conditional love song spot to express their need for each other in ways that the audience can perceive even if the characters can't.

If *The Producers* celebrates strangers with a shared goal and *Wicked* reveals two young women who hate each other on sight but will nonetheless grow up by growing to understand each other, *The Book of Mormon* gives us a pair who are, reluctantly, willing to accept the hand that's been dealt them by forces greater than themselves. They are Mormon missionaries about to be sent—as a badly matched pair—to Uganda. Baby-faced, handsome, and self-involved to a pathological degree, Elder Price was hoping for an assignment in Orlando with a cool companion. Instead he's paired with the über-schlub Elder Cunningham, who combines ineptitude and insecurity in ways that are bound to be toxic—especially in war-torn Africa. It's not a good situation for either young man, but in "You and Me (But Mostly Me)" the writers, Robert Lopez, Trey Parker, and Matt Stone, let each elder blindly assume it's all going to be okay.

"*You and me, but mostly me, are gonna change the world forever,*" Price sings, combining naïveté, arrogance, and narcissism with breathtaking efficiency. " '*Cause I can do most anything,*" he asserts, to which Cunningham replies, "*And I can stand next to you and watch!*" As Yente the Matchmaker says under different circumstances, it's a perfect match.

*Mormon* coolly borrows bits and pieces from about a dozen old musicals, and takes at least one page from *Gypsy*: its characters exactly switch places between the beginning of the evening and the end. Price wants nothing but to change the world—or so he thinks. The disheveled Cunningham only wants a best friend. At the final curtain, it is Cunningham who has changed the world and Price who has acquired enough humility to gain a best friend. As it is in *Gypsy*, it's a deeply satisfying structural knot. And "You and Me (But Mostly Me)" sets it up by merging (as one might expect in a twenty-first-century musical) the I Want with the conditional love song. By the time it concludes, we're set up for a satisfying array of personal, religious, and global catastrophes, which will all, of course, end happily—and ascend to heaven by creating a whole new religion.

# 5. Put On Your Sunday Clothes

*The Noise*

An awful lot has been accomplished by the time a traditional musical reaches the third or fourth song slot, and the audience has been asked to do a lot of work. We get the milieu, the time, the place, the style, and the point of view. We meet the hero and learn what's on his or her mind, which defines the hill to be climbed. We get the romance started and come to understand its challenges. We get the big picture of what the story's to be about and begin to understand the details. Time for recess.

Depending on the choices the authors have made about how much to tell how quickly, and given that this whole enterprise is supposed to be fun, a pure expression of energy is usually called for at this moment. This is where, in some senses, the musical departs from the world of logic and begins to respond to the biorhythms of the thousand or so people who paid their money to sit in the dark—the collective living, breathing thing that Oscar Hammerstein dubbed "the big black giant," and Mike Nichols and Neil Simon used to refer to, less poetically, as "the 900 Jews." Whoever they are, they are fused into one being by this time, and they probably need a little energy boost, a little fun, a little relaxation to restore their concentration and curiosity; they need to hear a big sound, and they probably need to watch some people dance.

Musicals depend on these rhythmic energy shifts. Quiet thoughtfulness must be followed by noisy energy, and vice versa.

In *South Pacific*, after twenty minutes or so of watching Nellie Forbush and Emile de Becque angsting about the possibilities of having a life together and bridging their not inconsiderable differences, and hoping that some enchanted evening something good will happen to them, wouldn't you like to take a break and hear a chorus of sailors sing "Bloody Mary" and "There's Nothin' Like a Dame"? Luckily, that's just what *South Pacific* has planned for you—a day at the beach, even in World War II.

This being Rodgers and Hammerstein, the scene is not without its own form of theatrical nourishment. R&H, in particular, lived by that old Puritan dictum "Waste not, want not." Even recess had a meaning and a purpose. The first song introduces the show's subplot (though we don't know it yet) as the mercenary Pacific Islands native Bloody Mary tries to sell junk souvenirs to the sailors. She and her daughter Liat will be the fulcrum of the show's secondary story. And the second number merely expresses, with lively vulgarity, the desire of men far from home for some female companionship and all that it implies. The song, rousing and mildly comic, may not appear to have much on its mind, but don't forget that for audiences in 1949, the loneliness, the deprivation, and the fear that home might never be glimpsed again were all raw and recent memories. Whether they had spent World War II on the front line or the home front, people watching the original production of *South Pacific* bore the scars of war. The men remembered the emotion, and the women appreciated hearing about it from R&H, since many of their husbands wouldn't talk about it. The number was funny, but somehow touching as well. And it bridged a story gap: by the end of the scene, Lieutenant Cable, who will fall in love with Bloody Mary's daughter, has arrived. But first, the noise.

Not all creators are as scrupulous, and there are some wildly entertaining production numbers that barely scratch the surface of storytelling utility. They're worth a look, though, because they reinforce one of the basic ideas that guide the building of Broadway musicals: the energy in a theater has to move in both directions. The audience reacts to shifts in tone and mood and tempo by sending out its own bursts of

applause, laughter, and even tears. It's a vital, living part of the equation. And the performers and creators need to control the flow, keep
the connection alive. Theater is about engagement in the moment. And it
doesn't take more than one black hole for the whole apparatus to stop
breathing. Standing against the back rail during a rough early preview
of *Guys and Dolls*, the director, Jerry Zaks, turned to a companion after
a weak scene transition—a scene transition, mind you—and said one
ugly word: "Death." He was speaking literally. The connection was lost.
The plug was pulled; the 900 Jews were suddenly dozing comfortably.
And the show, that night at least, expired shortly thereafter. Recognizing
the fatality pushed Zaks to go back to work and make sure it never happened again.

The recharging of the audience needn't be as meaningful as it is in *South
Pacific* or a couple of other shows that we'll look at presently. Sometimes
it's a recharge, plain and simple. Though it serves no real purpose, in the
classic B musical *Li'l Abner*, a subsidiary character named Marryin'
Sam turns to a chorus girl in the town square and proclaims, "Honey,
it's high time you knew that our town was founded by that beloved
man a-settin' up there on that beloved horse, Jubilation T. Cornpone."
This portends the noise: Sam is going to sing a jaunty comedy number
by Gene de Paul and Johnny Mercer about the worst Confederate general
in history, and make us laugh at some classic Mercer lyrics, and before
long the entire town is going to be dancing, and the whole thing, nonsensical as it is, is going to bring down the house. When it's done, the
story will start again. Audiences in the '50s expected that and loved it.
"Shoeless Joe from Hannibal, Mo." from *Damn Yankees* works the same
way. Ditto "With a Little Bit of Luck" from *My Fair Lady*, "A Bushel
and a Peck" from *Guys and Dolls*, and, though it's sung by a barbershop
quartet and not the entire company, "Standing on the Corner" from *The
Most Happy Fella*. Just give us a treat.

More recently, *The Book of Mormon* made the choice to have a pair of
noisy numbers in this spot—"Hasa Diga Eebowai" and "Turn It Off."

The twinning of the two numbers is justified by the two populations, African and American, that *Mormon*'s plot deals with. The creators were unable to resist either one or to make a choice between them. The first is a gleeful—some would say blasphemous—look at life in Uganda, and a poke in the eye at *The Lion King*'s "Hakuna Matata." The second delivers a kick in the pants to both the audience and Mormon philosophy, and even has an unexpected tap break (Mormons tap; they really do). The double recess is forgivable in a sense because each population gets a turn to celebrate its own somewhat unlikely way of dealing with life's disappointments. The numbers have exactly the same subject—how to deal with what life dishes out—yet the treatment couldn't be more different. They are really a complementary set. And if we're paying close attention, they accomplish something else, Rodgers and Hammerstein–style: they tell us how unlikely it is that the Mormons (who just want to ignore all their worst fears and concerns) will be able to be even slightly useful to the Africans, whose problems, needless to say, are legion and require a frank confrontation with the dire facts, not to mention immediate action beyond the bounds of spiritual uplift.

There's no narrative story material in any of these numbers, however; they make a joyful noise instead. And they perform another useful function: they introduce us to subsidiary characters who will figure in the plot or subplot. We meet some new folks, and we're happy to meet them because they, too, contribute to the energy boost. We want to know more about them. Our interest is rekindled.

And, truth to tell, it doesn't have to be a particularly joyful noise—just noisy. Serious musicals with a lot on their mind indulge in the practice, including classics like *South Pacific* and modern successes like *Spring Awakening*, where a song called "The Bitch of Living" serves the purpose.

*Spring Awakening* is based on Frank Wedekind's scandalous (at the time) turn-of-the-century play about teenage rebellion, which exposed the sexual exploits of young people at a time when no one spoke aloud about such things. In the musical, adult authority figures serve to destroy budding lives in a repressive society. The show is set in the late nineteenth century, but the style is entirely twenty-first century: handheld microphones, ambiguous clothing, and a score that is as often real rock as it is "theater music." After the requisite opening and preliminary numbers, the just-postadolescent ensemble gathers to bemoan "the bitch of living," in a song by Duncan Sheik and Steven Sater that would not be out of place in any rock concert venue but was a bit of a shock on Broadway (though not the biggest shock in this particular score). The details are about what you'd expect of a song called "The Bitch of Living" sung by angry, horny teens, but the value of the number is in its placement, a sour number in the sweet spot that is nonetheless an energy high. While other seriously intended musicals have sometimes used the spot to accomplish multiple goals, *Spring Awakening* is content to use it as a kind of antimasque to "Jubilation T. Cornpone," by which I mean no disrespect. The noise is enough, if it's a good enough noise.

One of the best of all such noises is Jerry Herman's "Put On Your Sunday Clothes" from *Hello, Dolly!* The show doesn't exactly fit the classic template, at least not without a stretch. Dolly Gallagher Levi, a busybody matchmaker from Yonkers, has explained in an opening number that her purpose in life is to bring people together in romance. And in dialogue she's told us that her immediate purpose is to find a husband for herself. Then we meet the obvious candidate, the misanthropic Horace Vandergelder, skinflint merchant. So the ultimate goal of the story is more or less set up, but there's no real I Want song for Dolly (Vandergelder expresses his desire in "It Takes a Woman"), and no conditional love song. Still, we're at about the same place in the story as if there had been. And the adventure to follow is about to begin when Dolly, with her assistant Ermengarde and Horace's two provincial clerks, set off from Yonkers for a day in the faraway big city—that would be Manhattan.

The number that takes them there starts modestly enough, though the fact that it's a kind of banjo-driven strut should tip us off that this piece of music might have room to expand. The lyric is simple and concise; it describes the ambition of everyone involved to *live* before it's too late, and in this sense it *is* a kind of an I Want song. It is rather a small song if you just play through it once, extolling the virtues of dressing up, going out, and seeking romance and glamour in the big city. But the creators of *Dolly!*, led by the director-choreographer Gower Champion, had big plans. The number is a kind of rite of passage, and the noise is not simply aural but also visual. We go from the modest Yonkers train station to the train and get the tour of the lower Hudson Valley in an ever-elaborating display of costumes and sets (a moving train! a passing cityscape!) as Dolly and her little brood of adventurers set out on a hunt for the adventure that might bring them lifelong happiness. The provincial becomes urban; the drudgery of everyday living is suddenly injected with infinite promise and beauty. Drear turns to joy, right in front of our eyes. What makes these five minutes or so of theater so exhilarating? It's not just the song or just the costume changes or the escalating excitement of the moving scenery or just the increasing noise made by the increasingly large number of singers. It's not even simply that the whole megillah is massively impressive in its totality. It's all of that, plus, in a leading role, what Jerome Robbins called "the rate of release of ideas." Champion understood that as soon as the audience has understood a visual idea and taken pleasure from it, another idea has to be presented. As soon as the sound of a trio has been enjoyed, the quartet has to enter, then the octet, then the entire company.

Timing is everything. If an idea overstays its welcome, the audience gets bored. If a new idea intrudes before the last one has been fully digested, the audience will be denied the proper introduction of a new pleasure and become confused or frustrated. But in "Put On Your Sunday Clothes," the rate of release is perfect, resulting in a catapulting delight. Like a great lover, the number has an instinct for escalating the audience's pleasure at the right moment. In the original production of *Dolly!*, that audience, having little or no idea of how many tricks Champion and company had up their sleeves, was left breathless—the number set off the joy buzzer and the crowd erupted. At its conclusion, *Dolly!*'s merry band of explorers had escaped the provinces and arrived in the most beautiful place in the world; life teemed with limitless possibilities. This, the audience told itself, is why there are musicals.

At almost exactly the same moment, Robbins was working on another version of the rate of release, but with a far different ambition. *Dolly!*

opened in January 1964. *Fiddler on the Roof* premiered a mere eight months later, and the two of them dominated the street for most of the next decade. *Fiddler* has a heavier heart than *Dolly!*, but it is still a musical, and still plays, more or less, by the rules. Its leading couple has been married for decades, so there is no conditional love song, but after Tevye the milkman leads the classic and exemplary opening number, we meet his three marriageable daughters, who have their I Want song ("Matchmaker, Matchmaker"). Then Tevye, beleaguered by his life as an impoverished milkman, delivers *his* I Want moment with "If I Were a Rich Man" (which is not about wanting literal wealth, but wealth as a metaphor for an elevated, meaningful life). The plot has now arrived: Tevye's oldest daughter, Tzeitel, is in love with Motel, the poor tailor, but Tevye's wife has entertained a proposal of marriage from Lazar Wolf, the wealthy butcher. The marriage will solve myriad difficulties but, of course, be a tragedy for Tzeitel and Motel.

Nonetheless, Tevye goes off to the local tavern, where he and Lazar Wolf consummate a deal. Immediately, a spontaneous celebration erupts: the noise.

It's important to understand that *Fiddler*'s entire world is shadowed by the presence of Russian gentiles lurking in a little Jewish village. Before the theatergoer's evening is over, the village will have been eradicated by order of the czar, but at this point, early in the show, the threat feels more theoretical than real. Here is where Robbins, with the songwriters Jerry Bock and Sheldon Harnick, uses the noise to raise the stakes. No one in the little village of Anatevka has any Sunday clothes to put on (in Anatevka they'd be Saturday clothes, of course), yet the number, "To Life," appears to have a similar purpose to the one in *Hello, Dolly!*: to celebrate life's possibilities. It's a rare moment when a small group of Jewish peasants can genuinely enjoy a tiny blast of optimism. The number begins with Tevye and Lazar Wolf, and soon adds a singing ensemble chanting a Hebraic melody. Then they are dancing, and the number is building excitement.

And then it stops. It stops because hidden in a corner of this little shtetl tavern is a group of Russian soldiers who have been minding their own business but who want to join in the fun. The music shifts, and where there was a klezmer-style clarinet there is suddenly a mandolin instead. We're no longer in that up-tempo minor-key wail so familiar to bar mitzvah attendees the world over; we're very much in the land of Russian folk music and the balalaika. And although the Russians seem to bear no ill intent to anyone in the room, there is a vague sense of danger that has completely replaced the joy that was unconfined only a moment earlier. The Jews retreat. The Russians advance. Their style of dance is different, too—a little too aggressive and a little too fueled by vodka. Suddenly we're aware that something very bad might happen.

But nothing does. Eventually, the Jews join the Russians. The Russians, having asserted their right to be dominant parties even as guests in a Jewish tavern, relent, and everyone dances together—sort of. "To Life" builds to a frantic, drunken climax, and for one more day, peace has been maintained. But the world has been shaken, too.

As "Put On Your Sunday Clothes" is classic Gower Champion, "To Life" is classic Jerome Robbins—the two men are almost living emblems of the masks of comedy and tragedy. The former fabricates an entirely original world of pure joy from the most reliable of musical comedy materials. The latter sees the dark edges and lengthening shadows of a cultural clash that is fraught with danger—also using classic musical comedy materials. Yet both understand that by telling their story at exactly the right pace, by concealing and then revealing the story elements, by reeling the audience in, neither dawdling nor racing, by having enough ammunition and using it wisely, they cause an actual experience to engulf the building. The show's heartbeat accelerates, and that energy tumbles across the footlights and into the house. Pixilated by color, light, and melody, or threatened with danger and potential violence, the audience still experiences the thrill of witnessing a genuine theatrical event happening in real time, and its spirit is lifted. Not all showstoppers are happy. Not all of them mean much of anything. Some are inane, while others portend deep human tragedy to follow. Or great hope. Or aspiration. What they have in common is this: the ones in this spot all make a lot of noise.

# 6. Bushwhacking 1: Second Couples

The moment comes in every life, alas, when it is time to be kicked out of the nest. For a musical theater story, that moment usually arrives right after the noise. Recess is over. And back in the classroom, something strange has happened. All the prior work has set the show on a unique course. Opening numbers tend to follow one of two paths. I Want songs are easy to describe, as are conditional love songs, and even the noise. But by the time all of that has happened, a particular and unique show has taken shape, and the time has come for it to wander off and find its own place in the world. The show leaves the prescribed trail and begins to bushwhack its way through the unknown thicket of its own making. This is a good thing. The formula begins to break down. This is often where the machines are separated from the animals.

In fact, most shows can be broken down into three acts (but are performed in two), with the first two acts crammed together in what we now call Act 1. The first half of Act 1 is the expositional piece: Where are we? What's the world of the show like? Who's the protagonist? What's her problem and how does she plan to solve it? What's she up against? What's the era, the attitude, the point of view? Once these things have been established (which often takes less than half the running time of Act 1), the journey begins in earnest, with complications, unexpected twists, and secondary characters who cause trouble or turn the story in different directions. This is really a second act. Intermission doesn't come until the basic quest has been sufficiently messed with so that it seems no simple or satisfactory outcome is possible.

The moment of demarcation may or may not be obvious, but it's fun to go looking for it. The first act of *Sweeney Todd*, for instance, ends when Anthony sings the first version of "Johanna." Sweeney has met and teamed up with Mrs. Lovett. He's told the story of how he got shanghaied to Australia on a false charge by a corrupt judge who wanted to steal his young, beautiful wife. Mrs. Lovett has explained that the wife took poison but the evil judge still has Sweeney's daughter, Johanna, imprisoned. We've learned that the judge has erotic designs on the by now almost adult daughter, and then Anthony, the sailor who rescued Sweeney at sea, sees the daughter in the judge's window and falls instantly in love with her. This inextricably links together all the principal characters and sets up a natural tension. Can Sweeney rescue the daughter and destroy the judge? Or will the sailor steal her away before Sweeney has time to act? Or will the judge destroy them both and keep the daughter for his own nefarious purposes? Can Mrs. Lovett lay her hands on Sweeney, on whom she seems to have developed a secret crush, or will she lose out to Sweeney's obsession with the judge and the daughter? The story is tightly wound up and ready to be sprung. Anthony sings "Johanna," which concludes with crashing, passionate chords that sound almost like "curtain down" music, and the next thing we see is a complete stranger with an Italian accent setting up shop as a barber in a nearby street. The action has shifted. The second part of Act 1 has begun. The first monkey wrench is about to be thrown.

How these second parts of Act 1 develop is a lot harder to characterize than how the first parts do. The beginnings of shows have such specific requirements that they tend to explain themselves. Once the story has wandered off, who knows what complications will ensue?

As a result, laying out a song plot for the late middle of Act 1 isn't simple, because good shows are happily unpredictable. But it usually involves some of the following: a number for the villain, if there is one; a number for the star, if there is one; and some time spent with the major subplot, whatever it might be. In the Golden Age, and often even now, it usually involves a second romantic couple.

The second couple is an age-old device, of course. Shakespeare used it a lot (think *Much Ado About Nothing*), and operettas in the 1920s usually had them—a soubrette and a comedian—principally to provide laughs, since the leading couple had to sing like birds, and actors who could do that tended to be stiff and humorless. By the time Hammerstein got to *Oklahoma!* the idea was virtually obligatory—hence Ado Annie and Will Parker (*Oklahoma!*), Carrie Pipperidge and Mr. Snow (*Carousel*), Liat and Lieutenant Cable (*South Pacific*), and Tuptim and Lun Tha (*The King and I*). The structure remained unchanged as Hammerstein laid out his librettos, but the intention evolved quickly into something more sophisticated and challenging than it had ever been.

Ado Annie and Will Parker are really in the shadow of operetta, there to provide comedy and up-tempo fun. But in *Carousel*, Carrie and Mr. Snow have a deeper purpose, which is to hold up a reverse mirror to the main romance, to make manifest the values that the main couple has rejected: a conventional marriage, hard work and prosperity, a legacy of success, and a proper and rising place in society. The two characters also demonstrate, of course, the flip side of that equation: sexual and conversational boredom, narrow-mindedness, and the stultifying life that a proper and rising place in society brings. Julie and Billy, driven recklessly by erotic love and a need to escape their own dead-end lives, wouldn't make the same choice even if it were available to them, but they are forced to confront it right in front of them—and so is the audience. The second couple is comic, and maybe even endearing, but their values are hopelessly middle class, dull, and exclusionary. Both couples are doomed to a destined outcome, in a sense, but only one—the conventional one—can survive as a couple. That's part of *Carousel*'s power—the greater the passion, the greater the danger.

In Frank Loesser's *Guys and Dolls*, the couples are split evenly—it's hard to tell which one comes first. Based principally on two Damon Runyon short stories, each a full-blown romance, the musical version does keep to the operetta model in one sense: Sky Masterson and Sarah Brown are the romantic ones with the legit voices, while Nathan Detroit and Miss Adelaide are the comics. But Abe Burrows, who wrote the book and was just beginning to emerge from the radio sketch comedy world, used a structure common to radio and, later, to classic TV sitcom writing. He began the show with all four characters, then methodically switched focus, bouncing between the two couples—and the two plots—scene by scene. First couple A, then couple B, then couple A, then couple B, reuniting them at the end. If you call Sky and Sarah's plot the Mission plot and Nathan and Adelaide's plot the Crap Game plot, the show lays out neatly, as shown in the chart opposite.

Note the way the plotting begins to throw characters from the two different plots together in Act 2 but still maintains a focus on bouncing from plot to plot. Lest we grow tired of seeing Nathan always paired with Adelaide, and Sky with Sarah, in Act 2 we get a scene with Nathan and Sky, and another with Adelaide and Sarah. It keeps us off balance just enough.

In Loesser's next show, *The Most Happy Fella*, for which he wrote the book himself, he took the operetta convention both forward and backward, employing it while lampooning it. In the process, he created what is probably the only successful musical with two different scores.

*Happy Fella* is almost an opera. Tony, the middle-aged Napa Valley grape farmer, and Rosabella, his mail-order bride, have big gorgeous arias to thrill audiences with; even Joe, the ranch hand who impregnates Rosabella, needs to have a booming baritone, which means Loesser didn't ask that he also have wit. By contrast, the "comic" couple, Cleo and Herman, needs to sing loud, but in a musical comedy manner. (Auditioning Susan Johnson, who eventually got the part of Cleo, Loesser told her, "Sing like someone's chasing you.") Loesser wrote for the characters in their own style, ignoring the idea of overall unity. Accordingly, Cleo and Herman's songs might have come from an entirely different musical than those written for Tony, Rosabella, and Joe. Stylistically, *The Most Happy Fella* is a mash-up of Puccini and *The Pajama Game*, except that in both styles, Loesser always sounds like himself, melodically and harmonically as well as lyrically. This score-within-a-score technique was met with skepticism by some critics of the day (and still comes up when the show is revived), but Loesser was essentially amplifying a pattern established by Victor Herbert, Sigmund Romberg, and Rudolf Friml back in the day. They, too, wrote in

# GUYS AND DOLLS
## Act 1

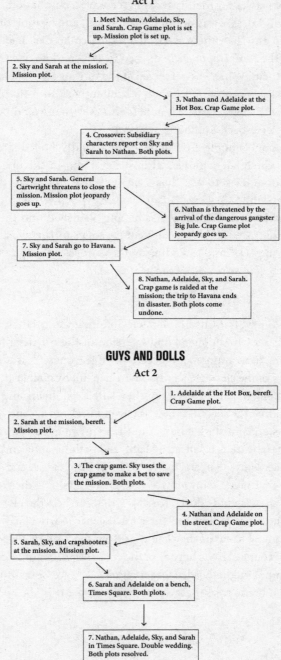

1. Meet Nathan, Adelaide, Sky, and Sarah. Crap Game plot is set up. Mission plot is set up.

2. Sky and Sarah at the mission. Mission plot.

3. Nathan and Adelaide at the Hot Box. Crap Game plot.

4. Crossover: Subsidiary characters report on Sky and Sarah to Nathan. Both plots.

5. Sky and Sarah. General Cartwright threatens to close the mission. Mission plot jeopardy goes up.

6. Nathan is threatened by the arrival of the dangerous gangster Big Jule. Crap Game plot jeopardy goes up.

7. Sky and Sarah go to Havana. Mission plot.

8. Nathan, Adelaide, Sky, and Sarah. Crap game is raided at the mission; the trip to Havana ends in disaster. Both plots come undone.

# GUYS AND DOLLS
## Act 2

1. Adelaide at the Hot Box, bereft. Crap Game plot.

2. Sarah at the mission, bereft. Mission plot.

3. The crap game. Sky uses the crap game to make a bet to save the mission. Both plots.

4. Nathan and Adelaide on the street. Crap Game plot.

5. Sarah, Sky, and crapshooters at the mission. Mission plot.

6. Sarah and Adelaide on a bench, Times Square. Both plots.

7. Nathan, Adelaide, Sky, and Sarah in Times Square. Double wedding. Both plots resolved.

two distinct styles for their two distinct couples, but the contrast was a delicate one. Loesser was nothing if not brash, and he took the idea all the way. In any case, the American operetta composers had been forgotten by the time *Happy Fella* opened in 1956 and no one thought to reference them. What was perceived at the time as an experiment was, in some ways, nothing more than a brilliantly skillful tip of the hat, executed with characteristic boldness in a way that would never have occurred to Herbert, Romberg, or Friml.

The second couple in *Happy Fella* actually had distinguished material, which such couples almost never did in the operetta era. "Lover, Come Back to Me" has long survived its source, 1927's *The New Moon*, while "Try Her Out at Dances," which was written for the comic lead in the same show, has happily vanished into the mists of time. By contrast, the best second-couple songs in *Happy Fella*, "Ooh, My Feet," "Big 'D,'" and "Standing on the Corner," are still a part of our consciousness if we're fans of the genre.

As for *Sweeney Todd* itself, Stephen Sondheim and Hugh Wheeler, working from Christopher Bond's version of the nineteenth-century melodrama, took a more jaundiced look at the operetta tradition. The psychology of the characters is distinguished not by nuance (it's a melodrama, after all) but by the way they sing. Sondheim and Wheeler make sure that the second couple's state of mind—innocent, naïve, and hopeful—stands in stark contrast to the main couple's cynicism, rage, and madness. Dark is balanced by light, and both Johanna and the sailor have mid-act solos—"Green Finch and Linnet Bird" for her and "Johanna" for him—that give definition to their characters and their dilemma. They also share a giddy duet, "Kiss Me," that furthers the plot and clues us in to the possible limits of their intelligence, particularly hers. The songs are about as far as they could be from the kind that were written for second couples in the heyday of the convention, but one could argue that Johanna's addle-headed observations do owe something to the kinds of soubrette roles that were typical of comedy in the operetta era.

What distinguishes these second-couple songs that populate the middle third of the first act? People tend to refer to them as "Ado Annie songs," and, to be sure, Annie and Will Parker have a couple of standard comedy numbers, "I Cain't Say No" and "Kansas City," early on in *Oklahoma!* Both are examples of what passed for comic erotica in 1943, or 1943's impression of 1906, and they've stood the test of time, at least as period pieces. Will's is about encountering indoor plumbing for the first time and going to a burlesque show in Kansas City, considered the big time if you lived in the Oklahoma Territory; Annie's is about a very mild and charming case of nymphomania.

But by the time of *The King and I*, R&H were well beyond focusing on the "comic" couple as necessarily comic. The progression is interesting and speaks to Hammerstein's conviction that there is no point in a subplot unless it illuminates the plot.* In *Carousel* (1945), Mr. Snow and Carrie are both comic and somewhat alarming, and slightly more integrated into the central story than are Ado Annie and Will Parker. Mr. Snow seems like an ambitious buffoon in the beginning (his big dream is of a fleet of herring boats), but as American business has proved countless times, buffoonery is no bar to wealth and power. And in the end, the prosperous Snow family displays a level of class consciousness and intolerance that turns them into implicit villains. In *South Pacific* (1949), Liat and Lieutenant Cable are in some ways more like Billy and Julie than like a typical second couple—eager for escape from two different repressive worlds and doomed by their dreams and their erotic awakening.

They are something new: the tragic second couple. R&H went a step further in *The King and I* (1951), introducing a second couple whose love is forbidden by the hidebound regime of the King. The slave girl

---

* To be fair, Hammerstein had been thinking about this since the latter part of his operetta career. In 1927's *Show Boat*, his earliest attempt to treat a serious subject in a musical, there are actually four couples. Magnolia and Gaylord Ravenal take the romantic leads, while Frank and Ellie, a specialty act on the show boat, fill out the soubrette/comedian responsibilities. Joe and Queenie, the African American couple, carry both entertainment and thematic work. But there is also the dissembling interracial couple—Julie and Steve, who personify the theme of racial disharmony and the dangers of challenging it. These are the real ancestors of Liat and Lieutenant Cable.

Tuptim sings "My Lord and Master," about her servitude, and she and her secret lover, Lun Tha, have a romantic duet, "We Kiss in a Shadow," that makes explicit how risky their love affair is, both during the middle of the act. In some respects R&H, by this moment, had turned the traditional subplot tone upside down, though they continued to use the device for the same purpose: to expose, through the second couple, the depth and shape of the problem being experienced by the first. Anna and the King are locked in a conflict over modernity. Tuptim and Lun Tha are threatened by the potentially fatal consequences of Anna losing the battle, their love forbidden by the ancient political caste systems over which the King continues to rule.*

Liat and Lieutenant Cable, and Lun Tha and Tuptim, represented a new kind of idea for second couples, and decades later the idea resurfaced in an entirely different context in, of all places, *Hairspray*.

By this point, the convention had worn out its welcome as a structural tool of modern musicals and was only occasionally on display. *Hairspray* embraced it with a vengeance and turned it back into comedy, but with a common theme.

Tracy Turnblad, *Hairspray*'s heroine, has a best friend, Penny, who is as pathologically shy as Tracy is bold. When Tracy reveals her plan to audition for *The Corny Collins Show*, Penny proudly says, "And I have to go *watch* you audition!" Penny has an awful, repressive mother and lives by trying to be invisible, until the moment when she meets Seaweed, a black student whose mom runs an R&B record store on the wrong side of town and hosts "Negro Day" once a month on *The Corny Collins Show*.

"Hey gal," Seaweed says, "I've seen you at the vending machines gettin' your Juicy Fruit."

---

* There is a practical consideration at work in *The King and I* as well. Neither Gertrude Lawrence nor Yul Brynner, who played the leads, was a particularly strong singer. In flipping the tone, if not the purpose, of the second couple, R&H could provide some lovely, and beautifully sung, ballads for the show instead of comic ditties.

"I'm up to two packs a day," she replies shyly, but feels something new stirring within.

"All that chewing must make your jaw pretty strong," Seaweed replies—a unique pickup line that, nonetheless, has the desired effect on the clueless Penny.

Seaweed and Penny are an interracial second couple like Lieutenant Cable and Liat, and they serve the same old function of amplifying and explicating the main couple's problem: how to confront bigotry in America (it's a big one). It's really the same problem Anna and the King were dealing with internationally—confronting progress in a world moving erratically forward—but in a different guise. Penny and Seaweed, like Tuptim and Lun Tha, and Liat and Lieutenant Cable before them, put a human face on the problem. This means Tracy is fighting for her best friend, not just for a cause, and that helps keep the show, which is, after all, a campy comedy, from getting didactic. Tracy doesn't have to make big statements about integration and liberty (though she makes a few hilarious ones), she just has to fight for Penny's right to be kissed by the man she loves, forbidden though that may be in the Baltimore of the early '60s.

Forbidden love, especially when the taboo is racial or religious, feels like a very American subject, but it serves a classic second-couple purpose in *Cabaret*, which is set in Berlin between the world wars. Written by Joe Masteroff (book) and John Kander and Fred Ebb (music and lyrics), it was the first of the producer-director Hal Prince's departures from the classic Golden Age style he had spent a decade producing. In 1964, Jerome Robbins announced his retirement from Broadway right after directing the Prince-produced *Fiddler on the Roof*. A year later, Prince produced Kander and Ebb's first musical, *Flora the Red Menace*, directed by George Abbott, who had given Prince his start and was now pushing eighty. Much as he revered Abbott, Prince knew that with *Flora*, he'd made a mistake. He wanted to push the musical into new territory; efficiently deploying the hoary conventions of the '50s, Abbott was the wrong man. And Robbins was back at City Ballet. Prince would have to do the job himself. *Cabaret* was something of an in-betweener, a transitional piece neither completely free from old conventions nor a slave to them. But one of its conventional paradigms that worked particularly well was the second couple.

They were played by Lotte Lenya and Jack Gilford—she a German émigré and the widow and chief interpreter of Kurt Weill, he an American vaudevillian. Both in the story and in real life, she was gentile, he Jewish. And they were older, not the young innocents to whom the roles were traditionally assigned. In a musical that chronicled the rise of Nazi Germany, their romance was destined to be brief and tragic. The main couple, an expat American writer named Clifford Bradshaw and an amoral carouser named Sally Bowles, promised excitement, but not warmth or tenderness. She was in it for kicks; he was a cool, sexually ambivalent outside observer. (In the subsequent film and later productions, Cliff's bisexuality was made explicit, but that would have been too big a reach in 1966.) To point up the hard edge of Cliff and Sally's doomed affair, the show offered an opposing portrait in the subplot: the warm, deeply human courtship of Fräulein Schneider and Herr Schultz.

Kander and Ebb, who had written some terrific and underappreciated songs for *Flora*, came into their own with *Cabaret*, providing a consistently first-rate score that alternated traditional "book songs" relating to the plot with cabaret numbers that explored the themes of louche Berlin falling inexorably under the spell of fascism. It was a dazzling display for the young songwriters. The songs that are best remembered are the cabaret numbers, particularly the title song and "Willkommen," an opening number in the mold of "Comedy Tonight" and "Tradition." But their songs for the second couple chart a perfect arc. Lenya's Fräulein Schneider endears us with a Weillesque "So What?" early in the first act, and then, in the classic midway spot in the act, there is a wonderful conditional love song about, of all things, a pineapple.

"It Couldn't Please Me More" is a charm duet, which both Lenya and Gilford used to create a three-way love affair—she with him, he with her, and the audience with both of them. Herr Schultz, the Jewish fruit dealer, brings Fräulein Schneider a pineapple as a gift, and they sing about it ruefully, shyly, complete with Hawaiian guitar accompaniment, although the pineapple's provenance isn't so glamorous:

SHE

*Ahh-ah-ah-ah-ah-ah, I can hear Hawaiian breezes blow*
*Ahh-ah-ah-ah-ah-ah . . .*

HE

*It's from California*

SHE

*Even so . . .*
*How am I to thank you?*

HE

*Kindly let it pass.*

SHE

*Would you like a slice?*

HE

*That might be nice,*
*But frankly, it would give me gas.*

Fräulein Schneider is "overwhelmed." But not as overwhelmed as she will be a scene or two later when Herr Schultz proposes marriage. In a simple but telling duet, they contemplate a modest but rosy future, and Ebb, the lyricist, turns into folk poetry the everyday speech of two working-class people who thought their lives were essentially done.

> *How the world can change*
> *It can change like that—*
> *Due to one little word:*
> *"Married."*
> *See a palace rise*
> *From a two-room flat*
> *Due to one little word:*
> *"Married."*

Somehow we know that it can't happen, and that it won't happen, which makes the modesty of their courtship heartbreaking in its directness and simplicity, and a perfect foil for the tart and alienated central relationship between Cliff and Sally.

Second-couple songs rarely get the kind of attention they are entitled to—of necessity, they exert less of a pull than the songs written for the main plot. We don't want them to upset the story architecture by seizing the stage too forcibly. They tend to do their work subversively, drawing our attention just long enough to add a layer of meaning to what the leading players are going through, while simultaneously providing some relief from it. Originally a comic device, they have evolved over the decades to play every conceivable supporting role—young, old, comic, tragic, and thematic. As time progresses, the adventurers, from Hammerstein to Loesser to Sondheim, Prince, and Kander and Ebb, keep asking them to do more, and to do it differently, but the basic architecture of the musical show is designed to contain multitudes.

# 7. Bushwhacking 2: Villains

Not every show has a villain, of course, but there must be adversarial forces if there is to be a contest worth watching. And not every villain has to sing. The murderous Warlord in *The Book of Mormon* is a perfect example. The authors, who had comedy galore everywhere else, may have considered giving a comedy solo to the vicious general with the unprintable (but I'll print it anyway) name of Butt-Fucking Naked, but letting villains sing funny tends to domesticate them. And this villain really needed to be scary, which is why, instead of singing, he shoots an innocent bystander in the face right in front of our eyes. Trey Parker and Matt Stone had command of how to tell their story, even though they were musical theater newcomers.

During a rehearsal, one of the veteran actors in the company talked about how two guys who had never tried it before were getting it so right with such seeming ease.

"The thing about these guys," he explained, "is that they've been telling a twenty-three-minute story a week for about twenty years on TV. You get good at it after a while. You have no idea what it's like for an actor to work with writers who just know how to tell a story—it's bred into them, and they have an answer for every question. We never doubt them; we have no reason to."

That said, in shows that aren't crazy comedies, it is possible to have the villain sing and actually gain stature in the process.

"A story is only as gripping as its villain," goes an old Hollywood saw, which is ironic, considering the blandness and predictability of so many Hollywood villains—at least the ones who are on-screen, as opposed to those who are running the studio. Generally speaking, villains are most compelling when, however terrible they are, we're forced to understand their point of view. If they seem like simple paper tigers, the audience is likely to lose interest.

Here again, *Oklahoma!* and *Sweeney Todd* are instructive. In the former, Jud, the sex-starved farmhand who wants desperately to get his hands on the heroine, has all the hallmarks of a generic baddie—he's unwashed, he lusts after pornography as well as actual women, and he isn't above trafficking in murder weapons. He's unquestionably a figure of the times (we're not so tough on porn enthusiasts these days, unless they're politicians), but even in this early version of the modern musical Hammerstein felt compelled to make sure we heard Jud's side of the story. In a song called "Lonely Room," Jud, alone in the outdoor shed he's forced to call home, ruminates frighteningly on his lot in life. There's no question we find him dangerous in this moment, but he is also somehow humanized.

"*The floor creaks, the door squeaks,*" he complains.

> *There's a field-mouse a-nibblin' on a broom,*
> *And I set by myself*
> *Like a cobweb on a shelf*
> *By myself in a lonely room.*

We're immediately captured by him in a way we didn't think we could be. There's poetry and self-loathing in the man in equal measure, and the power of his loneliness seems to have driven him mad. He's not just a baddie, he's ill, maybe more than ill, as Rodgers's creepy music makes clear. And the danger that's in him becomes immediately more powerful, more alarming than it has been, because we're tainted by it. We have to recognize him. He has dreams, just like the other characters in the piece, and just like us.

*But when there's a moon in my winder*
*And it slants down a beam 'crost my bed,*
*Then the shadder of a tree*
*Starts a-dancin' on the wall*
*And a dream starts a-dancin' in my head . . .*
*And the girl that I want*
*Ain't afraid of my arms,*
*And her own soft arms keep me warm.*
*And her long, yeller hair*
*Falls acrost my face,*
*Jist like the rain in a storm!*

What can you say about a man who expresses himself like this? *"Her long, yeller hair falls acrost my face, jist like the rain in a storm!"* he says, and we simply can't ignore that. He's a man for whom tenderness will never come, but he can imagine it easily and with a colorful gift for imagery. He's going to go off the deep end, if he hasn't already, and he's going to have to die. But the moral quandary that he presents is one of the reasons *Oklahoma!* is what it is—the golden door through which the musical play had to one day finally pass.

In *Sweeney Todd* (which also uses the phrase "yellow hair" to great effect), Judge Turpin stands in for Jud Fry. Unlike Jud, he's politically powerful—the most powerful character in the piece, in fact. But he, too, is overcome by lust and alarming sexual tastes. And Stephen Sondheim, with characteristic boldness, wrote him a villain's number (one of the three different songs in the show called "Johanna") in which he spies on his young ward, masturbates, and whips himself with a cat-o'-nine-tails. The number was cut from the original production, allegedly because the show was running long, but it's hard not to suspect an element of faintheartedness entered the argument. One can only imagine what commercial producers thought of the song—certainly it was the first time the American musical had ever featured an old man flagellating himself to orgasm on a Broadway stage. Is this what Cole Porter meant by "Anything Goes"? Perhaps, but he didn't say so explicitly.

In the years since that original production, the number has been restored and we've all gotten a little more accustomed to a wide-angle view of human sexual activity. But looked at without the filter of conventional censoriousness, "Johanna" is revealing and alarming in many of the same ways as "Lonely Room." It presents a character out of control, lost to his own fantasies, and crippled by an ambivalence that won't allow him to do the right thing, even as doubt engulfs him. He cries:

> *God, deliver me!*
> *Release me!*
> *Forgive me!*
> *Restrain me!*
> *Pervade me!*

But obsession, as with Jud, is the boss. And the outcome can only be fatal.

Villain numbers don't have to be scary, of course, and a far greater number of them were designed to be funny. In musical theater, the comedy villain dates back beyond the days of George M. Cohan, who wrote "Then I'd Be Satisfied with Life" at the turn of the century, a list song in which a fraudster ticks off the simple pleasures (*"All I need is fifty million dollars . . ."*) that would make him a happy man. But the appearance of comic villains has been more of an option than a staple of Broadway musicals, and most often the jokes in their songs, with some lucky exceptions, aren't that funny. What the songs do provide is a performance opportunity based on character—a chance for a good comic to have the stage all to herself or himself and display a unique gift and the craft that goes with it. The tradition probably evolved from vaudeville, and even in modern times it often feels like a throwback to earlier times. That's certainly the case with one of the most successful of them all, Miss Hannigan's "Little Girls," from *Annie*.

Dorothy Loudon originated the role of the dipsomaniacal mistress of the orphanage. Finally, after laboring in the Broadway fields since 1962, Loudon got a role worthy of her comic talents. She was loud, brassy, and slightly out of control, and could make pure, unmotivated meanness into something joyful to behold. Watching her drunkenly threaten a pack of defenseless little girls was inherently funny, so it doesn't really matter that the lyric to "Little Girls," on paper, is only fair. Loudon found the laughs, expanded them, savored them, and drop-kicked them all the way to the balcony. All she needed was a funny idea to work with, which "Little Girls" provides.

A similarly out-of-control baddie, the sadistic dentist in *Little Shop of Horrors*, gets his moment mid-act, and here the number is actually a witty send-up of the rebel-without-a-cause James Dean/Elvis types who were always threatening the sanctity of suburban teen-girl purity in early rock-and-roll America. The score, remember, tips its hat to those late-'50s and early-'60s chart hits that were knocking conventional show tunes off the hit parade, and "Dentist!" is a "He's a Rebel" pastiche that takes the genre into a kind of delicious netherworld. The Dentist (*"Here he comes, girls, the leader of the plaque!"*) simply sings his autobiography, relating how his proud mother, discovering his proclivity for twisting the heads off kittens and poisoning tropical fish, realizes that there is a budding professional in the house:

> *That's when my mama said,*
> *"You'll be a dentist!*
> *You have a talent for causing things pain.*
> *Son, be a dentist!*
> *People will pay you to be inhumane."*

Though he does, in fact, ride a motorcycle just like James Dean, the Dentist takes the convention into the land of reductio ad absurdum. He's a laughing gas addict, which should be funny, but he's also an actual sadist and misogynist, and within the confines of *Little Shop*'s loopy comic book world, he's genuinely dangerous. This combination of absurdity and earnestness accounts for a great deal of the show's appeal. It appears to be a cartoon, but it's lifted from *Faust*. It appears to be a camp comedy, but at the same time, it takes its characters and their moral and psychological dilemmas completely seriously. It's unique in this way: it lampoons itself while simultaneously selling itself to you as something that matters. Audiences grow to care for Seymour and Audrey, to empathize with Seymour's dilemma. His handshake with the devil actually affects us and makes us wonder what we would do, or what we've already done. The devil, in this case, is the plant, which also has a villain number in Act 1. But the secondary villain, the Dentist, in this strangely dark/light world, is as scary as Jud, and as funny as Miss Hannigan.

The Dentist's lyric is actually funnier than the one Howard Ashman wrote for the villainess of *The Little Mermaid*, the blowsy lady octopus named Ursula. But this reinforces the point that these songs don't generally survive on the strength of their punch lines. They're effective because they're character numbers for funny characters. We laugh at the kind of person who is singing, not at the quality of the jokes—at least usually. "Poor Unfortunate Souls" is a reasonably obvious number, but we love the idea of an evil lady octopus. Why? Because physically, a blobby, shapeless female baritone is a comic stereotype we can't resist, political incorrectness notwithstanding. Ursula the Octopus and Miss Hannigan are, for all intents and purposes, the same character. We want to think they're funny, and we're certainly willing to cut the lyricist a break in the service of our own amusement.

The Dentist is also a stereotype, of course, as comic villains tend to be, especially when the musicals in question—from *Annie* to *Little Shop*—are genre pieces. A less successful genre piece, 1966's *It's a Bird . . . It's a Plane . . . It's Superman*, featured a well-worn stereotypical villain—the mad scientist. In this case he's mad because he's lost the Nobel Prize ten times in a row, which is kind of funny to start with. His comedy number, "Revenge"—in the usual mid-act spot—is worth noting purely for the best joke in Lee Adams's lyric, which chronicles the scientists who have beaten him, concluding with Harold Urey.

"*The shocking thing about the matter is,*" he sings, "*my heavy hydrogen was heavier . . . than his!*"

For a musical comic book, the show had wit, though not quite consistently enough to survive.

The question every show with a villain has to answer is how much to expose. In a comedy, the villain is likely to be tweaked, to make us laugh. She or he remains at a safe distance, a type, not a person. *Little*

*Shop*, *Annie*, and *Superman* are all based on material rooted in comic strips, or at least in comic strip thinking. *Oklahoma!* and *Sweeney Todd* are sterner stuff, and in a drama, we're usually made to understand that there's a deeply troubled and complicated person struggling with demons. In either case, the decision of how to treat the villain is usually at its clearest when the villain takes center stage about two-thirds of the way through Act 1 and finally sings.

# 8. Bushwhacking 3: The Multiplot, and How It Thickens

In 1975, two new works—one literary, one cinematic—changed the rules for storytelling in America, and it was only a matter of time before Broadway woke up to the possibilities. E. L. Doctorow's novel *Ragtime* and Robert Altman's film *Nashville* appeared within months of each other, and each had the daring to look at narrative as if it were a form of plate spinning, trying to keep multiple stories moving at once, and letting them bounce off one another in continually surprising ways. Both works thrived on a new kind of energy, created by a constantly shuffling deck of protagonists and antagonists. Critics, audiences, and readers took notice—and took pleasure. Something new, it appeared, had arrived.

It only took Broadway eight years to catch up. In 1983, Stephen Sondheim, collaborating for the first time with James Lapine, moved off Broadway to experiment. He'd never really worked off Broadway before, but after the failure of *Merrily We Roll Along* had ended his long professional partnership with Hal Prince, Sondheim turned to a form of musical storytelling that would have been risky on Broadway even for him. And Lapine, who had begun his professional career as a visual designer and moved into the theater world as a practitioner of the off-Broadway nonprofit process—readings, workshops, and semiproduced productions that allowed for recalculation and recalibration outside the pressure of the commercial maelstrom—felt comfortable developing shows within institutions. Besides, *Sunday in the Park with George* needed that. It was a musical about a painting.

The painting, Georges Seurat's *A Sunday Afternoon on the Island of La Grand Jatte*, depicted the French bourgeoisie passing a sunny day on a small island in the Seine, apparently doing not much of anything. Lapine and Sondheim had the intriguing notion of trying to answer two questions in their musical: Who were these people—what were their lives really about? And who was Georges Seurat that he felt so compelled to depict them in an apparently documentary fashion—an elaborate snapshot of a community in repose that presented many more questions than it answered? True, the actual subject was the artist's insatiable need to create and connect. But there were lots of stories to tell along the way, and no one had done that in a narrative musical before.

The musical spends Act 1 answering Lapine and Sondheim's two questions, while Act 2, set a hundred years later, asks an updated set of the same questions, as Seurat's (fictional) grandson deals with the making of art in the 1980s, in a technological world and a community of arts funders, society types, and pretentious critics and kibitzers. In both acts, however, the dominant quest is the same: an artist is struggling to connect with a community and break through to an original statement about it. Needless to say, it's an unconventional work, and it took time to develop. It substitutes many stories for one, though it focuses on Georges and his mistress-model Dot more often than not. But it really is a multiplot affair like *Ragtime* and *Nashville*. Would the ricochet effect of one little story pushing another one into action create its own energy onstage? It had begun to work not only in novels and film but also in television, where it has since become a staple.

But it's more difficult in a musical, where forward motion is always threatened, if not brought to a halt, by the music and lyrics. Sondheim and Lapine solved this problem neatly by recognizing Seurat as an obsessively motivated artist, whose invention of pointillism and whose passion for completing the painting, despite the fact that no one thought it was any good (except for us—we know it takes up a whole wall at the Art Institute of Chicago), drive the action as relentlessly as they can. Also, the show has to compel an audience for only a little over an hour at a time. Since *Sunday in the Park* is really two intersecting one-acts, the audience isn't expected to stay on the ride for as long as it would in a traditional musical.

Yet for all its experimentation, the middle of *Sunday*'s first act finds its musical voice in a number of the same ways that traditional musicals do. It has not one second couple, but four or five of them. And one of them even functions as a kind of villain. He's an art critic, she's his snobby wife, and their utter conventionality and misapprehension of what Seurat is up to refract his obsessive drive to break through to something new. They are art-as-status-quo success, while Seurat, who is making art that pushes away from the present and into the future, refers to himself, with knowing irony, as "the loony with the palette."

Jules and Yvonne, as this second (or third, or fourth) couple is known, even have a small second-couple song that encapsulates their— and the Parisian world's—point of view about Seurat. It's called "No Life" and expresses an opinion of the painting Seurat is working on, which, of course, has had a long one. It's also a comment on Seurat himself, who seems to lack any social existence. In expressing their views, Jules and Yvonne manage to become stand-ins for the myopic conservatism of critics generally, something that may have brought Sondheim some pleasure, given the length of time it took for most of them to recognize his unique genius as a composer.

Critically, Sondheim had one of the easiest introductions into the Broadway world as a writer of words, and one of the hardest as a writer of music. Critics who noticed his lyrics for *West Side Story* (not all of them did) singled them out for their freshness. But his first full score, for *A Funny Thing Happened on the Way to the Forum*, was generally dismissed by the critical fraternity and wasn't even nominated for a Tony Award, though the nominators had to look pretty deeply into the land of flopdom to find a way to snub it (*Bravo Giovanni* got the fourth and final nomination. *Bravo Giovanni*?). His next score, for the unworkably experimental *Anyone Can Whistle*, established the musical voice that is now instantly recognizable. The music got a good review from a single critic, the former symphony trombonist Norman Nadel, who sort of knew a new voice when he heard one, though he had dismissed the

*Forum* score two years earlier. Nadel came around more quickly than most. Sondheim wasn't heard as a composer on Broadway again until 1970's *Company*, which, while greeted ecstatically in some corners, was viewed with suspicion by Clive Barnes of the *Times*; the music rattled him. It took Barnes's stunningly wrongheaded assessment of the *Follies* score before he finally caved in when *A Little Night Music* opened in 1973, eleven years after *Forum*. Today, all these scores—even *Whistle*—have become a part of the American theatrical pantheon, but it's hard not to imagine "No Life" as a little bit of revenge on critics everywhere for how long it took.

Unsurprisingly, perhaps, many of the critics were as buffaloed by the totality of *Sunday* as they had been by the scores for *Forum* and *Whistle*. It took a rave—followed by constant reminders—from the *Times*'s Frank Rich, who had long since replaced Barnes and his successor Richard Eder, to keep the show in the public eye. The Pulitzer Prize didn't hurt. The Tony was won by *La Cage aux Folles*, however. Admirably, the first Broadway musical about an (almost) openly gay couple, it had optimism, some very fat tunes, and a good old-fashioned plot.

Intentionally or not, *Sunday* led the way to a series of less convincing multiplot shows, including *Grand Hotel*, which had been in the works since the '50s but finally reached Broadway when the director Tommy Tune got involved in the late '80s (it opened in 1989). Based on the classic if somewhat tinny movie of the same name, and the novel that preceded it, *Grand Hotel* followed a number of stories all crossing paths at the Grand in Berlin between the wars. The stories, of a fake count who's really a jewel thief, an aging ballerina and her lovesick companion, a dying accountant, a ruined businessman, and the like, were melodramatic, sentimental, even camp. But they were enough of a springboard for Tune's stunning visual imagination and staging inventiveness, and the show—one of the last to be hammered together out of town with new writers arriving like the cavalry in Boston—ran for two and a half years.

*Titanic*, which won the Tony in 1998 in a very weak field, also followed multiple characters and stories, the ship itself functioning as the doomed protagonist. The book writer Peter Stone, in his Tony acceptance speech, thanked the critics "for their astonishing reviews." The reviews had mostly been terrible but were no doubt astonishing to Stone. And to the millions watching the telecast, he imparted an implied endorsement from the press. It was a moment more brilliantly conceived than anything in the show, alas, which nonetheless lumbered along for another unprofitable year on the strength of the win. *Ragtime*, based on the novel that began the whole multiplot trend, also made it to Broadway to some acclaim, but it couldn't sustain a profitable run, given its cost and the meandering quality of its storytelling. Despite a skilled set of collaborators doing some excellent work, the train seems to have stopped once too often, and too many audience members disembarked.

The most successful multiplot show didn't come along until the summer of 2003. *Avenue Q* thrived on the strength of a single brilliant concept: the Muppets on *Sesame Street* all grew up just like we did, and they have all the same intractable problems that we do. *Sesame Street* may have its virtues, the show seemed to say, but it doesn't solve anything in the long run. The idea was so good, and connected with audiences so strongly, that the show, which basically rings a set of mild variations on the theme, has proved immensely popular.

The multiplot show is bound to run into trouble in the middle of Act 1, because that's when the rules of all shows are loosened and the direct line between I Want and its outcome is allowed to slip the tether. Audiences want to be glued to their seats—an infelicitous cliché, but it perfectly describes the situation. When the glue is weak and runs off in all directions, the audience tends to do the same. In a multiplot affair, we may be fascinated by the setup and by the degree of difficulty that's presented at the start (*Ragtime* has one of the most brilliant opening numbers ever written), but watching the authors struggle to keep all the plates spinning is sometimes not so much fun. It's often an effortful job, and no one really wants to see them sweat, especially at these prices.

# 9. Adelaide's Lament

*Stars*

With all this necessary adventuring into the unknown, it becomes increasingly important as the act progresses not to ignore the known. Villains may need to sing, and second couples certainly do. Multiple subplots may make things too complicated—or not—and there's no doubt that audiences enjoy variety as the act progresses. But somewhere in the midst of all of this, we're going to want to hear from the protagonist or protagonists, loud and clear. If one or both are played by stars, it becomes doubly important that the show clear the decks for them.

In terms of plotting, it's generally a bad idea to spend more than one scene without revisiting the main story. A subplot scene may be appropriate, but two in a row constitute a mistake. We need to keep checking in with the hero, or the whole show gets quickly derailed.

If there is a bona fide star involved, this usually won't be a problem—stars are not shy about reminding producers, directors, and writers that they need to be seen and heard. No one did this more forcibly than Ethel Merman.

Merman starred as Annie Oakley in *Annie Get Your Gun*. She had nine songs. No one else had more than four. Irving Berlin, like a lot of songwriters, loved writing for Merman with her peerless clarion call of a voice and her perfect diction. But nine was a lot. The equally peerless Alfred Drake, starring in *Oklahoma!* three years before, had five, and only one was a solo. But Merman wasn't crazy about the idea of other people singing in her shows, and neither were audiences. They came to hear her, and, as her career progressed, she became more and more dominant. Ironically, in *Gypsy*, the young Gypsy Rose Lee says to her audience, "My mother—who got me into this business—always told me, Make them beg for more. And then, don't give it to them!" The real Rose Hovick may have believed in this dictum. The real Ethel Merman, who played Rose, did not. In *Gypsy* she had eight songs. On the cast album, "Small World," which is a duet in the show, becomes a Merman solo. Make of that what you will.*

Merman made clear that the appearance of the star, when a show has one, is what the audience is paying for. In addition to the opening number, and an I Want, and perhaps a conditional love song, likely the first act finale, not to mention a star-led production number and an "11 o'clock" in Act 2, there often needs to be an Act 1 solo, usually somewhere in the middle.

Part of the reason for subplot couples singing, villains singing, and other kinds of distractions is that the audience needs different forms of stimulation. So it's a balancing act—too much of a star is probably a bad idea and monotonous. But too little is worse. For songwriters, this spot in the middle of Act 1 is a golden opportunity. This doesn't have to be the most important song in the show or the most telling. Nothing is coming to a climax. Instead, it's an opportunity for a showcase: What does the star do best? Let's let her do that. What makes these songs unique is that they're tailored to the performer, often as much as or more than to the show's plot.

If I had to pick a favorite, it would be certainly be "Adelaide's Lament" from *Guys and Dolls*. Not that Vivian Blaine, who played the long-engaged and long-suffering fiancée of Nathan Detroit, was any

---

* There weren't a lot of Mermans, although Pearl Bailey had the same proclivities. In the short-lived *House of Flowers* she managed to sweep up a couple of songs intended for other performers and get them for herself. But, unlike Merman, she was a dominant force on Broadway only once—when she took over the leading role in *Hello, Dolly!*

competition for Merman in the star department. But she was the comic singing star of this particular vehicle. And Frank Loesser hit the mother lode with a number that won the audience's heart and set up the possibility that this brassy floor show performer actually had one of her own. And that it might break. It does, in a short reprise in Act 2. The song is actually the first important solo in a show that has featured an opening ballet, a male trio, an ensemble number for the men, another for the women, and a comic/romantic, I hate you/I love you conditional love song for the romantic leads. It's a first-class assortment, and the solo helps create continued variety.

"Adelaide's Lament" grows out of a unique comic situation: Adelaide's fourteen-year engagement to Nathan Detroit has left her with a stress-anxiety condition—a common cold that never goes away. This creates an opportunity for Loesser; he dreamed up a moment in which a working-class girl tries to decipher the complexities of a psychiatric tome about the physical manifestations of an unfulfilled romantic life. It was a perfect fit for Blaine, who specialized in playing the guileless-but-not-clueless blondes who were a fixture of '50s comedy. Here she struggles mightily. She can barely pronounce the words, but she gets the meaning: "*In other words,*" she says, after quoting the psycho-lingo of the text,

> You can spray her wherever you figure the
> Streptococci lurk
> You can give her a shot for whatever she's got
> But it just won't work
> If she's tired of gettin' the fisheye
> From the hotel clerk,
> A person can develop a cold.

The comedy grows from the contrast of a chorus girl grappling with a pedantic text. But it's more than comic—it's heartwarming because her struggle is so sincere and her triumph in understanding it is so well earned. To top it off, it even has good punch lines. In three minutes, we understand her completely, and we want her to win. We want Nathan to stop being such a boob and marry her, for God's sake. The "Lament" is, of course, an I Want song in disguise. It also stacks the jokes in order of quality, so that they keep topping each other. This is a key to the success of a comedy number. If the jokes get more familiar and less funny as the number goes along, it's doomed to disappoint. But in "Adelaide's Lament," Loesser is a master builder. Not only do the jokes get funnier, but also the desperation gets more real and more acute. Miss Adelaide begins the number as an eager but intimidated titmouse, gains confidence (and volume) as she realizes that she can understand this psychology book perfectly well and that it's all about her, and ends it with a clarion call—almost worthy of Merman herself—that brings down the house. The number is so completely crafted that the second-act reprise comes as a total surprise and, characteristically, contains the coup de grace of defeated expectations, which also happens to be the funniest image:

> *So much virus inside*
> *That her microscope slide*
> *Looks like a day at the zoo!*
> *Just from wanting her memories in writing*
> *And a story her folks can be told*
> *A person can . . . develop a cold.*

Miss Adelaide is the soul of *Guys and Dolls*, and while her solo is tailored to the performer's assets and the character's interests, it's also an indispensable asset to the show itself—a rare warm moment in a big, brassy musical.

Sometimes these songs are written for specific performers, but just as often the performer is cast for his or her ability to climb the hill of the number. Barbara Cook was a relatively minor figure on Broadway when she was cast as Cunegonde in *Candide*. "Glitter and Be Gay" was already written, and Cook got the part because the composer, Leonard Bernstein, believed she could make hay with it—it's a dazzling soprano aria about a formerly pure and virtuous heroine caving in to the pleasures of the flesh and the jewels that can decorate it. It's comic and difficult and entertainingly tricky, written to stop the show, which Cook did nightly. It's a classic mid-act star solo. Bernstein had already written another, tailored to Rosalind Russell's comic gifts and limited range in *Wonderful Town*. Playing the tough but romantically challenged Ruth Sherwood, Russell chronicled her mistakes and missteps in courtship on her way to potential old maidhood in "One Hundred Easy Ways." Funny and perplexed without a trace of self-pity or bitterness, it's a cousin to "Adelaide's Lament," though made of somewhat lesser metal. The lyric, by Betty Comden and Adolph Green, isn't as clever, nor is the struggle within the song as touching, but still, it gives a real established star a chance to go at it. Unlike Vivian Blaine, Russell was bona fide Hollywood royalty, and all she needed was a number that was good enough, that allowed her to do what her fans wanted her to do. And she got one—not a masterpiece but, like "Little Girls" in *Annie*, a big performance opportunity. Russell made it work for her, and in a later revival, Donna Murphy found gold in it too.

Julie Andrews and Rex Harrison—he a star, she a star in the making—each got one in *My Fair Lady*, and here the challenge was what you might call stacking each of their performance tracks correctly. Although Lerner and Loewe—and the director Moss Hart—found various ways of opening up Shaw's *Pygmalion* with glamorous settings and the occasional chorus number, the basic story remains intimate and largely involves two characters. They both sing a lot (to the degree that Harrison sings at all), and it was important to save the best, or at least the most emotionally full-hearted, for last. Andrews's numbers are carefully balanced one on top of another. "Wouldn't It Be Loverly" is a simple I Want, lovely but without fireworks. Her mid-act solo, "Just You Wait," is an angry comic tirade, in which she imagines her tormentor, Higgins, with his head on a platter and facing a firing squad. It establishes her fierce temper and her wit, with a dose of sadomasochism thrown in to keep things interesting. "I Could Have Danced All Night"—the closest thing the show has to a conditional love song—is pure Edwardian romance with a little sex in it. "Show Me," in Act 2, is an angry expression of desire for real physical love, and "Without You," her final number, is a defiant, strong, yet sad declaration of independence. Eliza has gone from snuffling flower girl looking for a warm stove to completely self-possessed Mayfair lady (hence the show's little-appreciated title pun) in a little over two hours, and we've watched the transformation in song, each song a step in a carefully constructed ladder.

Higgins, meanwhile, has his own ladder, beginning with "Why Can't the English?," a defiant comic I Want that shows him to be as passionate as he is intolerant. "I'm an Ordinary Man," *his* mid-act solo, demonstrates the challenge for anyone trying to worm her way into his emotional life—he's self-contained and unbreakable. And his galling pride in his own intolerance and upper-class self-satisfaction is really funny. "A Hymn to Him," in Act 2, shows him protesting too much on the same subjects, his temper at having lost Eliza getting the better of him, which signals to us, if not to him, that a dam might just break after all. And in "I've Grown Accustomed to Her Face," the dam breaks—well, it cracks. The man who was a self-contained prig discovers that he's human after all, that his heart, his brain, his nerves, and his sense of need are all connected and, perhaps, the connection is not to be avoided. By Higgins's straitened means of expression, he's saying, "I've fallen in love. Imagine that."

For both Eliza and Higgins, the mid-act solo is actually the least important step in the ladder, though there's certainly not much wrong with either song. They do less work than the songs that precede them and are less emotionally redolent than the ones that follow them. But they provide variety, coming after the noise ("With a Little Bit of Luck") and before the multivoiced teaching sequence ("The Rain in Spain"). And they give the stars one more chance to be stars and share a private moment with the audience.

Jay Binder, for many years the dean of Broadway casting directors, defined stars this way: "A star comes out onstage and every member of the audience feels that the star has a secret which is shared only with them. The star is looking directly at them, saying, 'You and I know something no one else in the room knows.' That's what's mesmerizing, and they do it to fifteen hundred people at the same time."

What the secret is, is anyone's guess and doesn't matter. And how the star manages to make every member of the audience believe that she's communing directly with him or her is a complete mystery. But you know it when it happens. A number in the middle of Act 1 reminds us of the secret, and that we share it.

One of the things that make it easier to share this one-on-one-ness is the physical life of the moment: there is no one onstage except the star. She's all ours. And the song needn't be spectacular or full of fireworks, like "Glitter and Be Gay" or the comparable "Rosabella," another operatic aria, performed by Robert Weede in *The Most Happy Fella*. Sometimes the star lets us in on the secret. Sometimes the secret is what the mid-act number is all about.

"Dividing Day," from *The Light in the Piazza*, is just such a moment—a heartbreaking discovery that the character makes and allows us to discover with her. It was performed in the original production by Victoria Clark, who isn't a star in the conventional sense any more than was Vivian Blaine, the original Miss Adelaide. But in that mid-act slot she, like Blaine, became one—at least for a moment. Her song appears to be the polar opposite of "Adelaide's Lament"—tragic, not comic; resigned, not defiant—but in some ways it's the same. Both are examinations of love and its consequences for women whose men—after many years—are nowhere to be found. The song is a hushed inner monologue about the death of love. The discovery is as unexpected for the character as it is for the audience. Margaret, a middle-aged woman on a trip to Italy with her daughter, has just intuited something about her husband. It's not an infidelity, or an addiction, or any other kind of public or private malfeasance. It's something he may not even recognize. But distance has created the lens through which Margaret can see with a different view of her own life, and suddenly there it is, right in front of her.

> *Dashing as the day we met*
> *Only there is something I don't recognize*
> *Though I cannot name it yet*
> *I know it*
>
> *Beautiful is what you are*
> *Only somehow wearing a frightening disguise*

*I can see the winter in your eyes now*
*Telling me*

*"Thank you*
*We're done here*
*Not much to say*
*We are together*
*But I have had dividing day"*

She puzzles over where and when it happened, how she could have missed it, and how it could have occurred, but comes up empty. All she has is the strength to name it, in Adam Guettel's memorable phrase.

*So when . . . when was this day*
*Was it on the church step*
*Suddenly you're out of love*
*Does it go creeping slowly*
*When was your dividing day?*

*I can see the winter in your eyes now*
*Telling me:*
*"Margaret*
*We did it*
*You curtsied, I bowed*
*We are together*
*But no more love*
*No more love allowed"*

She continues to speculate, and continues to come up empty.

*When was*
*When was*
*When was dividing day?*

By naming it, like an annual day of mourning, Margaret gives it stature and lets us know that it is to be respected, catastrophic as it is.

And, of course, it is shared and commemorated by a lot of people over the course of a lifetime, which makes it worthy of a name, and of a song. The lyric doesn't snap and pop with the classic lyricist's sense of rhythm—it's almost prose, but that's part of what gives it power—it seems naked of conventional artifice. And it tells. It has the ability to stop the breath of any audience, and the authenticity of its emotion is one of the reasons we go to the theater—to see the skin of human life peeled back and the nervous system and heart revealed. On the one hand, we're almost ashamed to be eavesdropping on such a private discovery. On the other, she is holding up the mirror in the most artful yet direct way. That's what makes it a star moment, as well as an important piece of theater. Like Miss Adelaide, Ruth Sherwood, and even Cunegonde and Eliza Doolittle, Margaret has paused the play itself to tell us something that she now understands for the first time. And she's told us at just the right time.

But, looked at mechanically, it's a mid-act solo for the star, neither more nor less.

# 10. Tevye's Dream

*Tent Poles*

In a good show, an hour into the first act we're deep into the story and living life along with the characters. The protagonists, the antagonist, the subplot couple, and any other supporting players have crashed into each other in combustible ways, and things are complicated. From the opening number to the I Want to the conditional love song to the presentation of the ensemble (long known in the business as "merry villagers") to all the obstacles standing in the way of a happy outcome, the authors have led us on quite a long and circuitous ride. The hero is still far from achieving his or her goal—probably further than at the beginning. And, frankly, we're starting to get a little weary. Our energy begins to flag. We realize we may need a drink and a bathroom pretty soon, but there's still another ten minutes of story—one or two scenes—before intermission. Almost every show solves this problem in the same way—with a high-energy number that gets everyone's blood pumping hard enough to get us to the first-act curtain.

Tent poles keep the roof from caving in on the audience. They may or may not be relevant to the story—the best ones in the most unified shows usually are, of course. But, as with the noise, it's not a requirement that they be anything but energizing. This is another one of those places where musicals are allowed—even required—to defy the logic of storytelling and operate on the other part of the brain—the part that responds to color and light, rhythm and pace.

The "Havana" sequence in *Guys and Dolls* is a classic example, and like so much about that almost perfectly structured show, it seems in some ways random. The number that precedes it, the title song, is a brilliant little vaudeville turn sung by two minor characters, commenting on the war between the sexes, but it neither furthers the plot nor reveals character. It's like Brecht touring the borscht belt. You could actually cut it, and you might never know it had been there. Of course, it's a great song, it is the title song (one suspects it was written before the show's book), it's a perfect encapsulation of the theme, and it covers a somewhat vague time lapse, which gives Sky Masterson the opportunity to get the reluctant Sarah Brown down to Cuba.

Once we see them strolling the boulevards of Old Havana, however, it seems the jig is up for Nathan Detroit—his bet is lost. He won't get the $1,000 he needs to buy off Joey Biltmore and hold his floating crap game in the garage, and his very life may be in danger from a particularly trigger-happy crapshooter who is looking for action and won't take no for an answer. We feel sorry for Nathan but happy for Sky— and at the moment, Nathan's story is on hold. Sky is in Havana with a buttoned-up "mission doll" whose behavior is true to form—she's got a sightseeing book and is dragging him from one ancient ruin to another, much to his consternation. This is not how Sky usually spends time in Havana. Finally, he draws her into a bar and gets her to drink a couple of dulce de leches, and suddenly, she loosens up.

Then, not surprisingly, a band starts playing and people start dancing (this is Cuba, after all). Like the title song, this might seem arbitrary, but the plot is complicated, the characters have all gotten themselves in one kind of trouble or another, and frankly it's a welcome relief to have some up-tempo Latinish music. The ensemble, suddenly all Cuban (the costume department's problem), starts to rumba across the floor; Sky and Sarah join in. Sarah gets picked off by a particularly attractive and supple dancer and then finds herself the object of a jealous battle between two dancers we've never met before. Mayhem ensues. Punches are thrown. Sarah is delighted. The music turns wilder, Sarah begins to get into the fight, the alcohol in her bloodstream fueling her newfound sense of freedom, and the next thing we know, we're in the midst of a full-fledged high-energy brawl. Sky comes to the rescue, and at the number's conclusion (to thunderous applause), he is throwing Sarah over his shoulder and hauling her out of the bar and back onto the street. He quickly discovers that she doesn't want him to put her down on the ground. She's deliriously happy, not to mention just plain delirious. What happens next onstage will be saved for the next chapter, but what has happened already has occurred mainly on the other side of the footlights. The audience is renewed, refreshed, and ready for one or two more of whatever the show is serving.

That's the way it works. But it's not always like "Havana," which has music and dance but no words. As with opening numbers, there are a handful of variations. "Havana," without a word spoken or sung, has brought a reluctant couple together physically and emotionally, with consequences still to come that neither of them anticipates. It has actually furthered the plot. But that was hardly required.

In the same spot in *Hello, Dolly!*, we are on the point of having the whole story ruined if the skinflint merchant Horace Vandergelder discovers that his clerks, who are supposed to be at home working, have escaped to the big city and are hiding in the very hat shop he and Dolly Levi have stopped into. He's about to open the cabinet in which the two clerks have secreted themselves when Dolly, desperate to protect them, bursts into an anthem about American virtues, called "Motherhood March." It's not a masterpiece of songwriting, and not even a very logical thing to do under the circumstances, though it does distract Horace from the discovery he was about to make. But the main thing it does is pick up the tempo, get fifteen hundred pairs of toes tapping, put a smile on fifteen hundred faces, and stave off whatever indications of ennui were beginning to overtake the generally happy audience. "Motherhood" is a classic tent pole in the category of "meeting the minimum basic requirements." The song that precedes it, "Ribbons Down My Back," is a beautiful and rueful ballad. The song that follows is called "Dancing," and while it develops into a lovely waltz number, a waltz is, by definition, not high wattage, unless it's a jazz waltz like "The Last Midnight." "Motherhood" covers for both numbers, though it's the weakest of the three. It has a job to do and it does it.

It's easy to spot these numbers, some greater than others: "Cool" in *West Side Story*, "Pick-a-Little, Talk-a-Little" from *The Music Man*, "N.Y.C." from *Annie*, and, in the modern era, "Keep It Gay" from *The Producers*, with its unmotivated celebration of gay pop culture from the Choreographer's Ball to the Village People. Tent poles are usually fun. They're usually up-tempo, too, though "One Short Day," from *Wicked*, in which we finally arrive at the Emerald City, is a midtempo pop-rock odyssey, which suddenly morphs into double time as the gates open, and backs down with the introduction of the Wizard himself. By the end of it, we're willing to sit still for another little while and see what the Wizard has to say.

*Hamilton* makes a tent pole out of the entire American Revolution—a bold step and hardly a "fun" number. But the kinetic excitement of watching a real showman figure out how to do a war in one extended number manages to thrill and reignite an audience that has already been sitting for a long time and processed a surprisingly large number of events. The show brings all its resources to bear in one explosive sequence comprising two numbers—"History Has Its Eyes on You" and "Yorktown"—at the end of which you'd think it would be time for intermission. But cannily, the number gives the audience enough energy to sustain it through a couple more scenes.

As is true with *Hamilton*, tent poles usually involve lots of people, too, but not always.

In Stephen Sondheim's *Company*, there is a showstopping turn in this spot—but it's a solo. "Another Hundred People" was written for a specific performer—twenty-one-year-old Pamela Myers, who auditioned for the show but didn't suit any of the roles in it. The character she played was reimagined around her; the number was created for her, too. And it was in the second act. As Sondheim recalls in his lyric collection *Finishing the Hat*, the number was cut after a three-hour first preview in Boston. In a last-ditch attempt to save it, he refashioned it, taking three short book scenes that George Furth had written and alternating a section of the song with a page or so of dialogue, so that the song covered a passage of time and grew more intense with each appearance. He then reinstalled it in the second-to-last spot in Act 1, and it went back into the show, where it's been ever since. There's little doubt that tent poles were the last things on his or his collaborators' minds as they worked frantically but systematically (such things are possible in the theater) to get the show ready for the Boston critics. But what they ended up with was a tent pole nonetheless. The character, one of the three young women the hero courts halfheartedly, is discovered alone onstage and sings, to a propulsive, shifting rhythm, about the unending daily arrival of young hopefuls to a big, exciting, cold city that doesn't care if they live or die. Each section drives harder than the previous one, thanks in part to some great Jonathan Tunick orchestrations, and in the end it tears the place apart.

In some respects, the number is a distant cousin of the title song in *Guys and Dolls*—it's a statement about the way things are from the point of view of a specific character, but the character is standing in for the authors. It's not a plot song. But unlike "Guys and Dolls," which is up-tempo, ingeniously funny, and harmless, "Another Hundred People" wounds as it excites—it causes audiences to sit up and take notice, and it gives a performer an opportunity to stop the show. In *Company*, numbers were shifted around a lot as the show found its form. Since it was essentially plotless—a show built around a subject instead of a story—the placement of the songs was in some ways up for grabs and ended up having more to do with controlling the biorhythms of the audience than with revealing specific story information at a specific time. (The final number, "Being Alive," is a notable exception, dealing as it does with an emotional dam finally breaking for the hero. It can go only at the end, but it was written out of town after most of the rest of the show had found its form.) As a result, "Another Hundred People," coming after the hero's heartbreaking confession of loneliness in "Someone Is Waiting," fit the bill at the one-hour mark. It roused the audience and raised the emotional stakes in a way that kept it alert for that last section of Act 1 still to come.

This underlines the reality that good musical theater writers rarely write to pattern, even though this book keeps describing the pattern they don't write to. The best writers are always trying to break the mold they perceive in the work of their predecessors and mentors, none more than Sondheim. And yet, when the dust settles, the result often fits the pattern anyhow. There's no logical explanation for this, but the best one I've heard came from a veteran producer who was reacting to the discovery that his own show was falling into line around the very commonplaces he was hoping to defy.

"The fact is," he said, "if we want to succeed, we're owned by the audience. And as many hot new ideas as we may have, the block of people who buy the tickets remains more or less the same—they're human beings, and they behave like human beings. So who are we to ask them to behave different? They want to know who the show's about? We better tell them. They want to know *what* it's about? We also have to tell them that—before they lose interest altogether. They want to pee at nine-twenty? We'd better arrange for that, too. We're charging a lot of money here, and the bathrooms are too small."


Perhaps the most perfectly realized of the tent poles is, not surprisingly, in a Jerome Robbins show. Robbins didn't seem to like energy for its own sake—in his mind it wasn't a commodity to be wasted. Also, he liked to use dance to tell a story. So his tent poles tend to be important to the plot, not a relief from it, none more than "Tevye's Dream." *Fiddler on the Roof*, by today's standards, is a long show. We're more than an hour into it when Tevye, the hero, is discovered in bed in the midst of a sleepless night, trying to solve a dilemma worthy of Solomon himself. He's promised his daughter's hand to the wealthy old butcher, but the girl is in love with the poor young tailor. And Tevye's wife, trying to make an advantageous match, is reveling in the prospect of her daughter's marriage to a rich merchant. Tevye loves his wife, but he can't possibly deny his daughter. Yet he daren't risk his wife's wrath. Or his daughter's eternal heartbreak. What to do?

We in the audience don't even really know what he's thinking about as we watch him puzzling restlessly in bed, his wife, Golde, sleeping peacefully beside him. But then we see him get an idea. Anyone lucky enough to see the original production of *Fiddler* early in its run had the privilege of watching the great comic actor Zero Mostel get this idea. His eyebrows rose to meet his comb-over, and his eyes turned into saucers the size of quail eggs. The man had an idea. But what was it?

In "Tevye's Dream," he awakens Golde by pretending to be in the throes of a horrifying nightmare. He knows she's superstitious, and once he's roused her from her slumber, he babbles breathlessly, knowing that eventually she will utter these magic words: "Tell me what you dreamt and I'll tell you what it meant."

With this opportunity, he launches into the tale, fabricated moment by moment and brought to life in vivid staging, of how their daughter's wedding is disrupted by the appearance of a ghost—Golde's long-dead grandmother, no less—who comes to warn them of the dire consequences of marrying the wrong man. Tevye lays it on thick, and Robbins creates a thrilling comic ballet, full of sound and fury, in which the message is never in doubt: marrying the wealthy butcher will lead to chaos and calamity—fire, brimstone, and God knows what else. The poor tailor is the man intended for their daughter—preordained, in fact, by *Golde's* ancestors, not Tevye's. Tevye's description of the events becomes more spectacular as Golde needs more and more convincing, and Robbins stirs things up until characters are levitating off the stage floor and wedding guests are shrieking and running for cover.

Golde, needless to say, comes around in the end, satisfied that it is her superior interpretive powers and her ancestors' wisdom that have made the difference. By the time the number ends, Golde has arrived where Tevye needs her to be—in favor of the tailor. The mother will be happy, the daughter will be (poor but) happy, the family will be preserved, and life will be permitted to go on, at least until the next crisis.

The number, like "Havana," solves a plot problem while it is making a loud and entertaining noise, and the audience, which may have been thinking about stirring, is ready for the wedding that (finally) brings down the curtain.

Robbins and George S. Kaufman, who directed *Guys and Dolls*, were—like Oscar Hammerstein—masters of the waste not, want not approach. Anything in a show that could do double or triple duty should be made to do so. As the producer Cy Feuer was fond of saying, "Everything in show business is twenty minutes too long." Search for economies wherever they can be found. The result will be a shapely elegance and grace in the storytelling, and the audience, knowingly or not, will appreciate the trouble you've taken for its benefit.

The "Havana" sequence is a tent pole that unites two unlikely lovers. "Tevye's Dream" is a tent pole that takes an audience on a journey through the hero's mind as he solves the main dilemma of the first act. Yet both also perform the basic duty of ramping up the heartbeat in an audience that is flagging. For Broadway theater from its inception, tent poles were the earliest form of pacemaker.

*Fiddler on the Roof* has one great tent pole. *Hairspray* has an entire first act filled with them. Why have one where a multitude might be available? The exuberant team of Marc Shaiman and Scott Wittman wrote some of the songs before there was a book, and the book underwent a number of fairly drastic rewrites before the show opened out of town. But the number of joyous, up-tempo numbers in Act 1, more, perhaps, than might have seemed wise, stayed pretty much the same throughout: "Mama, I'm a Big Girl Now," "Welcome to the '60s," "Run and Tell That!," "Big, Blonde, and Beautiful"—the songs keep topping each other and raising the tent progressively higher. It's hard to identify the actual structural tent pole (I vote for "Run and Tell That!," which is in the right place for one). An admirer of moderation in all things might object, but *Hairspray* celebrates the joy of excess. It only makes sense that the hits just kept on coming, and the show reflected a new reality in the audience as well. We've become excitement junkies with short attention spans. So what's Broadway to do?

The musical theater world is responding as you would expect. Some of this can be attributed to the way rock concerts work, and today's audiences are, for the most part, more familiar with live rock shows than they are with live musicals. Rock gins up excitement—that's its stock-in-trade. It often also exchanges romance for sex, as a post-'50s audience has also done. Volume levels are way up, the backbeat pounds relentlessly, random pyrotechnics create a sense of danger and ecstasy, and audiences lose themselves completely in the wall of sound.

This has been going on for decades, of course—people who came of age in the '60s are now frequently subject to what audiologists sometimes call "Jimi Hendrix hearing loss"—but it has arrived on Broadway fairly recently. For a long time Broadway fought a losing battle against rock, but so did American parents, churches, and pop singers. The opening of *Hair* in 1967 was the first shot across Broadway's bow, and it caused an uproar. A positive review in the *Times* that more or less demanded that other shows pay attention to America's new popular music caused anguish among songwriters and producers alike. Some of the traditional audience was offended in about equal measure by the nudity and the inanity of the lyrics. Traditional Broadway's very way of life was threatened, and Broadway fought back. Three years later, the Sondheim/Prince collaboration made a case for the musical theater's ability to continue to innovate and evolve without becoming a showcase for rock writers, but the first of their shows, *Company*, had at least a few rock elements. Everyone was worried.

While the war was going on, rock shows were becoming ever more theatrical. The relatively primitive psychedelia of Joe's Lights at the Fillmore East in the late '60s evolved into a whole new business involving carefully coordinated lighting effects and scenic patterns created by highly paid, highly skilled, and highly inventive designers. Rock stole from the theater, happily and with unabashed enthusiasm, while the theater was trying to fight off the onslaught of a new music and a new aesthetic.

But it couldn't, and didn't, want to fight off a new audience with money to spend. That audience's demands for fresher, more contemporary shows ultimately led to Broadway's waving the white flag.

On the fiftieth anniversary of the opening of *Oklahoma!* at the St. James Theatre, John Raitt, who had starred in the national tour in 1944, strode onto the stage and greeted an audience awaiting a preview of *The Who's Tommy*. This promised a dangerous disconnect.

"Hello, everybody," he boomed into a handheld mike, his rich baritone still in first-class condition. "I'm Bonnie Raitt's dad!"

The audience roared. They had no idea who he was, but they sure knew his daughter. Raitt then launched into *Oklahoma!*'s title song and soon had the whole audience—young, motley, ragged, and stoned—spelling along with him: "O-K-L-A-H-O-M-A, Oklahoma, yeow!"

The first peace treaty had just been signed and no one knew it. Revivals of *Oklahoma!* will no doubt be seen on Broadway again, as will *Gypsy*, *Guys and Dolls*, and *My Fair Lady*. But they'll be playing next door to a show with a hard backbeat and a phalanx of Fender guitars in the pit.

The entire mode of presentation on Broadway, in fact, has begun to shift toward the world of concert rock, and why wouldn't it? Broadway's a business, and pleasing audiences with a combination of the familiar and the exotic has always been its aim. Shows like *American Idiot* and *The Who's Tommy* adapted famous rock albums, and others celebrate rock icons from the Beatles to Janis Joplin. *Wicked*'s score is very rock friendly, and even shows that are based on classic plays, like *Spring Awakening*, have incorporated rock into their way of looking at a nineteenth-century world—it's our music now. It functions just as the classic show music that was incorporated into the nineteenth-century river towns of *Show Boat*, the rural Maine Coast in *Carousel*, or the Oklahoma Territory. We tell our stories in our own vernacular no matter when they are set, and that's always been true. But in whatever style— from operetta to hard rock, from "Motherhood March" to the Revolutionary War in rap—the audience needs a jolt, a tent pole, to get to the first-act curtain.

# 11. La Vie Bohème

*Curtain: Act 1*

**W**hen we left Sky Masterson, he was dragging Sarah Brown out of a Cuban nightclub. The two of them were headed toward the most typical kind of first-act curtain: the unraveling, in an instant, of everything everyone had planned. First-act curtains don't have to be that, and as time has gone on, they have grown more unorthodox, but *Guys and Dolls*, unsurprisingly, has a perfectly put-together traditional one that's worth taking a look at.

At the end of "Havana," we're still three songs away. And the three songs make up a suite, celebrating human courtship—as good a suite as you could hope to find. If you think of them as a single act of lovemaking, they encompass two lovers revealing themselves in ways they never have before, even to themselves, and then falling into each other's arms as much in gratitude as in heat.

It begins outside the nightclub, where Sky finally puts Sarah down in front of an old disused fountain on a moonlit empty street (the fountain is a nice rococo romantic touch in a show that doesn't have many). The simple question he asks her—"Are you all right?"—engenders an answer that surprises both of them. Sarah's had plenty to drink, and actually, she's more than all right. She's feeling something she's never felt before, or never allowed herself to. "Ask me how do I feel," she replies, beginning to sing.

*Ask me now that we're cozy and clinging.*
*Well, sir, all I can say, is if I were a bell I'd be ringing!*

Sarah has launched into a standard called "If I Were a Bell" that has been featured by everyone from Dinah Shore to the jazz pianist Red Garland. The song has an easy, insistent swing that suggests alcohol, moonlight, and unbuttoning. The unbuttoning is the important part.

Sarah is not unbuttoning her clothes, however; she's unbuttoning something much more important—maybe for the first time. She's saying, in effect, "Did you think I was a missionary? I don't blame you—I'm dressed like a missionary. Even I thought I was a missionary. But in this moment, I've realized I'm not a missionary. Strip away the missionary's uniform and you will discover a sensualist underneath. And the sensualist is who I actually am."

What a discovery! Everyone makes it at the same moment: Sky, Sarah, and the audience. Whoever you thought was inside those clothes, you were completely mistaken. By the end of the song, Sarah is emotionally naked, eager for what inevitably comes next, and as unashamed as Eve before the snake got to her. The song is a marvel of economy and transformation. It's a series of comparisons—"If I were a lamp I'd light . . . If I were a gate I'd be swinging . . . If I were a bridge I'd be burning"—that stay well on the pleasant side of decency but leave no doubt as to what's happening. Prim Sarah is ready for the life that she's shunned, that always scared her too much to even imagine what it might be.

Lovemaking, however, metaphorical or actual, is most easily achieved with two naked partners. Loesser doesn't shy away from this. The scene shifts back to Broadway, where we are carried by some transition music once "If I Were a Bell" is done. Sky escorts Sarah back to the mission as she asks him what time it is. Unsurprisingly, it's about 4:00 a.m.—they've been to Havana and back, after all. Sky, almost unprompted, begins to explain what he likes about 4:00 a.m. And, as was the case with Sarah, his armor falls completely away.

"*My time of day is the dark time,*" he sings. "*A couple of deals before dawn.*"

The first line is matter-of-fact enough, but the second achieves a certain unexpected beauty. And then, in a seductively chromatic melody that is far from the rest of the musical vocabulary in *Guys and Dolls*, Loesser turns Sky into a poet:

> *When the street belongs to the cop*
> *And the janitor with the mop*
> *And the grocery clerks are all gone.*
>
> *When the smell of the rain-washed pavement*
> *Comes up clean, and fresh, and cold*
> *And the streetlamp light*
> *Fills the gutter with gold,*
> *That's my time of day . . .*

Sky has just undergone the exact same transformation for himself, Sarah, and the audience that she did. In effect, he's telling her—and us—"You thought I was a hard-hearted gambler who saw only the cards and the dice and the wins and losses? That's what I thought too. But I'm not—I'm a poet. You're a beautiful sensualist, and I'm a man who appreciates beauty and sensuality in a way you could never have suspected."

They are two characters bared, and in the course of two musical numbers, we believe absolutely that they must have each other, that the possibilities are limitless.

Only the musical theater can do this in this way. The music seduces. And the lyrics compact big revelations into tiny packages. What would take pages in a play or chapters in a novel happens in magic time. And so, without a further word spoken, they begin to sing the show's most famous ballad, "I've Never Been in Love Before," because each of them has credibly demonstrated that it's true. They haven't been in love before, but now they are. Nothing they've experienced has prepared them, and yet (it's so often the way) they're prepared.

*But this is wine*
*That's all too strange and strong*
*I'm full of foolish song*
*And out my song must pour.*
*So please forgive*
*This helpless haze I'm in*
*I've really never been in love before.*

At this moment, everything should be in perfect harmony for couple number one, and indeed it is—except that Sky is leading Sarah back to the mission. And of course Sky has won his bet and Nathan has lost, which means that Nathan has no place to hold the crap game. By winning the bet, Sky has caused Sarah to abandon the mission for Havana. And, consequently, that's where Nathan is holding the game. The two would-be lovers turn a corner and find themselves in the middle of a police raid—and a Gordian knot of a plot tie-up. What is Sarah to do but to assume that Sky took her to Cuba to empty out the mission so that Nathan could have his game there? She's betrayed. In an instant, all is ruined. Nathan and his gamblers are chased from the mission by the cops, Sarah has—she thinks—been emotionally swindled by the first man she ever opened herself up to, Sky has lost the only woman he ever loved, and the roof has come crashing down—along with the curtain.

This is how a first act is supposed to end, though few do it as economically or as elegantly. One suspects, again, the hand of George S. Kaufman, the director and Broadway comedy's greatest dramaturg, and indeed his daughter Anne takes credit for the act's last line.

"What kind of a doll are you?" Sky asks, shocked and distraught that Sarah would blame him for the catastrophic circumstances.

"They had the question, but not the answer," asserts Anne Kaufman Schneider, who was a young woman at the time. "I just blurted out, 'I'm a mission doll!' And it's been that way ever since."

*Guys and Dolls* was not a star vehicle, which at least relieved its creators of finding a first-act curtain that would feature a big solo for the star. *Gypsy* doesn't have that luxury, yet among the classic musicals, it probably has the other most perfectly constructed first-act curtain.

Structurally, *Gypsy* is all about a power exchange that takes place over more than a decade. The power shifts from Madame Rose, the maniacally focused mother who insists that her daughter Baby June will be a star, to Louise, her second, apparently even less talented daughter, whose natural reticence and fearfulness make her an easy target for her mother's hostility. Madame Rose begins with all the power, Louise with none. The reversal does not even seem to have started by the end of Act 1, but the moment must come when the two of them are placed front and center, when we understand that the struggle is ultimately going to be not about the rise to stardom but about a daughter's well-earned revenge. For that to happen, both of them have to arrive at rock bottom, with nothing left to lose.

The story, remember, goes like this: Madame Rose wants Baby June to be a star. Louise wants a route of escape from the torture of pretending to still be a second-banana little girl in vaudeville when she's really a young woman reduced to playing the front end of a cow. For years she's harbored a secret crush on one of the boy dancers in the act, Tulsa. In the penultimate scene of the act, she catches him rehearsing an act different from the one he's performing in Madame Rose's troupe, and she senses that he, too, wants to escape. In a heartbreaking number called "All I Need Is the Girl," Tulsa teaches Louise the girl's part of the dance duet he's invented as his way out, and she's allowed to fantasize that they really are together in another time and place. The audience is also encouraged to think that this may be Louise's route of escape. She's not much of a dancer, but Tulsa encourages her and clearly cares for her in some way or other, and he's flattered by her attention. We can see her beginning to pin all her hopes on the scraps of evidence that are presented. He's always understood her better than the others have—he bought her books for her birthday a long time ago, and she hasn't forgotten. She points out their similarities. He takes her hand. He teaches her the dance, they blend; they seem, awkwardly, to actually be a duo. Maybe things will work.

The song itself is notable for staying neutral: it's a traditional showbiz lyric for a dance duet, though very well written. But the meaning of the scene is entirely in the action that the song allows to happen—Tulsa's increasing showmanship and Louise's complete seduction into the fantasy. Nothing in the lyric tells us this. But by the number's conclusion, Louise is actually energized for the first time in the show, and the audience is pinning a lot of hope on her possible rescue. Thank Jerome Robbins, once again, for understanding how dance can expose the human heart and tell a story all by itself.

But the next scene—the curtain scene—develops with a cunning virtually unique in the musical theater, and this time it is Arthur Laurents, the book writer, who has planted a time bomb, though no one has seen him do it.

We're at a railroad depot in Omaha (the vaudeville cards stage left and right bear only the ominous word TERMINAL). Madame Rose and Herbie, her lover and the act's business manager, are anxiously awaiting the arrival of June and Louise, and they're in the middle of an argument with two of the boys who have come to announce they're quitting the act along with the rest of the male contingent. The scene starts midcrisis, always a good idea in a musical, or anywhere else. The boys complain that they're too old. Employment is too spotty. They have to move on. Their explanation is logical enough, but Rose is suspicious. Something's not right. Then Louise rushes on with a note from June. Rose is reluctant to look at it, but Louise forces the issue:

"Momma, *read it!*" she says, raising her voice to her mother for the first time in the show.

One of the boys in the act summarizes its content: June has run off with Tulsa and gotten married. They're going to be a duo.

"It's a keen act. Ain't it, Louise?" one of the boys asks the heartbroken Louise.

"I didn't see it," says Louise, who is as close to dead inside as a person can be at that moment. Of course, she never has seen it, though she's danced it—once. And what she may mean is what theatergoers are also saying in that moment: "I didn't see it coming."

The consequences of this simple plot development touch virtually every aspect of *Gypsy*, but the important thing is this: Madame Rose's dream and Louise's dream have both crash-landed at exactly the same moment for exactly the same reason. There is no more Baby June, and no more Tulsa either. No stardom, no romance, no triumph for Rose, no escape for Louise. All prospects of happiness and fulfillment are gone for both of them. Each is at a moment that is, well, terminal. And it happens in an instant.

This is how an act traditionally ends: in a crisis that seems completely beyond redemption. It's why we come back for Act 2. In the case of *Gypsy*, however, the authors and the star have one final trick up their collective sleeve.

Herbie, who has wanted nothing more from the very beginning than to get out of show business and settle down, now sees *his* escape route. He puts on his best happy face and promises all of them a different life, a better life. A home life. For a moment, Rose seems to be considering the matter seriously, and Louise, who has always been deeply suspicious of Herbie's motives (he's sleeping with her mother, after all), suddenly throws herself into his arms at the suggestion. Allegiances are shifting with lightning speed.

"Yes! Momma, say yes!" she implores. She's actually talking to her mother like a person with a voice—and, as it turns out, it's the last time she's going to do any imploring, but, of course, we don't know that yet.

Rose ruminates, in one of Laurents's canniest speeches, that leads Herbie, Louise, and the audience to the conclusion that, miracle of miracles, maybe she's ready to wrap it up. Maybe she's done. Maybe she's come to her senses.

"This time, I'm apologizing," she says to Louise. "To you. I pushed you aside for her. I made everything only for her."

Louise protests, trying to protect her mother's feelings while almost basking in the joy of hearing her mother acknowledge the bitter truth she's lived with all her life.

We may expect any number of things to happen next—reconciliation, a marriage proposal from Herbie, a confession from Louise that all she's ever wanted was a few words of motherly love; we can speculate all we want. But what actually happens is, for those who have never encountered *Gypsy* before, not on our list of speculations.

"The boys walk because they think the act's finished," Madame Rose says. "They think they're nothing without her. Well she's nothing without *me!*"

We tolerate this—a little self-promotion seems reasonable under the circumstances, and we know Madame Rose is suffering a terrible defeat. So far the script is playing out in compelling but expected ways. But then it arrives: Madame Rose turns to Louise, her untalented, pathologically shy, gawky daughter, and says, "I'm her mother and I made her. And I can make you now! And I will, my baby, I swear I will! I'm going to *make* you a star!"

And to the horror of both Herbie and Louise, she begins to sing. The orchestra holds an ominous, pulsing chord created as a bed for Ethel Merman's trumpeting brag.

> *I had a dream*
> *A dream about you, Baby!*
> *It's gonna come true, Baby!*
> *They think that we're through, but, Baby . . .*

This is what the great screenwriting maven Robert McKee dubbed a gap. It's the gap that opens up between the expectations of the characters—the myriad potential things that might happen next—and what actually *does* happen next, which is none of them. Gaps are tremendous engines of drama. They throw the characters and the audience into energized emotional chaos by pulling out the rug: What can possibly happen now?!

The important thing about them is that they aren't on the menu of imagined outcomes. If you brought your same-sex partner home to your parents without ever having told them you were gay and announced that you were getting married, there is an array of potentially reasonable dramatic responses: your mother embraces you but your father cannot, or vice versa. You are banished from the house. You are welcomed by your more-progressive-than-you-thought parents. But if upon your announcing the impending nuptials, your father were to say, "Thank God! You're out! Now *I* can come out!"—well, that's a gap. When they're believable, they make for great theater.

In the case of *Gypsy*, the gap also creates an opportunity for the great Merman to take the stage, which, being Merman, she had to do at the end of the act. The song is "Everything's Coming Up Roses," and it quickly became an anthem of optimism and an American standard, superior to but not different in kind from "Hey, Look Me Over!" However, in the context of the show that gave it birth, it drips with irony, the blinkered manic declarations of self-delusion from a woman who has taken leave of her senses. As Madame Rose sings, Herbie and Louise cling to each other for safety, desperately afraid of where all this could possibly end. And *then* the curtain falls.

As late as the mid-1970s, John Raitt, who was almost sixty at the time, continued to tour in *Carousel*, playing in tents, civic centers, and even occasionally at county fairgrounds. He was happy to re-create the part that made him a star three decades earlier. Raitt loved to sing, and he loved for people to listen to him sing. He made one significant change in the play, however, with or without the permission of Richard Rodgers, who was still very much alive: he insisted that the first act end on the last note of Billy Bigelow's "Soliloquy," thus bringing down the house and the curtain at the same time. His idea may have been prescient, if self-interested. It's a rare musical in the twenty-first century that allows a first-act curtain to fall on anything but a showstopper.

That, however, is not the way *Carousel* was built. *Carousel* is among the first musicals to end its first act—at least as it was written—in anticipation of a crisis rather than after one has occurred. (To be fair, *Oklahoma!* hints at something similar, but it's done with a ballet and is not nearly as specific.)

Julie Jordan and Billy Bigelow have married, fated to do so by the iron hand of passion that gripped them on the park bench outside the carnival, but almost immediately, the marriage has run aground. Billy doesn't fit in with the tight-knit, provincial village of fishermen into which he's been introduced, and he spends his nights carousing with his friend Jigger Craigin, an ex-con with a nose for trouble. Julie has been as tolerant as she can be, and remains deeply in love, but she confesses to her friend Carrie that Billy, in his frustration, has hit her. For Carrie, who is married to the upright and ambitious Mr. Snow, Julie's marriage makes no sense. But Julie understands that in Billy's arms, she has something that Carrie can never have. Even in her misery, she's ablaze. She's scared of Billy, but she's in love with him. He's in love with her too, but he longs for the vagabond life of calliope music, cheap beer, and travel. There's an untutored poet inside him that's gradually being strangled by the tightening straps of rigid small-town life.

That small-town life, as the act begins to wind up, consists of preparations for a clambake on a nearby island, a clambake Billy has so far refused to attend. It's an annual ritual of the village, and Billy finds it both threatening and beneath him. He'd rather find a good saloon on the mainland.

Jigger, meanwhile, has concocted a plot for him and Billy to rob the mill owner, Mr. Bascombe, who will be bringing a few thousand dollars to a ship (that he also happens to own) that night. The plan is to take the money from Mr. Bascombe as he delivers it to the ship's vault.

Bascombe plays a significant part in the bench scene, offering Julie another chance at the mill if she'll just leave Billy behind (she declines). It's a prime example of the kind of architecture that keeps musicals shapely and all of a piece. Logically speaking, it's not especially likely that the owner of the mill would also be the owner of the ship that Jigger has sailed in on, but it's possible. It's even less likely that he would be out at midnight carrying a satchel of money. This coincidence is covered in a single line that slips by the audience almost unnoticed, however. Why bother to make Bascombe the intended victim in this robbery instead of some new character? It's important that the man who is going to be at risk is someone we know and already have feelings about—preferably negative ones. It gives us a rooting interest and makes us feel how the community is all interconnected. Bascombe is the town's richest man, an oppressor of local labor, a small-minded, tightfisted entrepreneur whose placid, churchgoing exterior hides a tyrant's soul. He's the man Mr. Snow is on his way to becoming. Surely Rodgers and Hammerstein could have created an additional character to carry the money—a chief accountant or bookkeeper or even a messenger—but this is better. This creates dramatic symmetry and pulls the story together.

Characters such as Bascombe are like the iron tie rods that run through the ridge beams of the shotgun houses in New Orleans. The houses were relatively cheaply constructed and given to settling and slippage over the years, so builders introduced an iron rod that ran crosswise, bolted at each side. Every few years, or when necessary, a homeowner can pull his own home together by tightening the bolts—pulling the house in on itself, turning the screws, so to speak. Thus the house stays waterproof, insulated, and strong enough to stand. The rods are rarely noticed but always functioning, creating tensile strength in the building. Bascombe is like a human tie rod, keeping *Carousel* shipshape.

This is one of the reasons that picaresque stories are hard to do as musicals. In shows like *Candide* and *Big River*, we keep leaving the secondary characters behind, never to be seen again. This, like the passive hero, tends to limit a musical's prospects. Audiences seem much more comfortable and nourished in a community that stays in the same place and where the people can be relied upon to take an ongoing part in the story. From *The Music Man* to *Fiddler* to *Sweeney Todd*, musicals thrive by taking audiences to a time and place and making them feel that—for a couple of hours, at least—they live there, too. *Carousel* gives us a community intact, disrupted by Billy, the force from outside whose very presence seems to ensure that there will be drama—just like Harold Hill or Sweeney or any other outsider entering a closed world.

*Carousel* needs tie rods not because it's a picaresque but because, like *Gypsy*, it covers a lot of chronological ground. In *Gypsy* the tie rods take two forms: the evolving but basically unchanging vaudeville act that we see being perpetually freshened up by Madame Rose but always reliably trading on corn and patriotism, and the musical leitmotifs that keep returning: "Let Me Entertain You" and the phrase "I had a dream!" No matter how often the show travels, it always carries the same baggage, literally and emotionally. The tie rods not only keep the show in shape, they keep the audience on the journey.

In any case, in *Carousel*, Jigger Craigin approaches Billy with his scheme, and Billy demurs. He hasn't sunk so low that he needs to pull a knife on someone. He sends Jigger packing—for the moment. Then Julie approaches and delivers a piece of news he wasn't expecting: she's pregnant. The ground shifts.

Billy is about to take on a level of responsibility willy-nilly that he has never thought about before. The eternally rebellious boy is going to be asked to be a man and behave like one. Implicit in this is the idea that raising a child is best done in one stable place—never Billy's milieu. Now what?

Rodgers and Hammerstein created from this circumstance one of the great showpieces of music theater, the "Soliloquy," an almost eight-minute rumination on impending fatherhood. It is perhaps the greatest example of Hammerstein's dictum that a song should be a miniature play, with its own movement, conflict, and resolution. Once Billy understands what's happened, it takes him four minutes of imagining the great things he and his unborn son may do together and separately—four minutes of fatherly braggadocio—before it occurs to him that he may not have a son at all. He may have a daughter.

He's awestruck by responsibility, an emotion with which he's largely unfamiliar. "What would I do with her?" he wonders. "What could I do *for* her? A bum—with no money."

Now the music shifts, and so does the nature of his thought process. By today's standards, Billy's musings on his "little girl, pink and white," may seem politically unacceptable, but for an untutored carousel barker of the late nineteenth century, they're apt enough. And then, after he's painted the rosiest possible picture of her, darker thoughts begin to intrude. Finally, after seven minutes, he confronts responsibility. It's not about the child at all—it's about the man.

As Rodgers's music stirs up a sense of resolve, Billy sings:

> *I got to get ready before she comes!*
> *I gotta make certain that she*
> *Won't be dragged up in slums*
> *With a lot o' bums—*
> *Like me!*
>
> *She's gotta be sheltered and fed, and dressed*
> *In the best that money can buy!*
> *I never knew how to get money,*
> *But I'll try—*
> *By God! I'll try!*
> *I'll go out and make it*

*Or steal it or take it*
*Or die!*

The lyric is prophetic, but we're hardly sure of what will happen, and on this moment, and after giving us his best high G, Raitt directed that the curtain should fall.

In the original show, however, that's not the end of the act. In a quick scene, Billy agrees to serve as Jigger's accomplice, and Jigger convinces him that their best plan would be for the two of them to go on the clambake with the villagers and then quietly "disappear" in time to go commit the robbery, returning immediately afterward. It will give them cover and an alibi. Billy runs into the kitchen for the knife they'll use to threaten Mr. Bascombe, and then the two of them rush to blend in with the other villagers as they head to the boats that will take them out for their annual revel. The curtain falls on a gentle reprise as this placid small-town population heads out for a well-earned evening of food and drink, and maybe some innocent necking and stargazing.

The audience, of course, knows what no one in the town, including Julie, does—that before the night is out something terrible and irreversible is bound to happen. And in that suspension, we are made to wait. If we care about the people in the story, the wait is heartbreaking, no matter how much we may need refreshment or a bathroom or, in the days of the original production, a smoke. It's unbearable because what can be more painful than bearing witness to innocence that is about to be destroyed by grim experience? It's like watching footage of President Kennedy's open limo turning into Dealey Plaza moments before the shots ring out. Although *Carousel* makes no claim to being witness to history, the emotional pull of watching the moments before a disaster—personal or global—is always the same. And, remarkable as it seems, it's actually more powerful than the "Soliloquy," and it's the proper ending for the act.

For many shows, the question of where to drop the curtain must have been difficult to answer. Is the anticipation harder to bear than the act itself? Is "What will happen?" better than "Look what just happened!"?

*West Side Story* used a variation of a classical technique to answer the question, the *finaletto*. *Finaletto* is a fancy opera term that refers to a piece of music that ends a scene. Often, it suggests a small cluster of reprises or intertwining songs. It doesn't end the whole show (that's the *finale ultimo*). A proper *finaletto* may take many forms, but it often manages to convey a group of differing points of view from different characters, letting us know that there are clearly defined conflicts and differences of opinion at this point in the story. But it also, by reprising familiar melodic strains in a small bouquet, reminds us of how these people feel and what they've been through emotionally. *Finaletti* were de rigueur in the operettas and musicals of the '20s and '30s but were still often in use in the '60s, though you find them less often today. And the shows that used them don't have to be high-minded just because the word is Italian; the first act of *How to Succeed* concludes with a *finaletto*—it's even labeled that way in the playbill. But the "Tonight Quintet" from *West Side Story* is probably the finest of them—except it doesn't end the act, and it's only partly a reprise.

Tony, as you may remember, has agreed to try to stop the planned rumble between the two rival street gangs, the Jets and the Sharks. He's also fallen in love with Maria, who has begged him to try to make peace between the gangs. Meanwhile, Anita, in love with the leader of the Sharks, is looking forward to a night of post-rumble sex with her presumably victorious lover, assuming the rumble actually takes place. A lot depends upon the rumble—if Tony can't stop it from happening. And the enormity of his task is made manifest by the energy of the two gangs as they sing the "Tonight Quintet," using a word ("tonight") that has so far been used only in the first version of the song, where it is plaintive and filled with ardor. Now, suddenly, it is combative and dangerous. And set to music that we've not heard before. It is interrupted by Maria and Tony, singing the original "Tonight" melody and words, restoring the sense of romantic passion that drives the love part of this love/hate equation. And then we hear from Anita, who is singing about sex, using the angular, edgy music of the Jets and Sharks, with lyrics that are far more carnal and less celestial than those Maria and Tony are singing. If Maria's love for Tony is celestial, Anita's passion for Bernardo is definitely of the earth. These five points of view combine in five voices that lay out the territory of what might happen—the sexual and romantic passions are just as potent as the hatred of the two gangs for each other. Passion raises the stakes for hatred, and vice versa. The cost of not stopping the rumble goes up exponentially as the "Quintet" builds to its climax. And because it feels like a classic *finaletto*, it's reasonable to expect that the curtain will fall on its final, percussive note, as we anticipate what this dangerous night will bring. But it doesn't.

Instead, all this propulsive energy is transferred to the site of the rumble itself, and dance takes over. In a short book scene, Tony actually brokers a compromise—a fair fight between the leaders of the two gangs—but it quickly deteriorates and, in one of Robbins's most famous theater ballets, all hell breaks loose. It ends when Bernardo, Anita's lover, stabs Riff, the leader of the Jets, and then, in what can only be described as a meta-gap, Tony kills Bernardo. Tony, who has vowed to find his way out of the world of gangs, blood sport, and racial animus, finds himself a murderer with a knife in his hand.

The geometry of this outcome is set up by the "Tonight Quintet," and now we know the outcome, at least for the moment. Anita will not have her night with Bernardo but will instead have her hatred of Tony and the Jets restoked. The gangs will remain at war. And Tony and Maria's love will be more sorely tested than either could imagine—because Bernardo is Maria's brother. The curtain falls not on anticipation but on all-but-certain tragedy.

*West Side Story* was Stephen Sondheim's first Broadway show as a lyricist; the opposite approach—using some of the same ideas—served him in one of his capstone achievements as a composer-lyricist fifteen years later. *West Side Story* was a gritty tragedy, while *A Little Night Music* was a frothy comic operetta, admittedly with some dark shadows lurking, as they tend to in Sondheim's work. Nonetheless, the show is an intricately constructed, sophisticated, largely comic work, created after the landmark achievement (but financial disappointment) of *Follies*.

"I told Steve we needed to return the investment on the next show," the producer-director Hal Prince recalled. "And turn a little profit. So we did."

In hindsight, *Night Music* is significantly more than just a hit, and one of its sweetest pleasures—especially if you admire puzzles and structural dazzle—is the number that brings down the first-act curtain, "A Weekend in the Country."

This time it's all about anticipation. An Act 2 lyric has the ensemble singing, *"Perpetual anticipation is good for the soul but it's bad for the heart."* While I can't say with any certainty what that means, the anticipation referred to is certainly sexual; the anticipation in "A Weekend in the Country" is sexual *and* theatrical. Like the "Tonight Quintet," it's about the unforeseeable outcome of diverse characters on a collision course. And, as with the "Quintet," there are five points of view. But the number itself couldn't be more different. No hint of a reprise-driven *finaletto* here—it's a whole new number with a whole new tempo. Where the "Tonight Quintet" treats rage, ardor, and danger, "A Weekend in the Country" is a frolic musically, and lyrically breathless. The danger it describes is of the heart, and there's some panic in it, but no one is likely to get killed. Remember, it's a comedy.

It begins when Desiree Armfeldt asks permission of her cantankerous wealthy mother to invite some people down to the mother's country house for the weekend. It's not an innocent move. Desiree invites her former lover, Fredrik Egerman, and his young, virgin bride, Anne, with the clear intention of creating an intriguing contrast between Anne's annoying innocence and her own appealing experience. This sets in motion, among other things, the downbeat of the number. The virgin bride, suspecting the earlier affair, is horrified, while her husband is flattered and intrigued. Anne seeks the counsel of her friend Charlotte, who advises her to be bold—youth will win out. Charlotte then gleefully reveals the plot to her husband, a caddish military man and Desiree's *current* lover. He, of course, insists on crashing the party. Finally, Egerman's son, studying for the priesthood, also joins in, talking himself into going along "to observe" the spectacle of human folly, though it's clear to everyone but him that he's in love with his stepmother, the virgin bride.

So there's a lot to look forward to, and Sondheim has a field day, piling expectation on anxiety on expectation as Egerman Sr., Egerman Jr., Charlotte and her husband, Anne, and even Petra, the housemaid, all make preparations to meet their romantic fates, weaving their points of view together at breakneck speed—though it's never hard to understand the lyrics. In six minutes, Sondheim creates an entire *agitato* playlet, revving up the audience for what might or might not be the door-slamming, secret-passageway, meet-me-in-the-library outcome of such a weekend. In the end, the ensemble joins in, carrying bag and baggage to the cars as the number comes to a surprisingly civilized if very *tutti* conclusion; the curtain falls on a virtual orgy of expectation and suspense.

This is plenty to get you through intermission and back to your seat. As another Sondheim hero marvels in another circumstance, "so many possibilities!"

In a significantly less elegant but more raucous fashion, *The Producers* takes the same tack. The show concerns the efforts of Max Bialystock and his newfound partner, Leo Bloom, to produce the biggest Broadway flop in history, raise much more money than they need, and keep whatever's left after the show opens and quickly closes. After all, with a flop, investors assume all the money is lost. The entire first act (once they come up with this scheme) involves assembling the elements of the show and raising the aforesaid money from unsuspecting lonely, rich, randy widows from "Little Old Lady Land," as Max calls it. He means the Upper East and West Sides of Manhattan. The closing number celebrates this accomplishment, with nary a word of concern about the obvious likelihood that the results will go horribly wrong, which seems inevitable to the rest of us.

In "A Weekend in the Country," the characters are filled with anxiety as well as anticipation as they set off for what they know will be an unpredictable and complicated fate. In *The Producers*, the participants are completely innocent of any possibility of mishap—they're delusionally enthusiastic about the terrible idea they've had and feel impervious to failure. In other words, they work in the theater.

*The Producers* hearkens back to the era of *How to Succeed*, so perhaps it makes sense that the finale is also a classic *finaletto* (though it's *not* called that in the playbill), comprising elements of songs that have peppered the first act. This makes sense from a dramaturgical point of view as well as being in period. Since the first act consists of Max and Leo assembling a script, a director, a design team, a spectacularly busty Swedish assistant, and myriad elderly backers, and since each new element has had its own musical number, we should be reminded of how the whole motley team was put together by hearing each one's music again. And that's just what happens. The cracks in the plaster are clear to the audience when we observe just how terrible every element of the show actually is going to be, but, of course, that's exactly what Max and Leo are hoping for. That it may go wrong in a different way—a way none of them can foresee—occurs to nobody but, perhaps, us. So we don't need a crisis, because the anticipation of one is deliciously ripe in the air and plenty to sustain us.

If *Gypsy, West Side Story, A Little Night Music,* and even *The Producers* are classically structured shows (well, *The Producers* sort of), Jonathan Larson's *Rent,* while based on a classic opera, was anything but. Larson worked for many years on what was to become his only significant contribution to the canon (he died at thirty-five just before it began previews) and had a difficult time taming the beast. Though it began as a collaboration with a playwright named Billy Aronson, Larson soon took over the project himself, writing book, music, and lyrics, and often getting tangled in the complexities of a story that was as much about a time and a place—the world of hipster artists on the Lower East Side at the height of the AIDS crisis—as it was about one specific character's dilemma. Reluctant to give up any of the many tributary story lines that he had created and/or adapted from Puccini's *La Bohème,* Larson needed help yet resisted offers to reshape the show into a conventional musical. It was, after all, about downtown bohemians living in ambitious, sometimes uncontrolled chaos. If form follows function, why not have a chaotic, uncontrolled evening of ambitious rock-operatic drama? Larson's reasoning made sense, but the show, in its earliest incarnations, was long and confusing, despite the obvious merits of his vision and his score. Its framing conflict, about the attempts of a community of artists, would-be artists, activists, and would-be activists to resist the takeover of their building by an ambitious former friend who has gentrification on his mind, meandered. But it served as a device for an examination of the lives of determined outsiders, most living with HIV, on borrowed time.

The off-Broadway New York Theatre Workshop developed the piece and eventually presented the premiere, which had been trimmed and rethought—if not always elegantly—to the point where it was wildly exciting to audiences and critics, both despite and because of its flirtations with indirection and even incoherence. Structurally, the show seemed to almost exactly mirror the state of mind of its various oddly connected, sometimes even disconnected characters. And since its story stubbornly resisted a simple description, Larson cleverly created a first-act curtain that encapsulated the underlying emotion of virtually every character in it: defiance in the face of certain defeat.

"La Vie Bohème" paid tribute to *La Bohème*, but more directly to the spirit that sustains outsider communities, dreamers, slackers, and those who would rather be lost in a dangerous world than found in a conventional one. The number invites the entire ensemble to plead the case, beginning with a statement that what they love and aspire to is already gone:

> *Bohemia? Bohemia's*
> *A fallacy in your head*
> *This is Calcutta*
> *Bohemia is dead*

What follows is a kind of list song, which owes a nod to both Sondheim's "A Little Priest" from *Sweeney Todd* and, strangely enough, James Rado and Gerome Ragni's "Ain't Got No" and "I Got Life" from *Hair*. Its gleeful death mask and its rhyme orgy are Sweeney's and its catalog of revolutionary values is straight from that other downtown musical.

> *To loving tension, no pension, to more than one dimension*
> *To starving for attention, hating convention,*
> *hating pretension*
> *Not to mention of course hating dear old mom and dad*

What makes "La Vie Bohème" an appropriate curtain moment, in addition to its energy and drive, is the sense of doom driving the heartbeat of it. Like every self-proclaimed creative outpost, the world of *Rent* portends plenty of heartbreak, illness, failure, and death, which somehow always seems to call for a celebration. "La Vie Bohème" is that celebration, made all the more poignant (as was noted continually in the months and years following the show's transfer to Broadway) by its creator's sudden demise in the midst of the process. We don't know how Act 2 will play out, but we're left with the sense that the entire structure of the community we've come to know and care about is on a precipice and not about to stop moving forward. Whether it will go completely over a cliff remains to be seen as the lights snap off onstage and come up on the audience—and that's plenty.

# 12. Intermission

**W**hen I was first taken to the theater, in 1955, intermission refreshments were limited to a watery form of orange drink served in a waxed cardboard carton. I have never understood why this should have been so. The theater owners, not above figuring out new and different ways to pick up a little extra something from a captive audience, could certainly have done better—heaven knows the movies were already selling a variety of products at inflated prices. But the Broadway theater, as it so often has, stubbornly resisted. The audience, made up almost entirely of New Yorkers who were inured to this pathetic reality, made do with orange drink and, slightly later, a similarly packaged (and similarly watered-down) version of lemonade. In an early—thus far unrepeated—act of petty crime, I stole one of these drinks from the refrigerator that stood across from the men's room door in the basement of the Eugene O'Neill Theatre during a matinee of *A Thousand Clowns* in 1961.

Jason Robards made me do it. In *A Thousand Clowns* he played Murray Burns, the writer of an awful kiddie TV show called *Chuckles the Chipmunk*. Murray has just quit his job and is spending his unemployed days making fun of the conventional workforce; shouting at the world from his window; seducing an adorable social worker who has come to threaten him with the removal to a foster home of Nick, the nephew he is raising; and generally imparting his unconventional values to the boy, who was exactly my age. Murray's message seemed to be that the world was wrong and he was right, and if he felt like doing something, he just did it, without apology.

I took the bait. I had seen the refrigerator before taking my seat at the beginning of the play, and I was seated on an aisle in the rear of the theater—perfectly positioned to be the first one down the stairs when the first-act curtain fell.

It was a revolutionary act: I thought the theater should be doing better with concessions, and charging less, and that its failure to do either entitled me to express my dissatisfaction in an act of sticky-fingered protest. And I was thirsty. Capitalism was a bad thing anyhow, though not as bad as the orange drink, which, I admit, tasted a little better when you had boosted it with lightning stealth.

I now work as senior vice president at Jujamcyn Theaters, which owns the Eugene O'Neill Theatre, and a trip down to the basement-level restroom is always tinged with a little nostalgia for that free carton of orange drink. This, apparently, is what persistence in a career amounts to.

The career would not have happened at all without the gambler's instinct of my first New York boss, Rocco Landesman.

In 1987, I was working as the dramaturg at the Mark Taper Forum in Los Angeles and had begun to understand what it meant to tell a story onstage. In hindsight, it's amazing that, as a daily theater critic in the early and mid-'80s, I had written about the subject with such authority from a perspective of almost complete ignorance. Thanks to the patience of the Taper's artistic director, Gordon Davidson—one of the legends of the not-for-profit arts movement—I eventually came to understand that theater is not the written word, it's the word made flesh. Sometimes a light cue can make you cry. Sometimes an actor turning toward or away from another actor can tell more of the story than all the words a playwright could think up. Onstage, the emotional ride is a moving target made up of countless words and deeds, of lights and scenery and costume color choices (they tell you where to look, and a lot about who's wearing them), pacing, cuing, and the sheer virtuosity of an actor clearing the emotional hurdles that a great role presents. I had to learn as much as I could, making as few mistakes as possible. And I had to come to accept that in the theater, the script is only the blueprint on which the theater makers depend. It was a little daunting. But at the end of it all, I still believed that, absent a credible blueprint, you almost couldn't build a house that would stand.

One other thing I began to learn at the Taper: how to relate to artists, particularly writers. Previously, I thought it perfectly acceptable to be cutting, sarcastic, even downright mean. In print. Critics rarely confront their targets face-to-face. Dramaturgs do. Sitting across from the great, underappreciated playwright Lanford Wilson in an L.A. bar, I got my first real lesson in dramaturgy. He taught it with a characteristic mix of gentleness and anger, masking hurt with pride and wit. And he did it, as he so often did back in the '80s, with a drink in his hand.

He was working on rewrites for his play *Burn This*, which was in previews at the Mark Taper. I was expounding, pretentiously, no doubt, on some line of dialogue in his play, and he was staring at me with a look that I later came to recognize as veiled incredulity. Finally I must have overstepped my bounds. He drained all but the last swallow of a margarita and then reared back and aimed the glass at my head.

He didn't throw it. He just held it in place like a man who was considering his options. Then he said, rather gently, "When speaking to a playwright whose work you care about, find a word other than 'cliché.'" Then he drained the last swallow and put the glass down on the table and we moved on.

Point taken.

One morning I read in *The New York Times* that Rocco Landesman was assuming the presidency of Jujamcyn Theaters, a company that owned five Broadway theaters. I knew who he was—a sort of legendary iconoclast who had sold his racehorses to produce the musical *Big River*, which, back in my days at the *Herald Examiner*, I had torn to pieces in a not very nice way during its tryout in La Jolla. Rocco was, and is, a Roger Miller fanatic, and his favorite American novel is *The Adventures of Huckleberry Finn*. He married one to the other and created a Broadway hit despite my dissenting opinion. (The way he did it is a story in itself. As Roger Miller later said, "Rocco Landesman made me an offer I couldn't understand.")

Rocco had gotten a Ph.D. in dramaturgy and criticism at Yale Drama School and run a small hedge fund. Despite his first name, he is Jewish, and from St. Louis, and has nothing to do with the Mafia. He claimed to keep $10,000 in his pocket at all times in case something interesting came up. He seemed an odd choice for this corporate position.

I went out to lunch with a friend at the Taper, and when I returned to the office I found a phone message in my in-box from Rocco Landesman.

"He's offering you a job," this friend of mine said to me as I stared uncomprehendingly at the message. That seemed unlikely, but it turned out to be true.

"I just took this job, running this company," he said on the phone. "We have five theaters and the only way we're ever going to fill them is to produce our own shows. Come to New York and produce shows."

Why me? I wanted to know.

"Well," he said, "you panned the hell out of *Big River* and a lot of what you said was pretty smart. I used your review to beat up the creatives and help fix the show. I think you're good at this."

Rocco, it turned out, is a hunch player when it comes to people, and a master of seduction. Being around him is like being in the center of a small lightning storm. He is creative, decisive, open to any idea that walks in the room, and an excellent judge of what is ingenious and what is foolish. He likes taking risks more than almost anything else, but he is canny in deciding which ones to take, especially in the theater. He is loyal, sometimes to a fault, and he is generous. He believes no meeting needs to be more than half an hour and keeps a parking meter in his office. As far as I know, he never had a meeting at Jujamcyn without keeping one eye on the stock ticker. But having even 70 percent of his attention is plenty. It was impossible not to come to New York and work for this man.

We sealed the deal over breakfast at the Carnegie Deli. This was in the summer of 1987, when there were still phone booths and no cell phones. As we walked out of the Carnegie, I headed for one of a pair of booths.

"I'd better call my wife," I said, slipping into one.

"I have to call my bookie," he said, slipping into the other.

Rocco, it turned out, made a habit of hiring people who panned him. A few years after I got to Jujamcyn, Paul Libin, the producing director of the legendary Circle in the Square Theatre, wrote a scathing letter to the *Times* attacking Rocco for some things he had written in an *Arts and Leisure* essay about Lincoln Center. Rocco's response was simple and decisive: he hired him. And so the modern-day incarnation of Jujamcyn was born—three guys from the not-for-profit world (Yale, the Taper, and the Circle) plunging into the shark tank of Broadway.

Back in 1987, Broadway had run into a deep ditch. Many theaters were empty, some of them for months, even years, at a time. The only shows that were making an impact were the British megamusicals. Times Square was a seedy, vaguely dangerous, and certainly unwelcoming neighborhood dotted with strip joints and porno theaters and littered with crack vials and used condoms. I loved it, actually, but it was hard to know whether the moment had come to write its obituary or dig in and work to revive its glory. We did neither. We started to do modestly the one thing we were able to do: produce shows.

When the Walt Disney Company bought and refurbished the New Amsterdam Theatre on Forty-second Street, even the most optimistic business interests could not have foreseen the resulting boom. *All* Forty-second Street followed suit. Peepland disappeared and McDonald's took over. Soon the blocks immediately to the north began to brighten. A Gap store appeared, and then a Swatch store. Within a few short years, Times Square had been utterly transformed. The M&M Store and the Hershey Store battled for dominance across the street from each other on two corners that had once featured entirely different kinds of candy purveyors. True, it was in some respects more like a midwestern mall than the unique showplace it had been in its heyday, or the tenderloin it had followed, but it was clean and well lit, commercial and safe. And the tourists began to come. Thanks to the relatively new (for the theater) field of market research, Broadway business folks learned that, for tourists, a Broadway show was the most highly prized destination and that *they didn't know which one they wanted to see*. This astonishing bit of news encouraged the industry to market itself as a brand of its own: not *Phantom* or *Beauty and the Beast*, but simply *BROADWAY*. Everyone could get a piece. Like the physical landscape, the show business landscape was renewed. And like the physical land- scape, it became more generic and less eccentric, less unusual, less New York. Suddenly, we were genuinely in a national and international business, for better and worse. For shows like *The Lion King*, it spelled infinite life. For others like *The Producers*, which Jujamcyn hosted at the St. James Theatre, it meant that once the New Yorkers had roared at its urban, Jewish wit, its days were numbered.

Rocco's days at Jujamcyn were numbered too, it turned out. When Barack Obama was elected president, Rocco decided that he needed to become the chairman of the National Endowment for the Arts so he could shake things up in a larger arena, and he is a very determined man. He worked tirelessly to get the job and said goodbye, selling the company to Jordan Roth, a young producer with a wide-ranging interest in the theater business as a whole, not just in individual productions.

For a moment, it felt odd working for a man who was a little more than half my age, but not for long. Jordan had vision born of another generation, which he managed to make refreshing rather than intimi- dating. He also did two things for which I'll be forever grateful, both of them completely unexpected. The first was to gently but firmly sepa- rate me from a growing reluctance to embrace the next generation of theater makers and their sense of what a Broadway musical could be. My natural artistic tendencies are conservative, and subconsciously I was beginning to wonder whether the era of shows I grew up with was the only one I could take real pleasure in. It was Jordan's passionate enthusiasm for productions like *Fela!*, *Spring Awakening*, and *Ameri- can Idiot* that made me look again. If the Jujamcyn of the late '80s and '90s had pushed the envelope with *Jelly's Last Jam*, *M. Butterfly*, *The Producers*, and *Angels in America*, why should we assume that that was as far as it could be pushed? We were young again—well, Jordan was— and I could rejoin the cavalry, which I happily did.

Jordan's other prime interest when he took the reins at Jujamcyn was the industry's public image. We were a famously rude business.

We were kind of delighted by our cranky box office personnel, our loud and vaguely exasperated ushers, our indifferent ticket takers. They were part of our New York profile—like the wise-ass Lindy's waiters or the know-it-all cabdrivers regularly parodied in the movies of the '40s. They were part of New York's gruff, unfeeling big-city lovability— back then. And our audiences were also a crowd of gruff, impermeable New Yorkers—back then. Jordan, coming of age much later than the rest of us, understood just how much things had changed. He had watched carefully how the hotel industry and particularly the restaurant business—largely inspired by the restaurateur Danny Meyer— had revolutionized the way they treated their staff and customers, and determined that Broadway needed to get with the program. The audience was now a national and international one. They were under no obligation to be charmed by this uniquely surly part of the New York Experience. He instituted a top-down and bottom-up rethinking of how Jujamcyn would train and monitor its employees, with a commitment to making the entire experience a happier one for ourselves, theatergoers, and theater makers. It was a grand adventure. The industry as a whole was initially skeptical, which delighted us all even more. There's hardly a happier feeling than waiting for others to catch up. Eventually, they came along, which was fun to watch from our imagined perch. All of this created a strong sense that Broadway was moving dynamically, and why in the world would anyone want to miss that? My passions were rekindled, and I'll always be grateful.

Of course, with the new, improved Broadway, the concessions available at intermission—already long since upgraded from crappy orange drink and lemonade—expanded markedly once again, though the prices, to be fair, do remain shocking.

Still, you can now buy a Courvoisier in a cup with a lid, and you can bring it back to your seat and enjoy it during Act 2, surrounded, as you will be, not merely by New Yorkers, but by theatergoers from all over the world. It's often a wise purchase, may I say—as the lights begin to dim and the entr'acte begins.

# 13. Clambake

*Curtain Up: Act 2*

Cole Porter reportedly said that for his new show, 1929's *Fifty Million Frenchmen*, he was putting the two best songs in the first fifteen minutes. Why? Because he was so irritated with his society friends coming to see his work "fashionably late" that he wanted to make sure they'd miss them and be damn sorry they did.

"You Do Something to Me" and "You've Got That Thing" became standards, apparently without the endorsement of Porter's friends (though the rest of *Fifty Million Frenchmen* has rarely been heard from since). But does anyone come to theater "fashionably late" anymore? Does anyone "linger in the lobby" before Act 2, as the title of a 1925 Gershwin song from *Lady, Be Good!* suggests they might?

The habit dates from another time, when the theater had a different audience, and when understanding the plot and characters of a musical show was hardly the point. Broadway was, for many society types, just another night on the town, and the play was often somewhat incidental to the overall experience, which might include a cocktail party and dinner before, or cocktails before and dinner after, with dancing, and a midnight floor show. And a visit to a speakeasy that might last until dawn. Those days are long over, and yet one aspect of writing for the theater has barely changed since the flapper era. As if we were still lingering in the lobby, most second acts begin with something virtually expendable: the song that has nothing to do with anything. Also, in case you are there to hear it, it's usually light and entertaining.

The reasons for the light and entertaining part of the tradition are easy to justify. First acts tend to end with a crisis and are often a downer. The two lovers have discovered they have betrayed or been betrayed, and will never have another word to say to each other. Or the protesters outside a local TV station have been beaten with truncheons and arrested. Or the hero is broke and needy, and has decided to commit a robbery that we know will ruin his life. It's all very grim and unpleasant, at least by musical theater standards. So the authors feel an obligation to welcome you back in for Act 2 in a way that suggests the worst is, perhaps, over—"Welcome back, dear audience," they seem to be saying. "We're really here to entertain you after all. We're glad you stayed, and we hope you are too." Theater makers today tend to refer to this moment as "one for nothing"—a gift to the audience, and, in some cases, to the songwriters as well.

Hence "Take Back Your Mink" at the beginning of Act 2 of *Guys and Dolls*, "Big Dollhouse" from *Hairspray*, and "This Was a Real Nice Clambake" from *Carousel*, among others.

A lot of good songs have occupied this spot, though it's unlikely they were placed there for spite, as Porter may have done with the opening numbers in *Fifty Million Frenchmen*. Instead, the slot seems to have given songwriters a certain kind of freedom, a recess from the demands of storytelling and character exploration. There's a high pleasure quotient in many of these numbers, as if the writers, like the audience, had been refreshed by intermission (no orange drink for them, one can assume). As a particularly classic example, give a listen to "Together, Wherever We Go" from *Gypsy*. It's the only tension-free moment in the entire show, even though the characters bicker as they sing. (It's not really the first number in the act; that's a variation on the tired vaudeville routine that appears throughout the show. But it *feels* like the first number.)

Frank Loesser seems to have had particular fun with "Take Back Your Mink," which is a disposable nightclub number from *Guys and Dolls*. After Sky Masterson's Cuban adventure with Sarah Brown has ended in disaster at the end of Act 1, the Act 2 curtain rises on Miss

Adelaide and the Hot Box girls doing a mild strip to a song that is all about handing back shiny gifts to a sugar daddy who actually expected to trade them for sex. The removal of the items constitutes the strip. The likelihood that the outraged Hot Box girls have never before encountered such a proposition from a sugar daddy is absolutely nil, which makes their expression of shock and horror a good joke, if somewhat politically incorrect by today's standards. The Hot Box girls, in fact, seem to know enough about fur coats and how they should be treated to conclude the number with the lyric

> *So take back your mink*
> *Those old worn-out pelts*
> *And tell them to hollanderize it*
> *For somebody else.*

As the decades have rushed by, this lyric, along with others in Loesser's flavorful postwar argot, has become progressively more mysterious to audiences. What does it mean to hollanderize a mink? Eventually the line was changed to "and go shorten the sleeves for somebody else," which doesn't sit on the music quite as elegantly and is certainly less colorful. But at the time *Guys and Dolls* was produced in 1949, audiences understood the lyric perfectly well, as they did the references to casting a "sheep's eye" at a girl you were mooning over, or owning suits with "two pair of pants," not to mention the Yiddish "*So nu?*" which forms the basis of an entire number.

As to the two pair of pants, men's stores well into the '60s often sold suits to middle-class white-collar workers with a jacket and two pair of pants, reasoning that the jacket would be hung in an office closet each day while the bookkeeper or assembly line supervisor sat at his desk. The slacks would need cleaning more often than the jacket—hence the spare pair. In the 1933 Marx Brothers movie *Duck Soup*, Groucho interrogates Chico at a war crimes trial by asking him, "Isn't it true you tried to sell Freedonia's secret war code and plans?"

"Sure," Chico replies, "I sold a code and two pair of plans," a joke that leaves today's audiences similarly at a loss.

Loesser was no punster, but he was particularly adept at using

colloquialism to create a particular—in this case Runyonesque—
landscape; only Johnny Mercer could compete with him on that front.
Sky Masterson, twitting Sarah Brown's ultraconventional idea of an
ideal man, sings, *"And you'll know at a glance by the two pair of pants."*

But what, a modern audience is entitled to ask, was hollanderizing?
When *Guys and Dolls* was revived in 1992 with Nathan Lane playing
Nathan Detroit, *The New York Times* ran an article about Loesser's
use of colloquial expressions, which engendered a somewhat startling
response in the letters column:

> To the Editor:
> A. Hollander & Sons, based in Newark and named for my
> great-grandfather Adolph, were the world's largest fur dressers
> and dyers, listed on the New York Stock Exchange . . . The
> Hollanders specialized in making cheap furs look expensive,
> especially mink-dyed muskrat. But was that Hollanderizing?
> Well, no.
> Hollanderizing was a cleaning process for many types of furs.
> It involved sawdust and other agents to remove the grime that fur
> accumulated during a winter of wear. For many women, it was a
> spring ritual to take their coats to a furrier, who would send them
> to be Hollanderized.
> Although Hollanderizing has gone the way of the Studebaker,
> it is nice to be a slightly mysterious footnote to Broadway history.
> This is gratifying to the present family members, notably my aunt
> Leslie Hollander of Asbury Park, N.J., who has a long memory.
> —JANE HOLLANDER Long Branch, N.J., July 8, 1992

So Miss Adelaide and the other Hot Box girls knew their way around
a mink, and knew their way around generally, as did Mr. Loesser. Yet
the number itself is hardly germane to the story of *Guys and Dolls*. It's a
throwaway, easily ignored, but written with a virtuoso's keen observa-
tion and enjoyment of detail.

The same might be said for *Carousel*'s "This Was a Real Nice Clambake," which features the novelty of the entire chorus of performers
singing it while lying on their backs, virtually overcome by an overdose

of steamers and lobsters. It's a number about the pleasures of being sated, and Rodgers and Hammerstein knew that audiences might miss it, or miss part of it, without missing anything much. But it serves as an antidote to the dramatic end of Act 1, and the stasis in the number is setting a trap: what follows is all action. There's to be an attempted seduction, which today might be considered a rape, a foiled robbery, and a suicide coming up. Beginning the act with the lulling three-quarter tempo of "Clambake" makes audiences feel secure and sated themselves, happy to be there, which ensures that they will be startled out of their lethargy in exactly the right way by the plot.

Among the classic shows, this pattern was all but ubiquitous. *Finian's Rainbow*'s Act 2 opens with a satirical revue number called "When the Idle Poor Become the Idle Rich"; *Gentlemen Prefer Blondes*, like *Guys and Dolls*, features a nightclub turn, as does *On the Town*. *Kiss Me, Kate* lets us enjoy three dancer-singers working out on "Too Darn Hot" for no particular reason. *The Music Man* gives us a rehearsal for the town's Ice Cream Sociable called, of all things, "Shipoopi," while *The Pajama Game* takes us to a party at the Union Hall featuring entertainment: "Steam Heat." The lesser-known *Paint Your Wagon*, a musical about the California Gold Rush, features a number called "Hand Me Down That Can of Beans," which sounds like it's going to be a reworking of "This Was a Real Nice Clambake," but with a less appetizing menu.

*Porgy and Bess*, which was as boldly experimental as any musical theater event had ever been when it opened in 1935, was presented in three acts and steered clear of the tradition, a sign, perhaps, that it wanted to be taken more seriously than the shows surrounding it at the time. But when it was revised for Broadway in 2012, it was telescoped into two acts, and Act 2 opened with "It Ain't Necessarily So," a classic fun-if-you-happen-to-catch-it number. *Porgy*, it seems, was being brought to heel for a less adventurous audience.

In modern times, with the audience all back in its seats and paying attention, theater makers began to insert plot or thematic information into these numbers without really changing the tone of the numbers themselves, and in some cases actually using the tone for ironic comment. Still wanting to seduce audiences into a sense of well-being, they began to try to eat their cake and have it too.

*Hello, Dolly!*'s second act opens with "Elegance," sung by four subsidiary characters out on the town, and it certainly sounds like a typical opener—very soft shoe and dripping charm. But it contains at least a hint of future conflict—the two girls think the two boys are millionaires, and the boys are playing up this lie in every way they can, while the audience enjoys the fact that this will no doubt cause more and more trouble as the evening wears on. So there's a hint of plot, but nothing too specific or crucial. (The number, credited to Jerry Herman, was actually ghosted by Bob Merrill when no one could figure out how the act should open.)

*Company* opens its second act with two numbers telescoped into one—"Side by Side by Side." The number begins as a charming soft-shoe takeoff on "Side by Side" and then morphs into a real barn burner, including a tap break, that goes on for so long that the cast pretends to be more and more out of breath as it progresses, and completely exhausted by its conclusion. By turns charming and intentionally overlively, it is dripping with irony. First "Side by Side by Side" adds one more "by side" to the number it is tipping its hat to, thereby showing us a couple and a third wheel, the show's uncommitted protagonist, Bobby. Then, in the second section, which could be a whole new song called "What Would We Do Without You?," the tap break shows us all the couples taking turns, with Bobby doing his part and then handing the break off to an empty follow spot and dead silence. In the course of the two halves of the number, we see him as both one too many and one too few, the natural number in a show about marriage being two, not three, not one. And yet, despite this remarkable display of theatrical thematic storytelling—we know he's going to have to become part of a pair or be forever alone—the number *sounds* like two charming, brainless second-act openers back to back: an embarrassment of riches.

If *Company*'s second-act opener made all its points in action rather than words, Sondheim's magnum opus, *Sweeney Todd*, took the opposite approach, while still honoring the tradition and pushing it forward.

"God, That's Good!" gets *Sweeney*'s second act off to a roaring start with an ensemble-driven number about how tasty Miss Lovett's meat pies are, never mind what they're made of. But as the number progresses, more and more plot gets inserted into it, and it develops into a complex musical scene, in which Sweeney's custom-made barber chair arrives and is installed and tested out, using a stack of books to simulate the path his victims will soon be taking from the second-floor barbershop to the revenue-generating bake house in the basement, and thence to the tables where the customers will extol their flavor. The tempo and tone of the number keep refreshing themselves, while these story intervals keep interrupting. Yet when all is said and done, the number reverts to a great big cheerful celebration again, the irony having deepened: we've come to observe exactly how Sweeney's victims end up as ingredients in the pies the general public is enjoying with such relish. It's a bright-as-paint advertisement for the joys of cannibalism.

But many modern shows, less ambitious ones perhaps, have declined to challenge the tradition, with no real harm done. *Annie* begins its second act with actual story material—the hunt for the poor orphan's parents is being taken to a new level by broadcasting it to the entire country over the radio. That's how we come to meet Bert Healy, a character we'll never hear from again, who, after presenting the plea, launches into "You're Never Fully Dressed Without a Smile," a classic example of the genre. The scene shifts from the radio station to the orphanage, where all the orphans do their own version of the number for no particular reason except to bring down the house, which a claque of little girls can certainly do. Mission accomplished.

"The Big Dollhouse" in *Hairspray* also follows the rules, though *Hairspray* is in most respects a shaggier, more informal show than *Annie*. But it does tend to observe the niceties when it can, and "The Big Dollhouse" gives us two minutes of lively women-behind-bars camp, as the protesters who have challenged the segregationist policies of *The Corny Collins Show* bemoan their fate, moments before they are all released from prison. We didn't really need to hear from them. The number is there purely for entertainment purposes and was summarily clipped out of the film version of the musical. Almost no one noticed.

Whereas *Hairspray* showed a surprising amount of respect and affection for classic forms, the bold *Sunday in the Park with George* rarely did. Yet in some ways it also chose to follow the rules at the top of the second act, though with a more complicated intent.

*Sunday* faced a particularly interesting problem: its second act begins a century after its first act ends. To link the two, Sondheim wrote a sophisticated comedy number called "It's Hot up Here." The curtain rises on Seurat's now-famous painting, inhabited by real actors, posed as if frozen in time, just as they were when the curtain came down on Act 1. But as they sing about the frustrations of being stuck in a painting instead of being able to continue their real lives, audiences begin to realize that it is not the people who are singing, it's the painting—and it has been hanging someplace for a very long time. This connects us back to Act 1 and also leads us into the ensuing scene, set in Chicago's Art Institute, where the actual painting hangs, comfortably locating us in modern times. Yet despite this highly original transition, the number itself follows tradition in one important way—there's not a single piece of information in it that we really need to hear to understand the story.

Of course, we do want to understand the story, and we may also have some fear that, having taken off a quarter hour to use the bathroom and check e-mail and messages, we may be momentarily disoriented and at a loss—more than audiences would have been half a century ago, when the distractions were fewer and less likely to be as intrusive as the information system everyone now has in his or her pocket or purse. Hence it's no surprise that *Hamilton*, which breaks so many rules and observes so many others, opens its second act with a sly, though possibly unintentional, tip of the hat to the tradition. Its second-act opener is called "What'd I Miss?"

# 14. Suddenly Seymour

*The Candy Dish*

I f the materials that open second acts are among the easiest to predict and describe, what happens next is significantly more imponderable. By the time a story has come this far, if it's worth anything at all, it has developed its own path and has no choice but to follow it. Still, there are a few reliable paradigms that carry audiences through to the big confrontations, climaxes, and celebrations still to come.

The term "second-act trouble," which every theater professional knows, usually refers to something that begins to happen right around this spot. Creators trying out their new show discover that once they've welcomed the audience back, they don't have a secure way of leading them home. Part of the problem is pragmatic; if you think of a musical score as a candy dish filled with a variety of delights, you can imagine the disappointment of discovering that too many of the candies in the dish are weak variations of each other, as opposed to new and surprising inventions. By the time we get to the second song in Act 2, a fair number of treats have been sampled. And the invention can begin to flag. How many kinds of musical numbers are there? How many kinds of dance numbers? Aside from getting through the remains of the story, are there any styles of presentation or any emotional explorations that we haven't already dealt with? What's left besides the big battle at the end?

Sometimes second-act trouble is really first-act trouble—too much of the vocabulary has already been on display before intermission, or something that might be useful right about now has not been set up, and the audience gets confused. Or too many subplots have been unpacked in Act 1, and they are cumbersome and time-consuming to pack back up again. But today's shows, which have many technological advantages over the classic era of Broadway, lack one candy that used to reliably be present: a visit with the star.

In revues like *The Ziegfeld Follies*, there used to be a spot in the playbill that simply said "A Few Minutes with Beatrice Lillie" or "A Few Minutes with Bert Lahr." The notation encouraged the audience to imagine that the star they had come to see was going to simply improvise, or chat, or in some other way supply an intimate experience that would be unique. In truth, these "few minutes" events were largely scripted—an early version of a stand-up routine—but whether they were or weren't, they gave the crowd what it came for: a seemingly once-in-a-lifetime audience with theater royalty. The star could string together old bits of monologue, sing songs, or tell jokes, and no one would interrupt. There was no one onstage but the star.

As shows progressed from the pre-*Oklahoma!* era to the postwar period, these moments became integrated into the story and were no longer spontaneous or irrelevant, but in some sense they still functioned in the same way: they provided an opportunity for the audience to celebrate the star. And audiences were hungry for the opportunity. Whether it was Ezio Pinza singing "This Nearly Was Mine" in *South Pacific* or Zero Mostel relaxing from the anxiety of life in Anatevka long enough to share the comic duet "Do You Love Me?" with his costar Maria Karnilova, or Angela Lansbury doing the same thing with Bea Arthur in "Bosom Buddies" in *Mame*, these were a powerful element in why audiences came to the theater: they loved to spend time with the star, especially if the star let her hair down or opened her heart. And the moment usually came in the second slot in Act 2.

Barbara Cook, though not a superstar even at the height of her career as a leading lady, had such a moment singing "Ice Cream" in this spot in *She Loves Me*. All alone onstage, she got a chance to show off her spectacular Broadway soprano, go through the character's inner monologue as she discovers that she's fallen in love, and hit a great high note at the end. In the largely forgotten musical *It's a Bird . . . It's a Plane . . . It's Superman*, the title character, played by a complete nonstar named Bob Holiday, all alone onstage, had a big comic solo called "The Strongest Man in the World." Looking at the show today, you would think the part had been played by somebody important. And Mandy Patinkin, who was a star on the rise, took the slot in *Sunday in the Park with George* to display his Danny Kaye–like ability with the satirical tongue-twister "Putting It Together"—all alone onstage except for some cardboard cutouts of the people he was supposed to be dealing with. All these moments are designed to be especially delicious, and the more modern ones advance the plot, or at least the subject.

Sometimes, the show itself celebrated the star in this slot. Most famously, in "Hello, Dolly!," virtually everyone in the cast joined in to let the customers know that Carol Channing was the greatest, most adorable, most eccentric, and most important person who had ever walked down a staircase. The producer-director Hal Prince, according to William Goldman's *The Season*, turned down the opportunity to direct *Hello, Dolly!* in part because he couldn't figure out what the number was doing in the show. Dolly Levi, after all, wasn't someone who was likely to be celebrated by the entire staff of the Harmonia Gardens restaurant—she was a small-time shanty-Irish matchmaker from Yonkers. But Prince was thinking of the character. Jerry Herman, Gower Champion (who did direct and choreograph), and David Merrick (who produced) were focused on the star. And they gave the audience the (admittedly irrational) thrill of a lifetime in one of the greatest numbers ever wrapped around a title song. Who cared whether Dolly Levi was famous or obscure, rich or poor, welcome or unwelcome in a fashionable New York eatery? Carol Channing was famous, rich, and welcome on the stage of the St. James Theatre. The damn thing worked so well that Herman repeated it in *Mame* two years later, though he moved it to the end of Act 1. And again in *Mack and Mabel* (apparently against his better judgment) with "When Mabel Comes in the Room," which occupied the opening slot in Act 2. Why make the customers work when you can provide their ecstasy for them? They're sure to join in.

But these Jerry Herman shows were inadvertently making a larger point. What if the show had to celebrate the star because the star wasn't actually that big a star? Carol Channing was a damned big star, but was she Beatrice Lillie? Lillie was an international celebrity in the '20s and '30s. Elizabeth Taylor was the audience's idea of a star in 1964. The Beatles were *stars*. Carol Channing was a star only live on Broadway. Angela Lansbury? Same thing. And Bernadette Peters's Mabel Normand in *Mack and Mabel* could hardly compete with Liza Minnelli's Sally Bowles in the film of *Cabaret*. There had been a time when Broadway stars were bona fide superstars, celebrated with big pictorial profiles in magazines like *Life* and *Look*. But Broadway stars were dimming in the face of Hollywood's increasingly larger share of the market. (The magazines were going out of business, too.) TV had given us Lucy and Desi, and Archie Bunker was yet to come. And rock stars, beginning with Elvis, were the biggest stars of all. No Broadway performer could compete. Broadway royalty ruled a shrinking fiefdom, and producers were taking notice.

Coincidentally, a practical problem cropped up at exactly the same moment. Back in Bea Lillie's day, a star played a show for a season, the show was a success, and everyone moved on. But by the mid-'60s (and it's only gotten worse), shows were having a hard time recouping their costs in a single season, and stars weren't willing to stick around forever. The economics of Broadway made it harder and harder for a producer to depend upon a star to create a hit. Shows had to find ways to survive the departure of their original stars. *Fiddler* did it ingeniously, by letting Mostel go quickly, replacing him with a series of credible Tevyes, and making the show the star. *Dolly!* did it with a series of stunt replacements; by the time it had run its almost seven-year course on Broadway, the role had been played by everyone from Mary Martin and Ethel Merman to Betty Grable and Phyllis Diller, with a hugely successful interval in which Pearl Bailey and an entirely African American cast came in and retooled the whole enterprise. But all this ingenious casting and producing couldn't completely conceal the problem: Broadway stars were becoming a thing of the past in musicals, and musicals needed to be able to survive their departure, after a season, in order to be financially sustainable. The lesson was learned again when *The Producers* became instantaneously legendary in part because of the teaming of Nathan Lane and Matthew Broderick. The two left the show, business faltered, and they were invited back, for astronomical salaries, to pump up the grosses. Then they left again. The show was a substantial hit, but its run was a bit of a disappointment, given that it had opened in a blaze of glory.

The English superproducer Cameron Mackintosh solved the problem. He introduced a new kind of musical with a mechanical star. Beginning with *Cats*, in 1982 (1981 in London), Mackintosh produced a series of musicals—*Les Misérables*, *Phantom of the Opera*, and *Miss Saigon*—in which the spectacle of the production—a chandelier that crashed down from above, a helicopter that actually lifted off and flew away—utilized modern technology and theater craft to become the heart of the attraction. True, some of these shows had stars, or semistars, but the stars were never the point. The soft-core operatic scores and the special effects were the draw, and they easily survived the departure of the leading players. The productions were actually reminiscent in some ways of the operettas that had preceded the arrival of the Gershwins, Rodgers and Hart, and Cole Porter back in the '20s. It was almost as if the ghosts of Sigmund Romberg, Rudolf Friml, and the young Oscar Hammerstein had returned with their exotic, overripe tales of derring-do romance and their ballad-heavy "light classical" (now mixed with light rock) sound. The techniques for delivering battle, fire, and flood had changed, but the objectives had not—to put on a live spectacle that would deliver machine-driven thrills eight times a week no matter who was doing the singing and acting. It was a stroke of genius, and it has survived for decades now in megahits like *The Lion King* and megaflops like *Spider-Man: Turn Off the Dark*. Foolproof it is not, but when it works, there are fortunes to be made and thrills to be discovered without an identifiable human star anywhere in sight.

Star turns, of course, were never the only option for this slot, and today, with fewer and fewer real stars, they have become impractical. Finding a new flavor that the show hasn't already exploited, however, remains a prime motivation. Audiences would stick with things if they believed that the theater makers still had new tricks up their sleeve. No show proves this more definitively than *Gypsy*—a show that actually did have a real star in Ethel Merman. But by the time Act 2, Scene 2, came along, we'd had a lot of Merman: "Some People," "Small World," "You'll Never Get Away from Me," "Mr. Goldstone," and "Everything's Coming Up Roses." The creators knew they had only one more shot with that particular cannon, and they needed to save it for the end. Enter three new characters—over-the-hill strippers who are going to take over for a bit. Just when you think you've seen it all, it turns out the creators have been saving something for a rainy day.

The by-now-overgrown troupe of child vaudevillians has been booked by mistake into a burlesque house instead of a vaudeville house, which explains the presence of Tessie Tura, Mazeppa, and Electra, three broads who've seen better days. They encounter Louise, with whom Tessie has been forced to share a dressing room, and decide to give her a lesson in show business because she seems so naïve. In the process, the three of them demonstrate their strip technique in a riotous trio called "You Gotta Get a Gimmick," which, in any good production, stops the show in its tracks. The reasons are various—it's funny, it's telling, the lyrics are witty and vernacular, and it's tuneful. But one of the major reasons it works so well is simply this: it's completely new. New characters, new tone (raunchy), new subject (audience manipulation). It's incredibly refreshing.

And it turns the show around. Madame Rose, Merman's character, is nowhere to be found. Louise, who has just begun to assert herself, listens quietly, but she's an eager student. These women are actually giving her all the fuel she's going to need to efficiently take over—take over her mother, take over the show, and take control of her own life. Before the number, she's a child-woman. After it, she's all but prepped to become a sex goddess. And all she does is listen. This is one of those tricks that musical theater can play because it has unplugged a few of the most rational channels in the brains of theatergoers. They make the leap with ease. Music, lyrics, and movement create a story bridge.

Sometimes it's a new emotion from a familiar character that makes its appearance here. The question is, What hasn't the character shown us yet? What will be fresh? In *Hairspray*, Act 2 was cruising along, but something was missing as the show played its debut engagement at the

5th Avenue Theatre in Seattle. Someone remembered a mostly forgotten moment in *Guys and Dolls* called "Adelaide's Second Lament," in which the tough nightclub cutie sits in a chair and reprises her big comedy number from Act 1, but in a completely different, heartbroken tone. No longer frustrated, angry, and assertive, Miss Adelaide has come face-to-face with the likelihood that Nathan will never marry her, and she is just plain resigned and sad. Although the reprise finishes with a really good joke, the body of it is quiet and reflective, and not at all what you'd expect from this brassy character. And it gives the lighter-than-air show a moment of gravitas.

In spite of everything *Hairspray*'s heroine, Tracy Turnblad, had done up to this moment in Act 2, it became clear that the one thing she had never admitted was vulnerability. Audiences rooted for her because she was audacious, inventive, and unwilling to acknowledge that her heft made her an outcast. She was going to win no matter what. But even the toughest characters are entitled to show us their melancholy and insecurity for a minute—and the truth is, we want to see it. Marc Shaiman and Scott Wittman fashioned a short reprise of the show's opening number, "Good Morning Baltimore," that revealed Tracy's longing and her fear that perhaps she was not invincible after all. And the audience stopped admiring her and fell in love with her. In a show that embraces the style of a cartoon, it was a welcome surprise, and it turned a corner, just like "Adelaide's Second Lament."

Sometimes characters need a push to show us what they haven't been willing to show us. That's when it comes in handy to have a character lurking in the background who can force the issue in the nicest possible way. Every protagonist, particularly the toughest, can use a few minutes with Yoda to force them to look inward.

This makes for a nice change of pace not only for the character but also for the audience. No one expected a tender ballad like "More I Cannot Wish You" to turn up in *Guys and Dolls*, but that's the reason Sarah Brown has a grandfather—so he can give her a little grandfatherly advice in the form of a lilting Irish air. In the knockabout and noisy cartoon musical *Li'l Abner*, Marryin' Sam is called upon to comfort Daisy Mae about her advancing age and declining marriageability (she's just turned seventeen) and does so in a charming soft-shoe duet called "Past My Prime." Yoda comes in all shapes and sizes. There's the salty rehearsal pianist Jeanette Burmeister in *The Full Monty*, who doesn't even show up until late in Act 1, and Henry Higgins's mother, who's also a late arrival and doesn't sing. All these characters have the honor of unlocking something in the protagonist, usually in a tone we haven't heard before. *Hairspray* has Motormouth Maybelle, who is the show's guiding moral force and who succeeds largely for the reason that all Yoda-like characters do: she combines wisdom with a need to speak truth to power, or at least to characters who are more important in the story than she is.

*Hairspray*, as previously noted, owes more than a little to *Little Shop of Horrors*, that off-Broadway cartoon with a brain. Both shows are stylistically two-dimensional but deeply invested in their subjects: diversity in *Hairspray*, the cost of moral compromise in *Little Shop*. And if *Hairspray* begins to show its true colors with the brief "Baltimore" reprise, *Little Shop* takes this opportunity early in the second act to go all the way, with a song called "Suddenly Seymour," which is both a joke and not at all a joke. The title makes it sound like a joke. Seymour is a perfect schlub with a perfect schlub's name. The idea of a woman—any woman—feeling the intense passion for a schlub that's implied by the song's title is inherently funny, but why? As Motel the tailor says in *Fiddler*, "Even a poor tailor is entitled to a little happiness." By "a little happiness," he means a love that will last forever. And that's what "Suddenly Seymour" turns out to be about. Two lost souls on skid row pour their hearts out to each other, and though they do it in the show's unique vernacular (complete with a backup girl group), they beg to be taken seriously. Audrey, responding to Seymour's sudden discovery that he wants to take care of her, sings:

> *Nobody ever treated me kindly*
> *Daddy left early, Mama was poor*
> *I'd meet a man and I'd follow him blindly*
> *He'd snap his fingers, me I'd say, "Sure."*
> *Suddenly, Seymour is standing beside me*
> *He don't give me orders, he don't condescend*

*Suddenly, Seymour is here to provide me*
*Sweet understanding, Seymour's my friend.*

If Seymour doesn't condescend, why should we? We've been watching a living comic book for most of the evening, and we've been focusing on Seymour's relationship with a murderous, blood-sucking Venus flytrap that has come to conquer the world. The scenery and costumes are wittily tacky, and the characters often speak in cartoon bubbles. When the real human element enters, it turns the show around, and that, finally, is what the early part of a good second act is often about: confounding expectations and raising them.

*Little Shop* does it by revealing raw feelings in their full-throated glory. It exposes passion where we never suspected we'd find any. In an odd way, *My Fair Lady* does the same thing, though the two shows could hardly be more unrelated on the surface. But structurally, they face the same problem—each has run out of room to explore its original plot idea. In *Little Shop*, we've seen Seymour's discovery of the amazing plant turn the fortunes of Mushnik's flower shop around. All that's left is for Seymour to pay the horrifying bill for his Faustian bargain. In *My Fair Lady*, the entire first act is about whether Henry Higgins can win his bet to pass the Cockney flower girl Eliza Doolittle off as a high-born lady by teaching her to speak proper English. (Let's note in passing that both shows do have flowers in common, but that's about it.)

At the beginning of Act 2, we learn that Higgins has prevailed. The bet is won. Eliza has triumphed, and for all intents and purposes, the story is at an end. And it might actually stop right there, if not for the following exchange:

#### HIGGINS

I suppose it was only natural for you to be anxious, but it's all over now. There's nothing more to worry about.

#### ELIZA

There's nothing more for *you* to worry about. Oh, God, I wish I was dead.

HIGGINS

Why in Heaven's name, why? Listen to me, Eliza, all this irritation is purely subjective.

ELIZA

I don't understand. I'm too ignorant.

HIGGINS

It's only imagination. No one's hurting you. Nothing's wrong. You go to bed like a good girl and sleep it off. Have a little cry and say your prayers; that will make you comfortable.

ELIZA

I heard your prayers: "Thank God it's over!"

HIGGINS

Well, don't you thank God it's over? Now you can do what you like.

ELIZA

What am I fit for? What have you left me fit for? Where am I to go? What am I to do? What's to become of *me*?

Eliza has just galvanized the entire second act with five succinct questions. She's found the hill behind the hill and put her tormentor on notice. As in the Pygmalion myth, he's invented a new woman, and now he's responsible for her, which he can't accept. It never occurred to him that she was a human being, not simply the subject of an experiment. She gives him hell on his own silver platter. And then she runs away. And he misses her. The story is far from over.

Credit George Bernard Shaw for the structural smoothness with which this happens, but in its way, it's not so different from the disparate qualities of "You Gotta Get a Gimmick" or the "Good Morning Baltimore" reprise or "Suddenly Seymour." It fulfills the larger purpose of changing the game. And now the audience is hungry again.

# 15. All er Nothin'

*Beginning to Pack*

I f the audience is hungry, the theater makers are likely confounded. Second acts should come with a notice like the one you get when you order a deck chair from Home Depot: "Assembly Required." Often there are a few apparently extraneous parts in the box that don't seem to fit anywhere.

The reason for this is simple: subplots.

Subplots are part of the fun of a show, and subplot characters are often entertaining foils for the leading players. Every good storyteller understands that we need relief from the central plot from time to time. But whatever the subplot in a musical story—it's usually a romance that somehow reflects on the main couple's romance, and maybe there's also a villain, a clown, or both—it is often no further along at the end of Act 1 than the main story, which means it needs some stage time in Act 2 to come to its own conclusion. And by then, we may or may not be all that interested in a subplot. We start to yearn to know how the main story comes out.

No matter how compelling a subplot couple may be, you can't drift away from the main plot for long, or the show inevitably feels as though it has sailed into dead calm and stopped moving; it is no longer focused on its principal story and the audience gets restless and starts to cough. Why this is the universal response of bored people in the theater is an enduring mystery, but it's a good tip-off that you're in trouble, *real* second-act trouble. Coughing is, apparently, an involuntary response to disapproval of your musical's structure, though not the only potential one. One well-known producer made a list of alarms that are set off in the audience when things aren't going well that looked like this:

> Program rustling
> Coughing
> Yawning
> Sneezing (rare)
> Snoring (not as rare as you might hope)

This was in the days before texting, of course. It's important, then, that whatever happens to the subplot people, it has to happen in a couple of swift, efficient, entertaining strokes, separated by scenes involving the main characters. Alternatively, the two plots can collide in ingenious ways that keep things moving while keeping the main story in view.

It was permissible in the '40s and '50s for the subplot couple to have their own little story, and that story, while it might be in telling contrast to the central story, didn't have to intersect with it much. In *Oklahoma!*, Ado Annie and Will Parker run on a parallel track to Curly and Laurey. They are already romantically attached at the show's outset, but Will discovers that Annie has also been spending time with the Persian peddler Ali Hakim, a community outsider. Curly and Laurey, meanwhile, are meant for each other, but she's been spending time with the farmhand Jud Fry, a community outsider. Ali Hakim is comical, while Jud is dangerous. The two plots reflect each other, but each stands pretty much on its own. In Act 1, Will Parker gets a solo, and so does Ado Annie. But there's no time for that in Act 2—they share a single duet, "All er Nothin'." One number is enough for them to state their differences and patch them up. Ali Hakim leaves the territory (at least for a while) and we can turn our attention back to the matter at hand. Still, for all its trailblazing fame, it's permissible to find *Oklahoma!*'s subplot a little wearying by evening's end.

Hammerstein had been using this parallel track construction since his days as an operetta librettist in the '20s, but in his work with Rodgers, he moved swiftly toward integrating the second couple with the first. In *Carousel*, the integration is mostly thematic, with Carrie Pipperidge's dull, conventional, and prosperous marriage to Mr. Snow underlining the dangerous, passionate, but impoverished marital choice of her best friend Julie Jordan. Once again, the subplot gets a single song in Act 2. But in both *South Pacific* and *The King and I*, the subplot stories are directly related to the main plot, and the outcome of the principal characters' lives is tied deeply to the outcome of the subplot. And the subplot sings more, because it matters more and because it is never unhitched from the basic story, so we never feel we've stopped moving.

To tie the plot and the subplot together in a way that matters (which seemed more and more of a virtue as the form matured) requires proper planning in Act 1, which is another reason that second-act trouble is sometimes first-act trouble. If the whole mechanism is not set in motion properly to begin with, it's going to come back and bite you before the evening is over. No show handled this challenge better than *Guys and Dolls*, in which the couples are of equal weight and completely dependent upon each other because the bet that gets the plot rolling is between the men in each couple. So when Sky Masterson goes down in the sewer to place a new, life-changing bet in the middle of Act 2, he's arriving at the crap game run by Nathan Detroit. The event is about Sky's story, but it's taking place on Nathan's turf. If Sky wins his bet (which he does), he stands a chance to win back Sarah. But if Nathan is caught by Miss Adelaide running the crap game (which he is), all hell will break loose between them. The scene makes room for a terrific comedy bit involving the show's other subplot (about a dangerous gangster from Chicago named Big Jule who is ready to kill Nathan) and a terrific production dance number ("Luck Be a Lady") that energizes the audience as it waits in suspense on Sky's roll of the dice. So even within this one scene, the outcome of both plots swings one way and then another, the fate of both pairs of lovers always hanging in the balance. In a roughhouse show, it's an elegant stroke.

*Sweeney Todd* matches the elegance of *Guys and Dolls* in terms of sheer architectural beauty. Since Sweeney's mission is to reclaim his daughter and punish the judge who stole her, while the subplot involves the daughter's romance with the sailor who rescued Sweeney at sea, no one can make a move in either story without affecting both stories. There is something of Alfred Hitchcock in the plotting—the entire second act of *Sweeney* is about a knot tightening around the characters we care most about. As Sweeney loses his grip on reality, it seems more and more likely that his innocent daughter will suffer the consequences. In the first act, Sondheim provides a terrifying outcry called "Epiphany," in which Sweeney, wielding his straight razor, threatens everyone within reach, including the audience, as his rage overflows. But Act 2 contains something even more frightening: a detached, docile solo (the third song in the show called "Johanna") that shows us a Sweeney completely unhinged, living in a private world as he blandly slices throats and admits that his ability to focus on revenge is beginning to slip in and out of view as his mind falls apart. Not only is it a new flavor for the show, nothing remotely like it has ever been written for any show. It alerts us that the floor beneath our feet is beginning to tilt and we'll soon be in dramatic free fall. It's gruesome, but somehow placid.

It must be a coincidence that four of the most elegantly plotted musicals ever written—*Guys and Dolls, Gypsy, A Funny Thing Happened on the Way to the Forum*, and *Sweeney Todd*—are pieces in which elegance has no place in the tone or flavor of the story itself. They are shows about working rough-and-tumble types (or in the case of *Forum*, low comedians), for whom refinement isn't even a consideration. Yet they move with the grace of a ballet. For a musical that balances elegance in both architecture and tone, one has to turn to *A Little Night Music*. (It's worth noting that four of these five can count puzzle master Sondheim among the creative team.)

*Night Music* is the most like a puzzle box of all. The middle-aged Fredrick Egerman is married to a child bride of eighteen but still yearns for Desiree Armfeldt, a former lover of his own age. His son Henrik toys ineptly with the Egerman housemaid but lusts after his eighteen-year-old stepmother. Desiree, meanwhile, is engaged in an affair with a wooden-headed dragoon, whose wife is a schoolmate—and becomes a confidante—of the child bride's sister. In order for Fredrik to end up with Desiree, the dragoon must be dispatched back to his wife, the son must run off with his stepmother, and even the maid has to find a lover of her own. It's dizzying and wonderfully satisfying, but it took some doing to weave all the strands together—and the second act certainly has its challenges. In an arresting theatrical gesture in the middle of the act, the director, Hal Prince, staged a dinner party in which all the participants are present and all the story strands interweave in a striking way that allows us to keep track. A singular temper tantrum thrown by young Henrik about the questionable morality of everyone at the table launches the show into its final set of resolutions. The scene is practically the only one in which people remain static, seated or standing by the table, some facing upstage, and it has the feel of a slightly surrealistic tableau. It's a unique candy in the dish, and a memorable one that serves an efficient purpose in a striking way.

The working out of the various romances from this point on takes a little longer than we might wish, but that's the curse of plots and subplots. Still, the elegance of the plotting is matched by the elegance of the tone, the music and mood of the piece, which drapes the chaos of sexual insecurity and desire in the golden glow of perpetual sunset. It's an admirable feat accomplished by Sondheim, Prince, and the librettist Hugh Wheeler, who also provided the clockwork mechanism of *Sweeney Todd*'s book. To be fair, both works were based on underlying material that set up the structures for Wheeler to work with. *Night Music* owes a considerable debt to Ingmar Bergman, whose film *Smiles of a Summer Night* is its source, and *Sweeney Todd* follows the English playwright Christopher Bond's version of the old melodrama of the same name. But Wheeler, who was a veteran author of many mystery novels (written under a variety of pseudonyms), understood the joys of clockwork plotting—not to mention the thrill of violence and sex, in any tone. Like Larry Gelbart, who cowrote *Forum*'s book, he remains one of the unheralded heroes of the form. And like Hammerstein, he had greater success in adapting work than in inventing it out of whole cloth.

*Forum*'s plot is so intricate and unlikely that I won't even try to describe it. But it's based on the simple premise of a Roman slave who passionately yearns for liberty, and his young owner who passionately yearns for the girl next door. They strike a bargain: if the slave can deliver the girl, the master will grant him his freedom. From that point on—good luck. There's the boy's aging but randy father, his harridan mother, the girl's pompous military fiancé, a procurer, a second slave with a secret pornography collection (erotic pottery, no less) who has a tendency to panic, some cross-dressing, a nonexistent plague, a funeral pyre, a sweating horse—the list goes on. With the exception of its remarkable opening number, however, there's not a lot to be learned from the show as a paradigm; it's a unique invention that never started a trend.

Among these elegant five, *Gypsy* is the one that is shy of a traditional subplot. Instead, it places both strands of its story in the hands of one character—Madame Rose. Her drive to turn her kids into stars is the plot. Her romance with the candy-salesman-turned-agent Herbie is the subplot. But they're so neatly entwined that it's hard to separate them, and every scene that involves Herbie also involves the main story, because he's the love interest *and* the agent for the act. That gives the show a rush of energy and forward motion. But cannily, the librettist, Arthur Laurents, also creates variety by introducing individual miniplots and then quickly resolving them. In the first act, it's the story concerning Louise's crush on Tulsa, which crops up in the second-to-last scene in the act and is resolved one scene later when he runs off with Louise's sister, June. We never see either of them again. In the second act, the strippers provide a major event with "You Gotta Get a Gimmick," and Tessie and Louise even establish a bit of a relationship, but it hardly qualifies as a subplot. Yet there's a fascinating miniplot that introduces itself subtly and resolves almost invisibly, adding texture to the show and serving as a useful aid to our understanding of the main characters. The protagonist of this little plot is a wig.

In the first scene of Act 2 of *Gypsy*, Louise tries, and fails miserably, to imitate her sister's vaudeville act, decked out like a bargain-basement version of Baby June (who was pretty much a bargain-basement performer to begin with) in a blond wig. In frustration, and for the first time, she explodes at her mother, tossing the wig onto the ground and declaring, "I am not June. I am not a blonde!"

The wig is picked up by one of the girls Madame Rose has recruited to be in the new act, whose name is Agnes.

"Gee," she says. "I always wanted to be a blonde!"

Louise offers her the wig, but Madame Rose won't hear of it. Wigs are expensive.

But the moment, which serves as Louise's declaration of independence, also leads Louise and Herbie to concoct a scheme in which all the young girls will become blondes—a new way to sell the act as Louise and Her Hollywood Blondes. It's the first idea for the act that doesn't come from Rose. Still, Rose negotiates for billing and the act becomes Rose Louise and Her Hollywood Blondes. "All blondes except you—because you're the star!" Rose says to Louise.

So Louise, finally, gets to have her own identity, which turns out to be a dangerous thing for Madame Rose.

A lot has happened as a result of this wig, with more to come. Louise has begun to establish her own personhood and assert herself against her mother. The vaudeville act has been rechristened. And for the very first time an idea hatched by someone other than Rose has been accepted. We don't know it yet, but for Rose, the worm is beginning to turn; power is beginning to shift. For an inanimate object, the wig has been busy.

The troupe arrives at the burlesque theater, where they're going to have to compete with strippers and blue comedians, and Agnes has changed her name to Amanda—a name more suited to her new, glamorous exterior. She's an actress now, and the wig is still exerting an influence. The troupe survives its stint in burlesque right up to the last day, by which point Louise, who seems suddenly to be in charge of the troupe and almost in charge of her mother, forces Rose to look in the mirror and recognize reality. The act is finished, vaudeville is dead, and there's nothing to do but quit. This is the hardest pill Rose has ever swallowed, and it goes down hard. But Louise, suddenly empowered, won't give Rose any wiggle room. She and Herbie gang up on Rose, and finally she capitulates. After years of resisting, she agrees to quit, marry Herbie, and settle down.

On the last day, Herbie encounters "Amanda," who admits that she's going back to "Agnes."

"I have to go home and let my hair grow out," she says.

True, the wig has been retired, but it's had a full life. Agnes/Amanda's little adventure is a parallel of the whole story of *Gypsy*'s vaudeville troupe and of Madame Rose herself: grand, unrealistic (and unrealized) dreams, no talent, and a very rough landing. A less skilled librettist than Laurents might have left poor Agnes in Act 2, Scene 1, never to be seen again. But by keeping her encounter with the wig alive and giving it a neat little shape, he underlines the showbiz trajectory of *Gypsy*'s larger story.

This leaves only the official subplot of *Gypsy* to be packed up, and since the plot and subplot are so deeply tied together, it's easy for Laurents to land a punch to the gut. When the lead stripper at the theater is arrested, Rose changes her mind about retirement and volunteers Louise as a replacement. She simply can't accept show business defeat, even if she said she would, and will stop at nothing, and stoop to anything, to "walk away—a star" (there's that word again). That's the final straw for Herbie, who calls off the wedding. He understands, finally, that he'll never have Rose to himself, that show business—no matter how low, no matter how tawdry—will always win. And when the scales fall from his eyes and he says goodbye for good, the last subplot is neatly packed and put away—and we're ready for the main event.

# 16. The Small House of Joseph Smith, the American Moses

*The Main Event*

In most classic second acts there are two big blasts of energy—two showpieces that are designed to give the audience its money's worth. Generally, neither of them is the most important thing in the show, at least not in the sense of getting you to care about the characters and what happens to them. Instead, they're designed to impress and to thrill, which is a big part of why you're there in the first place. The first one comes early, or perhaps halfway through, and it's not always a production number—sometimes it's a charm piece like "You're Timeless to Me" in *Hairspray*. It can be a specialty like "You Gotta Get a Gimmick" in *Gypsy*. And sometimes it's the whole nine yards, like the spectacular "Waiters' Gallop" and the title song from *Hello, Dolly!* or the "Spooky Mormon Hell Dream" from *Book of Mormon*.

But if the first one is there to remind you of how much fun you are still having in Act 2, the second might be called the "main event"—in some sense you've been waiting all night for it. It's a promise fulfilled, even if the promise has never been fully articulated in advance. Although sometimes it has. Many classic shows make sure their plots are building up to a big gathering of some sort—the union rally in *The Pajama Game*, the Ice Cream Sociable in *The Music Man*, the "Miss Teenage Hairspray" contest at the Eventorium in *Hairspray*. It's getting late now, and there are really only three beats left in the act: the main event, the all-important result of it (also known as the next-to-last scene), and the finale. So this is often the biggest blowout in the show.

Sometimes it's called an "11 o'clock number," a term that theater people love to toss around, although it tends to mean whatever they want it to mean. Legitimately, an 11 o'clock number, if there is one, is a final star turn—"Rose's Turn" from *Gypsy* is the most vivid example. That one comes very late in the show, while others, like "Lot's Wife," from *Caroline, or Change*, come somewhat earlier, before the plot has really been sorted. And, of course, the curtain no longer goes up at 8:30 as it did for decades, so the term itself seems to be operating in an unfamiliar time zone. Still, "10:20 number" just doesn't have that theatrical ring one wants from a term of art.

If you've got a star with great charisma and great pipes, you're going to want one of these numbers. But, particularly today, that's often not the case, and the 11 o'clock number's appearances have been scattered in recent years, as has its placement. Some kind of main event, however, is still very much with us.

During the development of *The Producers*, everyone knew that the biggest production number in the show would be "Springtime for Hitler," Susan Stroman's reimagining of the stunningly vulgar and shocking comedy number in Mel Brooks's original movie. It's the big set piece in the film, it's the culmination of Brooks's basic tenet that laughing at something (Nazism, in this case) is the best way to destroy it, and since it's a musical comedy production number in the film to begin with, inevitably it was going to be the main event.

But it comes too early in the act.

True, it's not right at the beginning, but it's no more than halfway through, in terms of the number of plot turns it takes to finish the story. Yet it couldn't be moved entirely, and so it was pushed as late as possible and became the first big event in the act; something else had to be the second. It was inconceivable that the show would get all the way from "Springtime for Hitler" to the final curtain without at least one more major showstopper. And it couldn't be a production number because nothing could ever be expected to top "Springtime" in that department. What to do?

The answer turned out to be that ancient thing that had been keeping audiences happy since the days of Ziegfeld—"A Few Minutes with . . . ," in this case, Nathan Lane.

At an early reading of the show to interest potential producers and theater owners (read: "backers' audition"), Nathan Lane played Max, but a nonstar actor played Leo. It was clear that the book for the musical was a very substantial improvement on the original film in a number of respects, not the least of which was that it elevated the sexpot secretary, Ulla, from a burlesque-style one-scene joke into an actual character with whom both Max and Leo have a flirtation. Max's interest is entirely carnal and passing, whereas Leo actually tries a little tenderness, and Ulla falls.

The quality of the show was obvious at that reading, though the skeptics believed it was too much of an in-joke to interest anyone but theater people. They missed the universality of the story that had been wrought out of what had once been a modest-grossing but well-remembered cult movie.

Two other things came out of that reading: Max and Leo had to be played by equally important stars, a team worthy of jousting with each other for top honors. And the second act needed its second big event.

Matthew Broderick took on the role of Leo, solving problem number one. And Lane himself, experienced and consummate professional that he is, suggested how to solve problem number two. The audience was coming to see him play Max Bialystock, after all, and it was only appropriate that he get a few minutes alone with them. Call it ego if you must, but Lane was completely correct. Something had to be customized that would fulfill expectations and allow the star to be a star. Max and Leo are partners, but it is Max who is driving the story. Leo is small and lovable. Max is terrifyingly larger than life.

Brooks labored on a couple of new songs and new spots to put them, but they seemed relatively tame and inconsequential. And a reprise on its own wouldn't cut it. This had to be something new and big. A big new idea. And no one had one. Instead, they created a number that recycled the story so far and repurposed snippets of songs and dialogue that had already occurred. You couldn't call it a reprise, because it reprised not one number, but the entire show. It required very little in the way of new scenery—Max got hauled off to jail after the unexpected success of his musical revealed the fraud of how it had been financed, and Leo, who should also have been in jail, has run off to Rio with Ulla.

Alone and depressed, Max receives a cheerful postcard from Leo, which enrages him and sets off "Betrayed," a tour de force for a comic. Lane got to play, briefly, almost all the important characters in the show, play little scenes with himself, use multiple voices and vocal ranges, and generally create mayhem for five minutes. And the audience adored him. Problem solved. "Betrayed" also created a seemingly unmendable break between the two partners, the mending of which gave the show its satisfying conclusion.

The number was a nightly challenge, and Lane gave it his all, eventually wearing down his vocal cords. And it's not a number just anyone can make work, which makes the show tricky to remount. But it fulfilled the musical's destiny in an original way, helped make it famous, and got the show to its next-to-last scene.

Like *The Producers*, *Gypsy* is about a nonromantic relationship between two characters—mother and daughter, in this case—and faces a similar challenge in its second act. *Gypsy* needed to save Ethel Merman's final blast for the 11 o'clock spot, practically at the final curtain. *Gypsy* had an additional challenge; daughter Louise doesn't become an important character until almost the end of Act 1. Her sudden rise to power in Act 2 needs its own moment of glory. And if mother and daughter are ever going to meet face-to-face and have it out with each other, we need to see Louise actually become Gypsy Rose Lee.

The show had already done a brilliant time-lapse sequence in Act 1 using a strobe-light-flickering imitation of a silent movie to have the children in Madame Rose's troupe replaced, invisibly, but in front of the audience's eyes, with the older actors who would play them in late adolescence. Now the authors and director had to pull another rabbit out of the hat to get Louise from fledgling—and terrified—stripper in a tenth-rate midwestern burlesque house to queen of the striptease at the world-famous Minsky's in New York. They saw it as an opportunity for the main event, and, as with *The Producers* decades later, they retrofitted material that had already been heard in the show. They used "Let Me Entertain You" in an entirely new and shocking way. This, after all, had been Baby June's number, the kind of song a little kid sings when she's dragged out to entertain the relatives at Thanksgiving:

> *And if you're real good*
> *I'll make you feel good*
> *I want your spirits to climb*
> *So let me entertain you*
> *And we'll have a real good time.*

We've been hearing it all night but never imagined what it might mean if sung by a gorgeous young woman who is shedding her clothes in front of us. The joke's on us, but it's a sick joke, and worthy of Madame Rose's psychopathic tendencies.

The writers and the director-choreographer, Jerome Robbins, fashioned a montage that takes the audience across the country as Louise learns her craft, gains confidence, begins to inject a sense of humor into the act, and perfects the art of taking over the stage with body language and attitude. In a final burst of cheesy glory, we're presented with Gypsy Rose Lee at Minsky's, paying tribute to Eve in the Garden of Eden, complete with a chorus of semiclad showgirls hurling apples at the audience so that we might all take a bite, so to speak.

When the number begins, Louise is a kid who stumbles onto the stage, in a pinned-up dress and borrowed silk gloves that were supposed to be used at her mother's aborted wedding. By the number's conclusion, she has earned everything she has gotten—an astronomical salary, a mink or two, a photo story in *Vogue*, and an ornate dressing room, complete with private maid and obsequious press agent. And she waits in that dressing room, ready for the inevitable fight with her mother—for a next-to-last scene that will quickly deteriorate into possibly the most memorable shouting match in any musical.

The main event, remember, isn't the main event. It's a walloping preamble that gets us down to brass tacks.

*Guys and Dolls*, that tossed-together masterpiece, has perhaps the most irrelevant main event of all, and yet it satisfies more than most. It's a song that could easily have been snipped from the score and no one would have ever known—but what a loss to humanity that would be. "Sit Down, You're Rockin' the Boat" has absolutely no business in the show's plot—either of its plots. It's sung by a lovable but tertiary character, and its purpose is purely to entertain—to top, if possible, "Luck Be a Lady." This is one of the rare occasions in which both big noises in Act 2 are production numbers.

The setup is as arbitrary as can be. Sky Masterson has won his bet on a single roll of the dice at the conclusion of "Luck Be a Lady," and after Nathan Detroit has been appropriately upbraided by Miss Adelaide in the comedy number "Sue Me," we find ourselves at the Save-a-Soul Mission. All the gamblers from the sewer come trooping in for a soul-saving session—Sky's bet to save Sarah's reputation was that they'd have to report if he rolled a winner. Their presence is supposed to prove the viability of the mission itself, and the mission is the show's stake. If so many gamblers are interested in salvation, how can the sourpuss General Cartwright possibly justify closing the place? And as long as the place stays open, Sarah will be a heroine, have a reason to be grateful to Sky—and keep her job.

The problem is that someone—anyone—has to appear actually to be contrite. But the only thing these crapshooters are feeling bad about is that they lost this particular roll of the dice. So who, to save Sky's relationship with Sarah, is going to make something up on the spot? After a couple of failed attempts, it falls to Nicely-Nicely Johnson to think on his feet and give out with his glorious tenor voice. In the original production the rotund and irresistible Stubby Kaye played Nicely, and he got the call.

"It happened to me kinda funny . . . like a dream," he says, stalling for time. And then inspiration strikes. "That's it—a dream!"

> *I dreamed last night I got on the boat to heaven*
> *And by some chance I had brought my dice along . . .*

And that's all you really need to know, because a man on his way to heaven with a pair of (probably loaded) dice in his pocket is going to have a lot to answer for, especially if he's traveling with a boatload of the blessed. Nicely-Nicely tells the story of how he tried to gamble with these folks, and to get them drunk in the process, and how the little boat foundered in the waves and he was tossed out of it, certain to drown. And that's when he came to his own salvation.

> *And I said to myself sit down*
> *Sit down, you're rockin' the boat*
> *And the devil will drag you under*
> *With a soul so heavy*
> *You'll never float*
> *Sit down, sit down, sit down, sit down*
> *Sit down, you're rockin' the boat!*

By now the gamblers are up on their feet rocking and swaying and harmonizing on the thrillingly stormy sea of Frank Loesser's music and lyrics, and an aura of pure joy has descended upon the audience. (Insiders are welcome to kvell over the internal masculine rhyme of "heavy" and "never," though it's probably unintentional.)

The story of *Guys and Dolls* is hardly resolved, or even pushed along in any meaningful way. And the credibility of the moment does not bear close scrutiny. When the gamblers all take their seats at the end of the number, the plot is exactly where it was when Nicely-Nicely first stood up. But who cares? "Sit Down, You're Rockin' the Boat" remains one of the glories of the American musical's ability to lift a thousand people out of their troubles and their seats at the same time in a way that no other art form does it. It's a kind of salvation all by itself.

It's rare that a show can get away with this kind of an irrelevant moment this late in the evening. Like horses, who begin to accelerate as they approach the barn that serves as their home after a long ride, the audience is now eager for things to speed up and move in a straight line. If your subplots aren't packed up by now, God help you. It's time to cut to the chase, as movies literally do in this spot. But somehow "Sit

Down, You're Rockin' the Boat" defies this truism; sometimes it even earns an encore.

No show has had more fun creating a main event than *The Book of Mormon*, because it is a gleeful rip-off, unhidden but unacknowledged, of *The King and I*.

Strangely, but no doubt intentionally, these disparate shows, separated by more than half a century, have a lot in common, though one is a sometimes somber drama and the other a generally profane burlesque. One is from the Golden Age, the other distinctly postmodern, created by Trey Parker and Matt Stone, who invented *South Park*, and the songwriter Robert Lopez, of *Avenue Q* (and, later, *Frozen*). On the surface the shows are polar opposites in style and temperament, yet they share many of the same concerns, and in the end both profess an optimism based on faith. Both are about strangers in a strange land, and both deal with a culture clash beyond the ability of their characters to comprehend. Both trade in stereotypes, though the ones in *The King and I* are unintentional and went unnoticed back in 1951. Both are about white do-gooders in non-white worlds, trying their best to improve the natives without knowing much about how. *The King and I* boasts a certain confidence that the white people actually know best, however, while *The Book of Mormon* is equally certain that they don't have a clue. This is completely appropriate for the differing eras in which they were created, Hammerstein's confidence in enlightenment having been replaced over the years by an abiding sense of skepticism and irony about American values, not to mention American foreign policy from Vietnam forward. And yet things work out pretty much the same way in both shows.

*The King and I* concerns the efforts of an English schoolteacher, Anna Leonowens, to bring modern Western civilization to Siam in the 1860s. Anna has been summoned by the King, who recognizes that his country has to join the modern world but doesn't know how to accomplish the task. Once he finds out what it means to be modern, he doesn't like it—it threatens his authority and his methods of enforcing it. Anna is supposed to be teaching his many wives and children how to enter a new world, but the King fears that in this march toward progress, he's likely to be left behind. Anna and the King spar for most of the evening about Anna's demands for a house of her own, but the real argument is about what it means to be civilized, to live in a world of laws, justice, and human compassion.

Despite these ambitious subjects, the plot is often about the house. There has to be some kind of announced stake for their debate, and while the real stake is the soul of Siam, it's too abstract and pretentious to argue about. So the house keeps them tussling. Toward the end of the evening, in order to impress the King and show him what it means to escape from a world of slavery and oppression, Anna devises a dance theater entertainment based on *Uncle Tom's Cabin*. The nominal author of the piece is Tuptim, a young woman who has been given to the King as a wife but who is secretly in love with the scholar Lun Tha— they're the subplot couple.

This set piece—choreographed by Jerome Robbins—has been retitled "The Small House of Uncle Thomas" (there's that house again) and is performed by Anna's students, based on their somewhat eccentric reading of Harriet Beecher Stowe's novel. In the plot of *The King and I*, it serves multiple purposes, including an attempt to impress a delegation of English visitors and a cover for Tuptim and Lun Tha to flee—escape also being the subject of *Uncle Tom's Cabin*. It is a brilliant conceit, weaving the themes of *The King and I* through the story of Stowe's novel and staging a uniquely Western tale with uniquely Eastern theater and dance techniques, at least as understood by a Western choreographer. It's hugely ambitious, utterly successful, and justly famous. But its entertainment purpose is simply to be the main event.

Full of simple, elegant theatrical gestures, it's a fully realized minidrama of its own, sweetly funny, touching, and stunningly beautiful to look at and listen to. But it doesn't meet with the approval of the King, for whom it is performed, because even draped in beauty and wit, its revolutionary bones are all too easily revealed. And when Tuptim's attempted escape is discovered, we know there will be an awful price to pay, and everyone will finally have to come face-to-face with the conflict of cultures and characters. Anna and the King will have to stare each other down in a final confrontation, and it won't be about a house.

It's hard to overestimate the achievement of "The Small House of Uncle Thomas," and yet, structurally, it is no more or less than true to form. The main event leads to the essence of the conflict. And since the essence is likely to be plainspoken and unadorned, "The Small House of Uncle Thomas," like "Sit Down, You're Rockin' the Boat," takes on the responsibility of providing some pre-essence excitement.

*The King and I* opened on March 29, 1951. Flash forward sixty years, practically to the day. On March 24, 2011, "The Small House of Uncle Thomas" returned to Broadway in recognizable but thoroughly fractured form as "Joseph Smith American Moses," the main event of *The Book of Mormon*.

*Mormon* concerns a couple of young Mormon missionaries, Elder Price and Elder Cunningham, who have been sent to Uganda, much as Miss Anna is sent to Siam. And the two of them, in various ways, have made a lot of assumptions about the life and people, all of them wildly off target. Elder Price is shallow and narcissistic; Elder Cunningham is frumpy and antisocial, and given to solving problems by making stuff up. When Elder Price deserts the mission in disgust, Elder Cunningham is left on his own to cope with a population and a set of problems he knows nothing about. But he's too eager to please, and in an attempt to be liked, he begins to invent passages from the Book of Mormon that will actually speak to the Ugandans about their own problems. In Cunningham's version of the Book, there are passages about AIDS, about tribal superstitions that it can be cured by having sex with newborns or frogs, about chronic diarrhea, and about superhuman figures who can help—all of them stolen from *Star Wars* and *Star Trek*. Suddenly the people, who have thus far found the intrusion of the Mormons an annoyance and an insult, start to take interest. Perhaps Mormonism is useful in their lives after all.

Eventually they become converts, but to what, exactly? Elder Cunningham's teachings are a wild and unlikely grab bag of ideas pulled from sci-fi movies, TV shows, comics, and whatever else he can remember about the detritus he wasted his youth consuming. It all comes in handy, the Ugandans never having heard of Yoda or the starship

*Enterprise.* Soon he finds himself with a lovely Ugandan girlfriend and a flock of followers. The Mormon leadership back home is so impressed by the reports of progress in Uganda that they deem it necessary to pay a visit. And to entertain them, a play is created, detailing the life of the Mormon founder Joseph Smith and incorporating Mormon teachings— entirely invented, in this case, not by Joseph Smith but by Elder Cunningham himself, borrowing heavily from multiple sources.

The idea of doing a play within a play is hardly new, of course. It dates back well before *The King and I,* at least to the late 1500s and Thomas Kyd's *The Spanish Tragedy,* and is a major feature of Shakespeare's *Hamlet.* But *Mormon*'s creators didn't want to just do a play within a play—they wanted to wreak a little extra havoc while they were at it. In the style of *South Park* and *The Simpsons, Mormon* takes delight in creating spot-on parodies of the pop culture that surrounds it, and takes down a number of Broadway musicals just for fun, including *Wicked, The Music Man,* and, vividly, *The Lion King.* When it came time to create the main event, "The Small House of Uncle Thomas" was a sitting duck.

The play's codirector and choreographer, Casey Nicholaw, is himself a man with a bent for parody—he once incorporated a small but unmistakable chunk of *Swan Lake* into a dance number in Stephen Sondheim's *Anyone Can Whistle.* And the opportunity to "do" Jerome Robbins was too ripe to pass up. He lifted some specifics involving sheets of China silk, onstage percussion instruments, and a set design that was a thatched hut version of its beautiful Siamese forebear, but had the greatest fun simply staging everything that Elder Cunningham had taught. Like the version of *Uncle Tom's Cabin* in "Small House," "Joseph Smith" was gleefully distorted, but this time twice: once through the lens of the local population's understanding and a second time by the fact that the Mormon story itself had been entirely exploded and reinvented by the man who taught it. (At least Anna had the good grace to *try* to get Uncle Tom's story right.)

In Cunningham's version of the story, Joseph Smith introduces himself by announcing that he has AIDS and is going to "fuck this baby" to be cured.

At this moment, God appears and commands: "Joseph Smith! Don't fuck a baby. I will cure your AIDS if you fuck this frog." God offers Joseph a stuffed frog, and we're off and running—downhill, needless to say. The Mormon authorities are appropriately appalled, but the performance continues into a vortex of profanity, sacrilege, and scatology. In about six minutes ("Small House" runs thirteen, not that it matters), the entire Mormon story is torn to shreds and replaced by one that, while it reaches an all-time high in vulgarity, is no more or less likely to be true than any other religious myth. And that, of course, is the entire point of the show itself. Elder Cunningham has invented a self-sufficient cosmology, full of chaotically assembled borrowings from other cosmologies and contemporary cultures and mores, as most religions are. He has inadvertently become Moses himself, with his own set of somewhat shocking tablets.

He has also brought the world down around his shoulders by letting this new cosmology out into the open, where it can only be rejected and vilified by those in charge, who fear the power of a myth that speaks to the people more effectively than their own. In this neatest trick in *Mormon*'s entire bag of tricks, we actually see how a religion gets created—more or less by mistake. "Joseph Smith American Moses" handles its main event chores dazzlingly, including the obligation to entertain and energize us while creating the greatest possible jeopardy for the characters we care most about. It tweaks one of the icons of the Golden Age and leaves the audience sated but still in suspense. The piper, as always in a well-constructed story, has yet to be paid, and it is time for the next-to-last scene.

# 17. I Thought You Did It for Me, Momma

*The Next-to-Last Scene*

In his great theatrical memoir *Act One*, Moss Hart tells the—somewhat self-created—story of his entrance into the world of Broadway in the 1920s, and spends the last part of the book describing the shaping of his first hit collaboration with George S. Kaufman, *Once in a Lifetime*. This was back in the day when Broadway shows tried out in places like Atlantic City and Philadelphia, and wholesale changes were made overnight in an atmosphere that was both exciting and chaotic. The entire enterprise amounted to a roll of the dice. If the show was in trouble and inspiration struck, it might be fixed. If the muses stubbornly refused to appear, another promising show ended up on the ash heap of theater history. The overall results were probably about the same as they are today, when plays are typically first developed and presented by regional theaters around the country, and Broadway producers shop for them by going and having a look. But the old-time tryout was much more romantic, at least in theory, if not in practice. As Larry Gelbart famously said during the disastrous and tortured tryout of *The Conquering Hero*, "If Hitler's alive, I hope he's out of town with a musical."

*Once in a Lifetime* was not a musical but a particularly promising comedy, dogged by third-act trouble. Days before it decamped from Philly to face audiences and critics on Forty-fifth Street, Hart came up with the scene that saved it, and his story is instructive and entertaining. As Hart tells it, the play's producer, the formidable Sam Harris, took Hart out for a drink a few nights before the end of the out-of-town run, got drunk, and told Hart, "I wish, kid, that this weren't such a noisy play. Just think about it. Except for those two minutes at the beginning of the first act, there isn't another spot in this whole play where two people sit down and talk quietly to each other."

Hart puzzled over this assessment—it could hardly be called an analysis—and made a bold move. He took the scene that he and Kaufman were proudest of having created—a rambunctious Hollywood farrago in a night spot called the Pigeon's Egg—and tossed it out the window. It was the biggest and most ambitious scene in the play, but also the noisiest, and it was late in the act. He threw out the most impressive, wittiest, and biggest set in the play—the set itself got laughs— and replaced it with an unprepossessing pair of seats on an eastbound Pullman car. The hugely populous Pigeon's Egg started out funny but gradually exhausted the audience, and the play had no real emotional payoff. Hart replaced it with two characters the audience actually cared about, who had a simple conversation. An attempt to top everything that had come before was replaced with something that didn't resemble anything else in the play—a heart-to-heart talk. And suddenly the play worked; it still works today, eighty-five years later. The young Moss Hart had inadvertently written a classic next-to-last scene.

*Act One* was a seminal book for me, as it was for a lot of theater people in my generation. But I never thought of it as an instruction manual until I got the chance to work on my first Broadway play, *M. Butterfly*. I had brought the play to New York in my suitcase when I moved east from Los Angeles to take the job at Jujamcyn, and I was eager to get involved in it—I admired its author, David Hwang, enormously and had been trying to get the play under way at the Mark Taper Forum when I suddenly changed jobs.

Based on a true incident, *M. Butterfly* had been commissioned by an independent, idiosyncratic producer named Stuart Ostrow, and he wanted to do the play directly on Broadway, not at a regional theater.

In other words, he wanted to try it out like *Once in a Lifetime*, although this route of march was already becoming unfashionable and unaffordable. But Ostrow had a vision for the piece that involved a lot of expensive production values, and he didn't think he'd get a first-class production from the Taper or any other regional theater, so he raised all the money for Broadway, booked a tryout at the National Theatre in Washington, D.C., and agreed to play Jujamcyn's Eugene O'Neill Theatre in return for a significant investment.

John Lithgow signed to star in the show as a French diplomat in China who falls hopelessly in love with a Peking Opera diva. In the course of the play, the diva becomes his lover and confidante, and listens to him pour out not only his heart but also a number of state secrets. And shockingly, the diva turns out to be not only a spy but a man. He/she was played by an amazing young actor named B. D. Wong.

The play opened in Washington to respectful mixed reviews and spotty business, but Ostrow was undaunted. He knew he had a hit on his hands—or behaved as if he did. He was an old-time impresario, with a strong stomach for risk and a lot of bravado. He was small of stature but had an ego that more than compensated, and he was great fun to be around.

During the third week of a four-week engagement in Washington, Ostrow called me on the phone.

"There's an emotional gap in the next-to-last scene," he said. "Can you look and listen?"

I hopped on a train and, during the ride down, remembered that section of *Act One*. Hart threw out a multilayered scene for a simpler, two-person one and saved the day. The problem I was pondering was this: David Hwang already had written a two-person scene in that very spot, so I couldn't see how Hart's lesson would be of any use. Still, I was trying to remain alert to the fact that these next-to-last scenes are best when kept simple and when they answer questions for the audience in a direct way.

As I watched the play that night, I thought I detected a parallel between Hart's problem and Hwang's. *Once in a Lifetime* had tried to use that penultimate moment to top everything that came before it— more scenery, costumes, characters, and gags than in any other spot in the show. Hwang had written a scene that *looked* simpler and, indeed, featured only two characters. But the language and ideas were dizzyingly complex, a pileup of political and philosophical notions that raced forward at an alarming pace—like Kaufman and Hart, he was trying to top himself. And audiences simply gave up on it in frustration. They were focused on something much simpler.

Over drinks after the show I gently and, I think, shyly (I was in awe of David Hwang; I still am) said I was puzzled by the audience's drift. He was too. Maybe, I said, the problem was that the scene was answering complicated thematic questions while the audience was wondering about a simple and literal one: How could a "sophisticated" French diplomat have fallen hopelessly in love with a Peking Opera diva and lived with her in the same bed for years without knowing she was a man? In the most literal terms: What made it credible, at least in the context of the play? Was there a way to answer this big metaphorical, apparently unanswerable question in a simple, human way that would set the audience's mind at rest and give it the release it was seeking and the opportunity to embrace the play's larger questions? I understood the whole play to be about how the West mistakes what the East is in the most fundamental way, but could this moment just be about two people instead? Could we settle the big dumb question before attacking the smart, complex ones?

"I can do that," David said casually. But he didn't say how.

He didn't throw out the scene, but he wrote a simple and startling line in the middle of it. The opera star has been revealed as a man—designer suit and all—and the diplomat is pressed to explain how this confusion could have continued for so many years. Was it deception, self-deception, or what? The diva needles him: How could it have been love? How could the lie have lived so long? How could a man, even an awkward, emotionally clumsy man, have clung to a fantasy so obviously implausible? How could a man love a woman so devoid of actual womanhood? The audience was right with him—that's what it was wondering too, so a spokesperson was up onstage who wasn't going to give up until the diplomat supplied the answer.

The diplomat, finally pressed to the wall, says without affect, "I'm a man who loved a woman created by a man. Everything else—simply falls short."

That line brought an audible sigh from the audience. Sitting in the dark, everyone got it. Whether the line bears close examination in terms of plausibility in the cold light of day isn't the point. The play had cast a spell and the audience was in the throes of it. It provided what all theatergoers want: an answer. It was the first time I ever saw what a dramaturg really does, and it was all about asking questions, not making suggestions.*

One other significant change occurred in between the D.C. tryout and the Broadway run, and it involved, of all things, the curtain call.

The play ends with the diplomat lying facedown on the stage floor, overwhelmed and destroyed by events, his face painted clown white in the style of the Peking Opera diva he loved. He is, in effect, a man unmanned, a shell. In the original staging, the lights went out, and when they came up for the curtain call, the ensemble took its bow, followed by the major characters in ascending order of importance, who finally brought the star, John Lithgow, his face cleansed, onstage for a well-deserved ovation. But the director, John Dexter, had a better, more unconventional idea—a cunning theater trick.

In New York, Lithgow collapsed into his swoon, fell to the floor, and remained motionless, as in D.C. But when the lights came back up for the bows, he was still there. Then he rose slowly, in a daze, apparently in character—or somewhere in between the character and the actor, a man very much exhausted by the journey he had just taken—his white makeup now smeared and smudged. He looked bedazzled and exhausted. And the audience, as one, rose to its feet.

---

* My first dramaturgical note, at age sixteen, was delivered, unasked for, to Al Selden, the producer of *Man of La Mancha*. His daughter and my sister were roommates at boarding school, and he invited our whole family up to see the show's tryout at the Goodspeed Opera House. When he asked how I liked the show, I advised him to cut "The Impossible Dream." I still think the world might be better for this, but it was a bad note as far as the show's success was concerned. And the song has sold millions, of course.

The dramaturgy helped. But never count show business out of the equation.

Nonetheless, it's essential that the audience has its moment with the Gordian knot of the play and the way it is untangled. A couple of characters need to come face-to-face and thrash it all out in simple language, and preferably quickly, at least in a musical. The evening is getting late, and we're ready to know the outcome of the story's central conflict. In classic playwriting, this is called "the obligatory scene," but that's too pretentious for musicals. In musicals we settle for "next-to-last scene," and it's not always—or even often—done in song. The main event earns the writers the opportunity to speak plainly for a few minutes.

But time is of the essence. No audience comes to musicals to listen to dialogue, though they understand there's likely to be a certain amount of it. Still, if everything is going to stop cold for a book scene at this point, it had better be good or short, preferably both. Contrarily, this is where *Gypsy*, as original as it is iconoclastic, places its longest scene between mother and daughter. Daring, but it works. Rose and Louise really have it out, in one of the more entertaining verbal battles in all of American playwriting. The subject is love and abandonment— how we project our failed dreams onto our children and how we tragically confuse their needs with our own.

Louise, now rechristened Gypsy Rose Lee, is in charge of her world, of her stardom, and of herself for the first time. Rose, who was once the boss, can't even get Louise to let her help put the costumes away. Louise is having a life beyond her wildest dreams, and for her mother it's a nightmare. She's been put out to pasture, and she knows it. And Louise is actually enjoying it—it's payback time. In constant combat, Rose and Louise review the tangled conflicts of their lives in corrosive detail. Finally, having lost the battle and the war, Rose shoots off one last salvo:

**ROSE**

All right, miss. But just one thing I want to know: All the working and pushing and fenagling, all the scheming and scrimping and lying awake nights figuring: How do we get from one town to the next? How do we all eat on a buck? How do I make an act out of *nothing*! What'd I do it for? You say I fought my whole life. I fought *your* whole life. So now tell me: What'd I do it for?

LOUISE

I thought you did it for me, Momma.

That's it. That's what the play is about. In one simple—if wordy—question and one terse answer, the entire evening is thrown into high relief, in a way that anyone can appreciate and be moved by.

When a playwright can nail a moment like that, two things are happening. First, the playwright is letting the audience know that he understands and is in complete control of his work, his subject, his reason for writing the play. That in itself is satisfying to an audience. Second, we are given the opportunity to rack back through the entire evening and see how it fits together. It's deeply pleasurable. We understand why we came to church.

And at its best—in plays and musicals—it often comes in the form of a question and an answer.

In *Fiddler on the Roof*, the question-and-answer moment is in the hands of two minor characters, the Rabbi and a young villager. During the course of the evening, the little village of Anatevka has been defined as being held together by tradition, and the traditions have crumbled from within, as Tevye's three adult daughters have taken their love lives into their own hands and made bolder and bolder choices about whom to love—the third of them breaking the final taboo by marrying outside the faith.

But there is equal pressure on Anatevka from without; the Russians have taken more and more from the Jews and finally seize their land and purge them. There is an edict from the authorities, and just like that, Anatevka is no more. Everyone gets out the wagons and donkeys and packs up what little they have and prepares to leave a town that will instantly disappear. A place they've called home for generations is now vanishing before our eyes. They are about to begin their wandering—off to America, to Europe, to Palestine—when a young villager turns to the Rabbi.

MENDEL

Rabbi, we've been waiting for the Messiah all our lives. Wouldn't this be a good time for him to come?

RABBI

We'll have to wait for him someplace else.

This is the point—the question-and-answer moment—where the 899 other Jews I first saw the show with in 1964 began to understand the scope of *Fiddler*'s subject. It's a song cue, but it makes you inhale sharply. Because "someplace else" means "everywhere" to these villagers—the entire diaspora, the world of Jews who had lost and found and kept in touch with each other since the day they packed their candlesticks and prayer shawls into carpetbags and trudged off to discover a new life. Again.

I was completely startled by this moment when I first heard it, though I had been brought up in suburban Stamford, Connecticut, and really had very little idea what it meant to be Jewish—my family was more zealous about assimilation than about Judaism itself. My father was also deeply affected, but he was a great needler and didn't trust sentiment. He pulled himself together quickly, and on the car ride home he said, "I don't understand the ending of that show. All those Jews standing in the aisles crying their eyes out. Every one of them the grandchild of someone who left Anatevka so sadly—they all came to the United States, became successful, and their grandchildren can afford to sit in orchestra seats at the biggest hit in town. What the hell are they crying about?!"

But he knew. His father had fled Minsk in 1895 at age five.

There was a deeper resonance to "someplace else." The line was being spoken by a simple man of God who had no idea of its implications— assimilation in the United States, a Holocaust in Europe, an unending struggle in what became Israel. There was more than a century of happy endings and tragic endings, and no real ending at all, in those two simple words. And that's one of the reasons *Fiddler* remains immortal.

The exchanges are not so simple in Meredith Willson's *The Music Man*, which can be read as a kind of country cousin to *Guys and Dolls*. Willson's Iowa townsfolk are flimflammed by Professor Harold Hill, a slick salesman with an apparent heart of tin, who vaguely resembles Sky Masterson in his firm belief that women are for momentary amusement, not for life commitment. His opposite number, Marian the librarian, is a kind of rural Sarah Brown, committed to keeping dangerous men at bay while she pursues her higher ideals, which include bringing culture to the benighted citizens of River City.

They're a perfect match for a musical or any romantic comedy—two people who can't possibly end up together but somehow do. That's the myth we love to believe in.

Under their armor, Marian is a pure romantic, and Harold is simply waiting for someone to awaken his true heart. But the armor is thick. The agent of the awakening is not Marian but her troubled, shy little brother, Winthrop, who is afraid to talk because he has a pronounced lisp.

Harold genuinely takes to Winthrop and feels for him, so he enlists him as the cornet player in the band that he's promoting—a band that will earn him some quick money in sales commissions but will never actually materialize, since Harold knows nothing about music. This is a fatal turn in Harold's life because his fondness for Winthrop is real, but the dream he sells the boy is a phony. Marian knows it—she's done her research on the professor's nonexistent credentials—but she loves him anyhow, because he has saved Winthrop. The question is: What will happen when the flimflam is revealed? How will Winthrop survive it, and what will Marian do with the love she's invested in this disreputable man?

The answer is interesting and comes not in a single question and answer but in a series of them with a surprising final punch. As Professor Hill is about to be hauled off and tarred and feathered by the local citizenry, Winthrop tries to run away, and Harold grabs him and holds him. Here's what happens:

WINTHROP

I won't listen! You won't tell the truth anyhow!

HAROLD

I would too. Tell you anything you want to know.

WINTHROP

Can you lead a band?

HAROLD

No.

WINTHROP

Are you a big liar?

HAROLD

Yes.

WINTHROP

Are you a dirty rotten crook?

HAROLD

Yes.

WINTHROP

Let me go, you big liar!

HAROLD

What's the matter? You wanted the truth, didn't you? Now, I'm bigger'n you and you're going to stand here and get it all so you might as well quit wiggling.

*(Winthrop finally stops, exhausted.)*

There are two things you're entitled to know. One, you're a wonderful kid. I thought so from the first. That's why I wanted you in the band, so you'd quit mopin' around feeling sorry for yourself.

WINTHROP
(*sarcastically*)

What band?


HAROLD

Kid, I always think there's a band.

And therein lies our ability not only to forgive Harold Hill but also to admire and celebrate him. He may be, in one sense, a snake-oil salesman. But in another sense, he believes it all himself, like any true salesman, or any true child. He believes there's a band. He believes a sullen, frightened ten-year-old boy can be saved, even though there's no evidence that it's true and no one else believes it. He believes it's worth doing, and he never questions why. In the process, he proves himself worthy. And, naturally, he and Marian fall in love, which is the real kicker. Because love is the one thing he's never believed in. "*There were bells on the hill,*" he sings to her in the show's final reprise, "*but I never heard them ringing.*"

And so, in a small, close-minded Iowa town, three souls have been saved by each other, in a next-to-last scene that is full of promise for the new, more enlightened America that *The Music Man* believes in. No wonder it outran *Gypsy*.

Famously, two of the show's best-known songs, "Seventy-six Trombones" and "Goodnight, My Someone," have the same melody, and Willson saw fit to show *how* Harold and Marian have fallen in love by intertwining them, each at its own tempo, and then switching off who sings what. So eventually Marian finds herself singing about a marching band while Harold is singing about love, and in that moment, both of them discover a world they never knew existed. In a show that features a simple, hometown approach, it's as neat and clean a turn as anyone could ask for.


Love, of course, is what a lot of these scenes are about, but since they are not the finale, they usually conclude with lovers parting, only to be reunited one scene later, having realized that the knowledge they've gained actually grants them permission to love. But sometimes the scenes don't even involve the romantic couple. After all, in the modest scene Moss Hart wrote for *Once in a Lifetime*, one of the characters was a relatively minor one, a playwright who was driven to a nervous break-down in Hollywood by underwork (good joke) and is on his way back to New York. He was originally played by George S. Kaufman himself. Like Winthrop, he was more catalytic than anything else. It really doesn't matter how the audience gets the news, as long as it gets it loud and clear from someone, and that usually requires dialogue—but not always.

In *Guys and Dolls*, also directed by Kaufman many years later, the two leading ladies take on the task. Kaufman was personally mortified by sentiment, and the book writer, Abe Burrows, didn't have much time for it either. The songwriter, Frank Loesser, had a huge capacity for it, but he didn't discover it until his next show, *The Most Happy Fella*. In *Guys and Dolls*, the authors and director were sticking with a wise-cracking tone and a masculine belief that honest emotion was more likely to cause trouble than not. That made for a bit of a conundrum when it came to the next-to-last scene. Usually, the idea is to speak plainly and from the heart—not a place these three were comfortable accessing. So they send Miss Adelaide out to a park bench at dawn to mourn the loss of Nathan Detroit, and there she encounters Sarah Brown, carrying a torch for Sky Masterson. And in another masculine joke that felt completely at home in the '50s, the women get to decide everything and set the trap that any man is likely to fall into. In the end, the gamblers and gangsters are going to be domesticated—that's what a 1949 audience expected. And in a sense that's what the show is about to begin with: the allure of 4:00 a.m. New York versus the practical life that gets lived out in the daytime. *Guys and Dolls* shows off all the color and flash and danger of the Broadway underworld, while keep-ing the audience, in reality, completely out of harm's way.

Adelaide and Sarah bemoan their fate and the impossibility of expect-ing their men to ever change into the sensitive, caring partners they'd like them to be. The very idea seems preposterous. And then it strikes them both virtually simultaneously that there is only one way to achieve what they're looking for, and it requires—of all things—placing a bet.

ADELAIDE

*You simply gotta gamble*

SARAH

*You get no guarantee*

ADELAIDE

*Now doesn't that kind of apply to you and I?*

SARAH

*You and me!*

ADELAIDE

*Why not?*

SARAH

*Why not what?*

ADELAIDE

*Marry the man today*
*Trouble though he may be*
*Much as he likes to play*
*Crazy and wild and free*

SARAH AND ADELAIDE

*Marry the man today,*
*rather than sigh in sorrow*

ADELAIDE

*Marry the man today*
*and change his ways tomorrow!*

Loesser could be funny and clear at the same time, and he handled the next-to-last-scene chores with relish. You might think that there is a missing scene in the show—the one where the two couples actually reconcile. But after "Marry the Man Today," it's entirely unnecessary.

The women's conviction is all we need to know about. The men will be helpless to resist the tidal wave that's coming at them. We're headed to a double wedding, and to hear about how each couple finally agreed to forgive and forget would only bore us. We can picture it all too clearly and don't need to witness it to believe it.

One of the shifts—some might say losses—in craftsmanship between the Golden Age shows and the more modern ones has taken place in the next-to-last-scene slot, and it's easy to see why. The really good traditional ones are a matter of formal rigor and craft as much as inspiration—and formal rigor and craft are virtues that have faded in most of American pop culture since the 1960s. An equally valid virtue, inspired improvisatory spontaneity, has replaced them. And, to be fair, the post-'60s audience doesn't expect the kind of tidiness that used to be an unquestioned virtue in theatrical writing. The well-made play has been long since eclipsed by the descendants of Beckett, Albee, Pinter, and Sam Shepard, and the same thing has happened with musicals. Even the most meticulous composer-lyricist, Stephen Sondheim, has most often found himself involved in experimental shows meant to push the form into the unknown, rather than to build the neatest house on the block. Reaching beyond Sondheim, writers like Jonathan Larson, Lin-Manuel Miranda, Jeanine Tesori, the team of Marc Shaiman and Scott Wittman, and all their various collaborators have most often found themselves solving dramatic problems without the kind of structural rigidity that was common a few decades earlier—or with only a nod to it.

In *Hairspray*, for instance, Shaiman and Wittman took the next-to-last scene out of the hands of the principals altogether and did something that almost felt like reparations for the stain of racism itself. They gave the most important thematic moment in the show to an African American subplot character. At the end of the day, *Hairspray* is about the struggle for acceptance, and although the show is a campy comedy, "struggle" is the operative word. Tracy Turnblad needs to be accepted for who she is—a plus-size heroine. Her mother is played by a man in a dress because in the original film, John Waters needed to include gender liberation as an element in a story that didn't really ever touch on the subject. But within the confines of the plot, it is African American acceptance that is driving things. Tracy lends her considerable heft in the push to integrate the Corny Collins dance show on TV. In the penultimate moment of the show, when Tracy has escaped from prison and taken refuge in the record store owned by Motormouth Maybelle, it is Motormouth who gets to tell us why we've been watching the show for two hours. *Hairspray* takes a hard left turn so that this subsidiary character can gather the theme to her ample bosom and give voice to the pain of being the eternal outsider. The moment is unusual in a number of ways: it's musical, not spoken; it becomes an ensemble number instead of a confrontation between two characters; and it radically shifts the tone of what has been, up to this point, an outlandish, jokey show. Things come to a completely serious full stop.

The song she sings, "I Know Where I've Been," could have been an anthem in a civil rights gospel concert, but here it stands, at the end of *Hairspray*. It confronts the problem the show has been teasing from the start: bigotry in all its manifestations. It's not so much a summation of an argument between protagonist and antagonist as it is a clear statement of the subject matter: this, it says, is what we've been fighting for all night long, and now we're going to go get it. It doesn't wink for a moment. And as soon as it concludes, the show goes right back where it's been—an intentionally tacky joy machine, but with a clear point. That one moment of removing the mask of comedy pulls the audience in, lets it know why the story is being told in the first place, and what it's really about. It's an unheralded key to the show's success.

I will freely admit, however, that it was a bone of contention in the show's construction, and that I fought like a dog to keep it out of the show. (I also tried to boo Bob Dylan off the stage at Newport in 1965. For shame.) The creative team believed in the moment, but the producers did not, at least not initially. The number replaced the militant, upbeat "Step On Up" with something much more somber. In part, it scared everyone who hadn't been involved in creating it. But the

*Hairspray* team could afford the luxury of arguing about this. The show had been so popular from its first industry exposure—a reading of the first act—that it felt like a hit no matter what. In those rare cases, it's fun to have a debate. That the authors actually won it was a lucky outcome, and, in hindsight, I was fortunate to be wrong. As Rocco Landesman is fond of saying, sometimes it's better to be lucky than smart.

If *Hairspray* was a plea to embrace diversity cloaked in transgressive comedy, Tony Kushner and Jeanine Tesori's *Caroline, or Change* treated some of the same issues in a different way and is one of the real under-recognized masterpieces of the post–Golden Age. Shaped by the director George C. Wolfe into an inspired theatrical whole that included a singing washer and dryer and a bus played by an actor who tolled out JFK's assasination like a church bell, it concerns a great doomed love between a middle-aged black maid in Louisiana and a ten-year-old Jewish boy whose mother has died, leaving him lonely and isolated. It's a parent-child love affair, but that doesn't make it any less impassioned than a romantic one, just a lot harder for the participants to articulate. Caroline, the maid, has to behave in a certain way. And Noah, the boy, only knows how to behave like a kid. They have no language to communicate the possibility that they are each other's saviors, so they settle for little moments of connection, as when Noah ritually lights Caroline's cigarettes.

It's a heartbreaking situation, fueled by Kushner's personal memories of growing up in Lake Charles, Louisiana, where Jim Crow intolerance and a tacit anti-Semitism drove all the social interactions, and economic inequalities informed every kind of behavior. In the world where Caroline is paid to take care of Noah, but lacks the time or financial wherewithal to see to her own three children, bad things are bound to happen.

The plot turns on a simple, seemingly trivial rule in Noah's house. Whatever money he leaves in his pants pocket belongs to Caroline if she finds it when she's doing the laundry. This is supposed to teach Noah to take more responsibility for his allowance. Quarters and dimes are supposed to change hands, but Caroline can never bring herself to take the money, even though change, for her, could change things.

Then, after a Hanukkah party in which Noah has been given a twenty-dollar bill by his grandfather, the bottom falls out of Noah's life. He leaves the twenty in his pocket, and this kind of money Caroline cannot resist. It speaks to everything in her—the inequality she lives with every day, Noah's heedless carelessness with money, the upper-middle-class atmosphere of her workplace, the basement to which she's largely confined while doing the laundry, the poverty of her own neighborhood, the needs of her own children. It's all suddenly intolerable, and she takes the bill, which, according to the rules, belongs to her.

As much as any romantic betrayal, this is a breaking point for two people who love and need each other but whose worlds are so utterly unalike that there is no way to bridge them back to each other. Besides, they don't even know they need each other until they are suddenly without. But Noah wants his money back, and he cracks. The son of progressive Jews in Louisiana who officially believe in the civil rights movement, he lashes out at the only parent figure he's ever felt connected to, using language he's no doubt heard on the street and in school:

> *I hate you! I hate you! I hate you!*
> *There's a bomb!*
> *President Johnson has built a bomb*
> *special made to kill all Negroes!*
> *I hate you, hate you, kill all Negroes! Really! For true!*
> *I hope he drops his bomb on you!*

Noah is a little boy, of course, and Caroline knows it. But this is simply beyond what she can bear. She replies:

> *Noah, hell is like this basement,*
> *only hotter than this, hotter than August,*
> *with the washer and the dryer and the boiler*
> *full blast, hell's hotter than goose fat,*
> *much hotter than that.*
> *Hell's so hot it makes flesh fry.*
>
> *And hell's where Jews go when they die.*

*Take your twenty dollars, baby.*
*So long, Noah, good-bye.*

It's a shocking moment of anger that exposes the rot of bigotry infecting the community across all social boundaries. It tears Caroline's world asunder, and Noah's too. This happens about two-thirds of the way through the act, and the remaining third deals with the consequences. Noah's stepmother has lost Caroline as a maid; worse, all her attempts to build a more positive relationship with this black servant than her neighbors would have done are proved worthless. Her already strained relationship with her Communist father is brought to the breaking point. Meanwhile, Caroline cuts herself off from her neighbors in shame over what she's done and, in an earlyish 11 o'clock number, pours her heart out to God. The number, called "Lot's Wife," is a gem of a performance piece but in some ways hard to understand, as Caroline attacks herself and—to the best of her ability—the economic norms in America that have brought her to such an uncontrollable state of anger and helplessness. Tesori's music ranges over a spectrum of emotions from deep anger to deep sorrow, and both music and lyrics end in pathos, with a plea.

"Lot's Wife" inevitably stopped *Caroline, or Change* in its tracks, but if you had asked the audience members who were giving the actress Tonya Pinkins a well-earned ovation exactly what the number was saying, some would have had a hard time doing so, at least in any detail. Kushner writes densely, and sometimes his work feels more like poetry than lyric writing. Nonetheless, the ending is crystal clear, as Caroline cries out:

*Caroline. Caroline.*

*From the evil she done, Lord,*
*set her free*
*set her free.*

*set me free.*
*Don't let my sorrow*
*make evil of me.*

This bloodletting doesn't cleanse Caroline, but it allows her to begin to rebuild her life. And Noah, who is as deeply ashamed as she is but better protected by socioeconomic circumstance, also begins to function again within his shattered family. Which brings us to the next-to-last scene. Here, Noah and Caroline are allowed to talk to each other, though they are in different spaces—Noah in his bedroom, Caroline at home. Each carries the other in his or her head. And unsurprisingly, perhaps, it is time for questions and answers. Not one big one—these two are so separated by history and circumstance that it is impossible for either to fully articulate the subject of a deep connection broken. Instead, there is a scattering of information that the audience must patch together. Noah apologizes to Caroline for hiding from her on her first day back at work, and she responds.

CAROLINE

*Someday you won't.*
*Someday we'll talk again.*
*Just gotta wait.*

NOAH

Will we be friends then?

CAROLINE

Weren't never friends.

That's the first question and answer. And later in the same sequence:

CAROLINE

*Noah,*
*Someday we'll talk again*
*but they's things we'll never say.*
*That sorrow deep inside you,*
*it's inside me too,*
*and it never go away.*
*You be OK.*
*You'll learn how to lose things . . .*

After a brief sung rumination on the peace of death, where there's no money and no sorrow left, Caroline admits that with that peace, you will miss things, miss connections, like the cigarette-lighting ritual. Then Noah asks his final question: "Do you miss sharing a cigarette?"

And Caroline replies, "You bet I do, Noah."

It's a long way from *Gypsy* or *The Music Man*. It's oblique, as it must be, because Caroline and Noah don't know how to use the same language or approach an issue directly. They're saying as much as they can to each other, and that's the tragedy, because they're trying to say "I love you" but never will. Still, at heart it is the same technique for making the same kind of a point as every question-and-answer sequence. In an exact reversal of *The Music Man*, in fact, neither of the souls is saved, and life simply sweeps by. It's an exchange between two people who will soon have nothing of each other but memories. At least Kushner remembered whatever parts of it are autobiographical deeply enough to write it down, and immortalize Caroline.

There is probably no better encapsulation of where the musical theater has been, and what it has come to, than the seemingly absurd contrast between *The Music Man* and *Caroline, or Change*. Both involve a young boy and an older parent figure, but the conclusions drawn by each are exactly opposite. Harold Hill's faith in dreams saves Winthrop, Marian, and himself. That's the world we once believed in and treasured. Caroline's admission that we have to "learn how to lose things" reflects a very different America, where dreams have all but vanished, where we admit out loud that struggle is constant and slow, and people—especially outsiders—are ground down by it.

In *The Season*, William Goldman's 1968 survey of how Broadway worked back then, the author claims that there are really three theaters operating side by side on Broadway: the musical, the play that tells you a myth you want to believe, and the play that tells you the truth you don't want to hear. In 1968, the musical was set aside—it was largely sunny and mythical. By now it's clear that Goldman's model has been reduced to two, because the musical theater has embraced both the optimistic myth and the darker truth, and *Hairspray* and *Caroline* can both set up shop virtually next door to each other. We sing about it all.

The most famous question-and-answer moment is worth noting simply for its eloquence, though it doesn't come from a musical at all—it's the second-to-last moment in Thornton Wilder's *Our Town*, which pretends to represent daily life in a small New Hampshire village while taking on many of the struggles of the entire human race (that's why it's called *Our Town*). In the third act, the heroine, Emily, who has died in childbirth, is offered the opportunity to return to earth for one day of her short life and relive it. The offer comes from a character known as the Stage Manager, who has led the audience through the entire panoply of small-town life without benefit of scenery or other stage effects. Emily chooses her thirteenth birthday, and it is suddenly revealed in all its ordinariness. After watching the distracted, routine behavior of her parents and herself as the day sweeps by, she begs to go back to the grave, away from human life, and then asks a question.

**EMILY**

Oh, earth, you're too wonderful for anybody to realize you. Do any human beings ever realize their life while they live it—every, every minute?

**STAGE MANAGER**

No. The saints and poets, maybe . . . they do some.

Wilder can be faulted for the latter part of the line, perhaps, in which he seems to be tipping his hat to himself, among others. But a one-word answer might have been too stark. Nonetheless, the money part of the line is the single word: No. The desire to savor life as it's lived is continually thwarted by distraction and devaluation—we don't know it is passing until it is too late. And that's what *Our Town* is really about—the missed connections, lost opportunities, misunderstandings, and prejudices that make up a life that is nonetheless all too brief and dotted—but only dotted—by happiness, tender moments, fellow feeling, and love. It's the right question and the right answer.

These simple exchanges, so easily uttered, are damnably difficult to devise. But when they work, the art that contains them tends to endure for a very long time.

# 18. You Can't Stop the Beat

### *The End*

Shows begin with infinite possibility. They conclude with all possibilities removed save one. The lovers unite. Or not. The quest is rewarded. Or not. Everyone lives happily ever after. Or not.

Among the Golden Age shows, this was often the spot for a celebratory—or not—11 o'clock: a star spot. Sometimes this was propulsive, like "Rose's Turn," sometimes reflective, like "I've Grown Accustomed to Her Face." The star has the stage to herself or himself, for the purpose of spending time with the audience while exposing an emotional core. Rose comes to grips with who she actually is—at least for a moment. Henry Higgins admits that he has feelings for another human being—to the degree that he's able to admit anything.

Often these numbers were followed by a very simple scene, usually a sweet or wry one, between lovers united, who were, in effect, bidding us good night. And then we could all get some rest.

It's not hard for these 11 o'clock moments to top the next-to-last scene, because they're almost always sung, while next-to-last scenes are usually spoken. So even though Madame Rose and Louise have had a perfectly written knock-down, drag-out fight in the dressing room in *Gypsy*, "Rose's Turn," Madame Rose's musical nervous breakdown that follows, easily tops it in excitement. Partly that's because it's thrilling on its own terms, but partly it's a matter of temperament. The next-to-last scene is patiently answering our questions about where and how and why the events of the show happened—and what it all means to the people we've invested in. The finale, not to put too fine a point on it, is the show's orgasm, which comes at the end in any good encounter—followed, for a moment, by a shared cigarette.

"Rose's Turn" wasn't so much written as mined. Late in rehearsal, the director-choreographer, Jerome Robbins, realized that the ballet he had planned, in which Rose would confront all the characters and crisis moments of her past, was wrong for the spot, so a new plan was concocted. Rose would sing about her gradual self-destruction, but defiantly, not reflectively. According to Stephen Sondheim, he and Robbins holed up one night in the long-abandoned rooftop theater that had once been home to Ziegfeld's Midnight Frolic shows. Located at the top of the New Amsterdam Theatre, it is now the executive offices of Disney's Broadway operation. Robbins played Rose. Sondheim played the piano and ad-libbed lyrics, which were refined over the next few days. Using snippets of music from the show by the composer Jule Styne (who was not present), they gradually stitched together what has become the signature 11 o'clock number of all time. Robbins moved around the stage, stalking Rose's past and present states of mind, while Sondheim plugged in jagged fragments of Styne's music, linking them with a few of his own inventions, until they had zeroed in on Rose's psychological profile—a woman abandoned by her mother, who had so tightly controlled her own children that they both have abandoned her, leaving her with nothing at all to cling to except scrapbooks and selective memory. It's possible that Rose might give up in despair at the end of the number, but even in total emotional disarray, she's indomitable and the mistress of denial. Having clocked all the defeats and disappointments of her life, she makes one brave if not entirely sane declaration: from now on, she'll be the star of her own life: "This time for me!" she shouts defiantly. "For me! For me! For me!"

When the show opened out of town in Philadelphia, it was at this moment that Louise interrupted her, and the two of them played out the last scene, a rapprochement that is sweet, though we know it won't last. Sondheim didn't want applause at the end of the number—he feared it would cut into the applause at the final curtain, which was only a moment away.

But Oscar Hammerstein, at Sondheim's request, came down to Philadelphia to see the show, and his one big note was "You've got to let them applaud for 'Rose's Turn.' If you don't, the audience won't listen to the last scene—it's coitus interruptus." Hammerstein felt that denying a star of Merman's stature in such a galvanic number was cruel—not only to Merman but also to the customers. All they wanted was to release their pent-up excitement and gratitude.

Merman got her applause, and that's how the show opened.

In 1973, Arthur Laurents directed his own production in the West End, starring Angela Lansbury, and added a new touch: he let Lansbury take a bow at the end of the number, and then kept her bowing as the applause gradually faded, no matter how long it lasted, until she was alone again, bowing to an imaginary audience in an empty theater. It was eerie and uncomfortable (and it echoed the atmosphere of Sondheim's 1971 *Follies*), and finally, in silence, we saw her for what she was—a woman consumed by fantasy and far over the edge. And then Louise entered.

That's how "Rose's Turn" has been ever since—topping itself in a moment for which credit must go to Robbins; Sondheim; Jule Styne, who wrote the tunes but not the piece itself; Oscar Hammerstein, who got on a train and saw something that could be improved; and Arthur Laurents, who wrote the book in the first place and then, fifteen years later, saw an even better way to stage it.

The little scene that follows is memorable on a number of counts, as Rose and Louise try to pretend that they're friends again, while all of us in the audience know that the bond is forever broken. Louise, in a rare moment of kindness bordering on blather, tells her mother that she really could have been the star. It's something that a mother might do for a disappointed daughter, and in this little moment, their reversal is complete: the child has become the mother, and the mother the child.

But childish or not, Rose is no fool. "If I could've been, I would've been," she replies. "And that's show business."

It's as cruel and accurate an assessment of the business as has ever been stated, and perhaps the briefest. It's also the one moment when

Rose faces the unvarnished truth. Like virtually everything else about *Gypsy*, it's a model of efficiency that pulls no punches.


Jerome Robbins doctored two shows after he directed and choreo-graphed *Gypsy*—*Forum* and *Funny Girl*. He also directed a couple of straight plays for the first time, one a hit (*Oh Dad, Poor Dad, Mama's Hung You in the Closet and I'm Feelin' So Sad*) and one a quick flop—Brecht's *Mother Courage and Her Children*. But when it came time to take on his next full musical project, *Fiddler on the Roof*, it was the Brecht play that proved most influential. *Mother Courage* is about a woman dragging a cart across a war zone, making what profit she can by selling to the miserable soldiers on both sides, and losing all her children to war in the process. Eventually there is no one to haul the huge, heavy cart but her, and that image of a human being dragging a wagon proved so powerful that Robbins couldn't leave it behind.

Anyone contemplating what *Fiddler* would be during its gestation period might have imagined that Zero Mostel, who created the role of Tevye, would have an 11 o'clock number. He had become a bona fide Broadway star in *Forum* and was a big draw in *Fiddler*'s advance sales. He was the protagonist. Why wouldn't Robbins and Bock and Har-nick do for Mostel what Robbins, Sondheim, and Styne had done for Merman?

The cart, I suspect, is why. Heaven knows Jerry Bock and Sheldon Harnick, *Fiddler*'s composer and lyricist, were capable of writing a showstopper. But that's not what was called for in *Fiddler*. Early in the show, Mostel enters hauling the cart, explaining to the audience that his horse has pulled up lame. The show wasn't going to pay for a live horse—it was a serious musical, not a spectacle—and the excuse seemed natural enough. But it was setting up the final event, when the entire commu-nity of Anatevka prepares to abandon the little village that has, until this moment, been held together by internal communal spirit, external pressure from the Russians to remain within its boundaries, and, of course, tradition.

The final stage direction reads as follows:

*The stage begins to revolve, and Tevye begins to pull the wagon in the opposite direction. The other villagers, including the Fiddler, join the circle. The revolve stops. There is a last moment together, and the villagers exit, at different times and in opposite directions, leaving the family on stage. Tevye begins to pull his wagon upstage, revealing the Fiddler, playing his theme. Tevye stops, turns, beckons to him. The Fiddler tucks his violin under his arm and follows the family upstage as the curtain falls.*

This has to be the quietest 11 o'clock moment in the history of the musical theater and, though entirely wordless, among the most eloquent. The diaspora is acknowledged, but the Fiddler, with his essential Jewish melody, travels with the family, wherever it goes.

As the Rabbi in Tony Kushner's *Angels in America* says at the funeral of an old Jewish émigré, "She was not a person, but a whole kind of person. The ones who crossed the ocean, who brought with us to America the villages of Russia and Lithuania . . . You can never make that crossing that she made, for such Great Voyages in this world do not any more exist. But every day of your lives, the miles of that voyage between that place and this one you cross. Every day. You understand me? In you that journey is."

And this is the reason that *Fiddler* lives on so easily. Robbins was saying in movement (not exactly dance) what Kushner puts so beautifully into words, and there is hardly an audience member—most especially, but not only, the Jews—who can escape the power of it. In *Fiddler*, the 11 o'clock moment cracks open not the protagonist's heart but the viewer's.

In *The King and I*, hearts are broken both literally and figuratively. This was an earlier Robbins collaboration, but, as was so often true, he made movement poetry out of a culture clash and a world in transition. From *West Side Story* to *Fiddler* and back to Siam in the nineteenth century, Robbins was questing for meaning in the seismic changes that cultures go through when things collide. The stakes are always high for people on the brink.

In *The King and I*, Siam stands on the precipice of inevitable modernity, and the change, when it comes, will kill the King. Miss Anna, who will bring the change, hates the King's authoritarian rule but admires his internal battle with it, and has fallen in love with the man himself. The moment, needless to say, is ripe with conflict and risk.

It's not actually the last moment of the show, or even really close, though it is the last new song—there are no fewer than three book scenes and a couple of reprises to follow. But Rodgers and Hammerstein had certainly earned the right to adjust the form to their requirements and were always breaking down formulas and creating new ones anyhow. So "Shall We Dance?" may not quite fit the mold, but it's still a classic 11 o'clock number for the stars—it just occurs a little earlier than you might expect.

Oddly, it's a kind of conditional love song that has transmigrated from its normal home early in the first act to a spot almost at the end of the play. But there are reasons for that. Conditional love songs generally happen when couples meet and feel the pull of romantic attraction. But Anna and the King come from such different worlds, and are embroiled in such a skein of disputes, that it takes almost all night for them to realize they have fallen. There are too many reasons why they can't, and it is from this fact that both the song and the dance derive power.

Unlike Curly and Laurey in *Oklahoma!* or Julie and Billy in *Carousel*, Anna and the King have no common ground at all that we can see. He's a king in an autocratic ancient Eastern society; she's a schoolteacher from a putatively modern and democratic one. He is in every normal respect the dominant one—a male ruler to whom everyone pays obeisance. She's a female who is supposed to know the limits of her station. But from the beginning, she's been struggling for the power position because she finds his ideas so backward and unfair. She also—though she can't admit it to herself—finds him magnificent. Even so, she believes that her advanced understanding of a free society should allow her to be in charge, or at least to transform his thinking, not the other way around. So it appears that what's at stake this late in the day is not their personal relationship but the social, political, and cultural direction of the world itself. Like *Carousel*'s "If I Loved You," in which the whole natural world seems to be conspiring to drive two powerless human beings into each other's arms, "Shall We Dance?" takes the global and makes it personal. This time it isn't the black sea and the stars in the sky and the cherry blossoms that fall on a windless night, it's the forces of democracy and enlightenment on the march that overtake this pair of almost lovers. And this is how the musical theater approaches the problem: with a polka.

After describing the typical English tea dance, in which every girl, her eyes cast downward, waits for the sight of "two black shoes—white waistcoat—a face!" Miss Anna sings to the King of what that experience is like—to meet a man, to try to find a way to know him a little better, and to resort to a social custom designed to solve the problem: a dance.

The King watches with fascination and becomes irritated when she stops dancing around the room by herself—so much so that he wrangles his way into the act, feigning disapproval but insisting anyhow. And soon, really for the first time in an almost three-hour-long musical, the two of them are joined not just physically but also in intent. They trade lines of the song carefully, keeping a verbal distance even as they become physically closer. They share precisely one word in the song: "romance."

After that, it's only a matter of time until the King insists upon holding Anna as he's seen Europeans holding each other—one arm around her waist and the other joined to hers just above their heads. And in that moment, the music takes off like a flock of birds, and they are lost in each other as they swirl madly around the room. Properly executed, it is more powerful than the signing of any peace treaty you can imagine. It tears up theatergoers because they can see not just a couple finally in love but also two societies finally seeing each other with loving eyes and raising the possibility that in a single dance the entire world might change, might move forward. Western social dancing in "Shall We Dance?" carries the weight of cultural imperialism as a world cracks open in front of us—in song and dance.

Musicals in general may be sentimental, mythologized, full of false optimism and showbiz glitz, but every now and then one features a moment that manages to be profound. That's what we wait for.

The moment doesn't last, alas. Because as soon as the number is finished, they are interrupted. The slave Tuptim has been captured, and within moments the King is threatening to beat her with a bull-whip. No society was ever actually transformed by a polka. But we've seen a glimpse of possibility, a die has been cast, and it's all worth it for that. We also know it's the end of something as well as the beginning. The King's heart fails him as he tries to bring himself to whip a helpless slave girl in front of a powerful English schoolteacher; he can't do it. He can't be the same king anymore and there is really no place for him to live. He dies trying to be a better king than he can be, and leaves the world to the next generation. Hammerstein was an optimist, even in death.

*The King and I* had as its subject the collision of worlds. The much more modest *She Loves Me* was a simple romantic comedy but was also about two lovers who didn't recognize each other until the last minute. It was so ingenuous, in fact, that it never had a real chance to become a smash hit, though its charms have endured and its craftsmanship is faultless. And it handled the task of bringing down the curtain in the loveliest possible way—by setting the lyric hook of one earlier song on the melodic hook of another.

The two most important words in the show are "dear friend." That's the way two members of a "lonely hearts club" address each other in letters that lead, eventually, to an abiding love. They don't know each other and have never even seen each other—or so they believe. Actually, they work side by side in a perfume shop, where they bicker and snipe at each other all day, every day, having no idea that their workday annoyance is aimed at the person they feel most tenderly toward during evening letter-writing sessions. It's probably an ancient premise, but in this case it is based on a Hungarian play by Miklós László, which also served as the source of the movies *The Shop Around the Corner, In the Good Old Summertime*, and *You've Got Mail*. It's a reliable notion.

In the Broadway version, Barbara Cook played Amalia Balash, who talks her way into a job at an elegant Budapest perfume shop against the wishes of the shop's manager, Georg Nowack, played by Daniel Massey. Cook's magnificent soprano was put to good use at the end of Act 1, when she goes to meet her unknown beloved, who never shows up. Actually, he does show up, but he sees that his daytime enemy is his nighttime romance, behaves terribly toward her rather than reveal the truth, and ducks out. Left alone, Cook sings a soaring but somehow contained ballad called "Dear Friend," and the curtain falls on her, alone at a table, her heart broken.

Early in Act 2, Georg, feeling guilty and confused, comes to visit her because she's called in sick, and he brings her a pint of ice cream as a peace offering. She tosses him out unceremoniously and decides to soothe her feelings by writing to her "dear friend."

"Dear Friend," she writes,

> *I am so sorry about last night—*
> *It was a nightmare in every way.*
> *But together you and I*
> *Will laugh at last night some day.*

At this point her concentration fails her, and she begins to think about the pint of ice cream that Georg has brought her, and how nice he's been to her, for the first time in her life. She suspects nothing. She's just puzzled, and something in her is stirring. She sings to herself:

> *Ice cream—*
> *He brought me ice cream—*
> *Vanilla ice cream.*
> *Imagine that!*

What follows is a spectacular solo called "Ice Cream." Just as "Dear Friend" manages to soar without losing control, "Ice Cream" manages to express ecstasy without ever leaving behind a sense of puzzlement. "What's happening to me?" Amalia seems to be asking herself. "And why has it been caused by a pint of vanilla?"

The two numbers seem unrelated—one heartbroken and the other full of expectation—but they share a significant link: each has a title that consists of two one-syllable words. And the lyricist, Sheldon Harnick, puts this seemingly insignificant fact to exquisite use in the show's final moment.

Amalia and Georg are united by it, in fact. Georg, bursting to tell Amalia the truth, understanding the risks involved, finally throws caution to the wind.

"You sounded—irresistible," he tells her.

"But you never *said* anything!" she replies.

"How could I? I knew how you felt about me . . ."

"But you didn't know! . . ." she insists. "What a shame we never spoke up . . ."

At this point, Georg reveals himself by quoting the letter Amalia was writing as the introductory verse of "Ice Cream." After all, no one could know of those words except Amalia's "dear friend."

> *I am so sorry about last night—*
> *It was a nightmare in every way.*
> *But together you and I*
> *Will laugh at last night some day.*

Amalia nearly bursts with relief and gratitude, and the song continues musically exactly the way it did the first time we heard it. Except that instead of singing

> *Ice cream—*
> *He brought me ice cream—*
> *Vanilla ice cream.*
> *Imagine that!*

she sings

> *Dear Friend—*
> *It's really true then . . .*
> *It's what I hoped for . . .*
> *That it was you!*

By creating a simple lyric that shares scansion with "Ice Cream" but references "Dear Friend," Harnick joins two unlikely musical companions as the plot joins two unlikely romantic companions. Sometimes genius lives in small places. The song races headlong to an embrace as the dam breaks. Love blooms like blossoms in spring, even though it's Christmas Eve and snow is falling. The orchestra swells—not with the melody of "Ice Cream," which we were expecting, but with the melody of "Dear Friend," and the tapestry of music and lyrics is complete. The entire event takes less than two minutes, yet it is as full a meal as we need. Like virtually everything else about *She Loves Me*, it doesn't announce itself or preen. It doesn't even draw attention to the fact that Harnick and Jerry Bock, the composer, have slyly substituted "dear friend" for "ice cream." And that's why the number can be so short. The weaving of musical ideas with the lyric swap does all the work necessary even if we're unaware of it. It expresses great tenderness and intimacy, and it is also startlingly efficient. Everything that needs to be said has been said, and every emotion has been covered by Bock's music. The words "dear friend," which brought down the first-act curtain in heartbreak, lead to the final curtain in romantic triumph. It's a kind of writing that happens only in musical theater. No other form has any use for it, because no other form has the opportunity to do things that way.

*She Loves Me* opened in 1963, more than a half century ago, and we are not as satisfied by tender, quiet curtain moments anymore. The rock concert, not to mention rock itself, has taught us to expect more visceral, high-energy climaxes, with maybe a megamix to follow. A megamix would not have suited *She Loves Me*, though it wasn't unusual in those days for a curtain call to include a brief ensemble reprise of a couple of the better tunes in the show.

Still, in the classic period, shows often resolved quietly, leaving the audience alone with the protagonist, the lovers, the characters we cared most about. But at a certain point things began to change, and the final curtain became an opportunity for something more kinetic and viscerally exciting. Today, closing numbers are like opening numbers. They come in two varieties: the intimate ones that tie a beautiful knot and the noisy ones that shoot the works. They may be reprises (more on that later) or new songs, but they head for the same place—a quiet "wow" or a riotous one.*

The riotous method is more forgiving. To do what *Fiddler* did, or *The King and I, She Loves Me*, or *Caroline, or Change*, requires that the creators thread the needle virtually perfectly and pierce the audience's heart in one way or another. These kinds of shows often want the curtain to fall, leaving the audience in tears, even if the ending is happy. The noisy ones have a different intent: to muscle an audience into submission, which is another kind of impact altogether.

No show has ever done this better than *Hairspray*, which did it out of necessity. Always a bit of a shaggy dog, *Hairspray* is really about three couples, not two, and contains three important villains, as well as an entire population of African American characters who are not included in the above listing. There's a lot to wrap up at the end, and the authors left most of it for the very last minute. The principal romance, the secondary romance, the political story (the racial integration of television), and the punishment of the villains were all left hanging as the show launched into its final number, thankfully called "You Can't Stop the Beat." The number was written before the enormity of its responsibility to bring all the strands of the plot to a conclusion was fully understood. And it was a doozy to begin with, with a title hook that morphs into an entirely new piece of music just when you think you've heard it all. This unexpected nugget of music and lyric (*"The motion of the ocean or the sun in the sky . . ."*) is so infectious that almost no human body is able to remain still when it is played. It causes a Broadway version of Saint Vitus's dance and was the number's secret weapon.

It's lucky they had it, because all attempts to wrap up most, or at least some, of the subplots in an orderly manner earlier on in the act had failed. So no one was going to have the luxury of stopping the beat before an awful lot had been accomplished. Luckily the song was a killer

---

* Among the most effective quiet ones, I'd count *Jelly's Last Jam* and *Caroline, or Change*, both brought to life through the imagination of the director George C. Wolfe. Lin-Manuel Miranda has acknowledged that it was *Caroline*'s last moment that inspired *Hamilton*'s—an unexpected left turn in which Hamilton's wife takes center stage after her husband's death, to conclude the evening in an unforgettable hush.

that got audiences up and rocking, and by continually extending it so that it covered the wrap-up of first one subplot, then another, then another, it got bigger and better. Every major character got a short solo chorus, including Harvey Fierstein's Edna in his spectacular super-sized red gown. Shaiman and Wittman wrote clever lyrics that gave us all the information we needed, credible or not (did the villainous Von Tussels *really* get converted into good people simply by the beat? Well, who cares, in the end?). And the audience wanted the number to go on forever, which certainly didn't hurt. No time for a wry or ironic scene at the end of this one—the stage exploded with streamers (shot from cannons) that reached all the way to the back of the house, and the lights went out. When the fireworks are over, they're over.

"You Can't Stop the Beat" was an entirely new song in *Hairspray*, but just as frequently shows rely on reprises of songs we've heard before to draw an emotional response. Sometimes they are songs that are repurposed with new or variant lyrics that cause them to set off different emotions from those we experienced with them the first time, as when Harold Hill and Marian Paroo revisit "Seventy-six Trombones" and "Goodnight, My Someone" in *The Music Man*, and love blooms, using two songs that we've previously associated with razzmatazz and loneliness, respectively. And sometimes, as in "Rose's Turn," the final number revists several portions of the score we've already heard to make an entirely new number. But no show revisits its score more thoroughly than *Sweeney Todd*, which spends its final thirteen minutes of narrative reexploring no fewer than sixteen musical numbers. The idea here is not to create new emotions with old tunes but, instead, to drive us headlong into a suspense climax. Stephen Sondheim uses the constant and unexpected shifting of music and lyrics the way Alfred Hitchcock uses visual montage to crank up the stakes and frighten us half to death.

Sixteen separate musical reprises (not to mention four murders) in thirteen minutes must be some kind of a modern-day record, but the idea of reprises at the end is a time-honored tradition and often an effective way of bringing the story to a satisfying conclusion. In the days of operetta and earlier musical comedy, the *finale ultimo* was almost always a set of interlocking reprises that brought the lovers together. This was not an 11 o'clock situation—there were no fireworks and not even quiet surprises. There was, instead, the satisfaction of inevitability. We like revisiting the tunes of a show, assuming it has good ones—even if, or especially if, we're getting a new twist on the old melody. Reprises are a feature of the finales of shows as varied as *Damn Yankees*, *The Most Happy Fella*, *She Loves Me*, and *Carousel*, though more modern shows tend to avoid them, fearing sentiment, which we didn't used to fear.

There was a more commercial impulse behind using reprises in the old days when show tunes were bestsellers. It was a way of locking a few tunes into the memory banks of the customers, which drove them to want to hear the songs again. This desire to monetize melody reached a satirically shameless zenith in Ira Gershwin's final lyric for *The Ziegfeld Follies of 1936*, in which the lead tenor for the evening crooned:

> *We hope you'll soon be dancing to the score*
> *It helps the sales at every music store*
> *As we start the finale, we'll mention once more*
> *We hope you'll soon be dancing to the score.*

What followed was a reprise of every important potential hit song in the show except "I Can't Get Started," which in fact was the only one to become a standard; for decades, it enriched eager would-be lovers' chances of success, not to mention the bank accounts of Gershwin and the composer, Vernon Duke.

Somewhere along the line, a third type of finale came into being: the moral admonishment. These may have begun with the finale of *Forum*, where a simple reprise of "Comedy Tonight" concludes with the lines

> *What is the moral?*
> *Must be a moral.*
> *Here is the moral, wrong or right:*

*Morals tomorrow:*
*Comedy tonight!*

It was sweet and an enjoyable way to conclude an evening of knock-about mayhem, but Stephen Sondheim turned it on its head at the conclusion of *Sweeney Todd*, which without its moral admonishment would end almost as quietly as *She Loves Me*, though, admittedly, with quite a different outcome. Instead, as soon as Sweeney's been done away with and the factory whistle blows, the cast stands and instructs the audience in a way that is positively Brechtian:

*Attend the tale of Sweeney Todd!*
*He served a dark and a vengeful god!*
*To seek revenge may lead to hell,*
*But everyone does it and seldom as well*
*As Sweeney,*
*As Sweeney Todd,*
*The demon barber of Fleet Street!*

Hardly "Comedy Tonight," but it's a different show.

Perhaps with the intent of a direct send-up, or perhaps just because their show also comes to an end with most of the principals dead on the floor, *Little Shop of Horrors* took the same path three seasons later. In this case, the cast has been sucked dry, so to speak, by a rapacious Venus flytrap known as Audrey II, which (who?) has come from outer space to conquer the world—a process that seems to be very much in the ascendant as the curtain is about to fall. But suddenly the cast recovers in time to tell us the rest of the tale and deliver an admonition to all of us:

*The plants proceeded to grow, and grow*
*And they did what they came here to do, which was essentially to*
*Eat Cleveland*
*And Des Moines*
*And Peoria*
*And New York*
*And where you live!*

*They may offer you fortune and fame*
*Love and money and instant acclaim*
*But whatever they offer you*
*Don't feed the plants!*

This presents not only an opportunity for moral instruction but also a rock anthem that is as infectious as it is—somehow—ridiculous. And also serious, as *Sweeney*'s chorus is. Revenge is real. Temptation is real.

So, as it turns out, is faith, which brings us to a closing number that brought all these ideas together—the "Hello" reprise that concludes *The Book of Mormon*.

Officially, this number is called "Tomorrow Is a Latter Day," and it's a rock groove not unrelated to "You Can't Stop the Beat" and "Don't Feed the Plants." Like both finales, it's a new number. Somehow the creators of *Mormon* intuited, however, that the big rock anthem had become a standard-issue finale for musicals in the twenty-first century and might be on the verge of cliché. Besides, they had one more big idea up their sleeve—the idea that brings the message home, just as in *Forum*, *Sweeney*, and *Little Shop*. From "Latter Day," they morph into a reprise of the opening number, "Hello," with new lyrics, like the "Comedy Tonight" finale or "The Ballad of Sweeney Todd." And although it never quite goes so far as to read us the moral in so many words, it introduces one, which sums up the idea of the entire show—that doctrinal faith may have its utterly noncredible side, may be full of holes and built on unfathomable tall tales and superstitions, but somehow that doesn't reduce its value. The show may treat Mormonism itself like a mechanical bear in a shooting gallery, but that doesn't mean you shouldn't believe in something.

The moment comes because Elder Arnold Cunningham has created, out of necessity and a fervid if shallow imagination, a cosmology that satisfies and gives hope to the Ugandans, even while it appalls the Mormon home office. He's mixed some chunks of Mormonism with common Ugandan cultural beliefs and a serious helping of American pop-culture schlock to create his own stew and, unwittingly, a brand-new doctrinal faith. What we don't quite get at first is that he's done what every great religious pioneer has done—used the old religion and belief system where it suits his purposes and worked forward from there, using whatever he's got, to create a new one that's relevant for the time and place he finds himself in. In effect, he has become the descendant of Moses, Jesus, Joseph Smith, and Brigham Young—because he's been called. And he's done it from his perch as the local outcast who becomes a charismatic leader. So it's perfectly logical that as the show circles around to its reprise of the opening number, the words are new. Where once we met this company of squeaky-clean missionaries singing

> *Hello!*
> *My name is Elder Price!*
> *And I would like to share with you the most amazing*
> *Book.*

> *Hello!*
> *My name is Elder Grant!*
> *It's a book about America a long long time ago*

we now find the Ugandans, some in Mormon uniform, some in traditional tribal garb, mixed in with the Mormon elders, in a pose that is eerily reminiscent of the opening tableau, with all the uniformity of that picture in happy tatters. As in *Hairspray*, the whiteness has been left behind. And they sing to us:

> *Hello!*
> *My name is Elder Mutumbo!*
> *And I would like to share with you the most amazing*
> *Book*

> *Hello!*
> *My name is Sister Kimbay!*
> *It's a book about a people who were poor and sad*
> *Like you!*

The number chatters along to its climax, introducing the "Prophet," Arnold Cunningham, and concludes with a joyful ode to the new church, the new members, and the promise of redemption:

> Join our family
> And set your spirit free
> We can fully guarantee
> That
> This book will change your life . . .
> The book of Arnold!
>
> Hello!!!

And with the show's apparent last line (except for the jubilant "Hello!!!"), the story has finally been told to its satisfying conclusion. We've seen a religion invented and a people saved. Or sort of saved, at least spiritually. But Gotswana, the doctor, who complains all night of having "maggots in my scrotum," actually gets the last line. After a quick celebratory restating of "Tomorrow Is a Latter Day" sung by the entire company, Gotswana has the last word—or words—of wisdom and warning to the newly ecstatic Ugandans: "*I still have maggots in my scrotum!*" he sings resonantly. And then the show's really over. *The Book of Mormon* gets to eat its cake and have it too, which makes some audiences angry—even the ones that love it. It gives value to faith and cheerfully admits that faith is no substitute for worldly things like food, shelter, and medicine. So what good is it? It's like art: we can't live without it, the show seems to be telling us, even if its purpose is unfathomable. And that's just the way it is.

*Mormon*'s finale may not be the greatest ever written, or the only one that has employed resources from the past, but in terms of where the musical theater stands at the moment, it's fair to say that no show has ever gathered more techniques and ideas from classic Broadway and put them in one place at one time. It's a finale that's a new number, a reprise, a rock anthem, a deliverer of moral judgment, and a perfect example of how new lyrics on a familiar melody can change the game completely. Practically the only things missing are Tevye and his cart.

That, in the end, is what the American musical theater has always done, just like every other form of commercial endeavor: tried to keep—or steal—the best of the past while continuing to invent as the world around it keeps changing. Although today's musicals bear so little resemblance to American operetta or the Jazz Age shows of Gershwin and Rodgers and Hart that it's hard to imagine they are natural offspring, the trail is there to follow. As musical tastes and social mores and taboos change, certain things fall away and others take their place, but the theater tries to keep up. It's a business, with customers and investors to satisfy, and inventors and manufacturers (otherwise known as theater artists) with continually evolving ideas. Still, having created a way of telling stories that involves a certain overall architecture, it hasn't, at its best, ever abandoned that aspect of what it does. Shows as disparate as *Wicked*, *Mormon*, *Hairspray*, and *Caroline* are, wittingly or unwittingly, using the building blocks that evolved beginning three-quarters of a century ago or more.

In some cases, we've circled back even farther. The musical plays introduced by Rodgers and Hammerstein led to the megahits of the '80s, like *Phantom* and *Les Miz*, which were in some ways still musical plays and in others resembled a second coming of Sigmund Romberg and Rudolf Friml, with their lush, sometimes overstuffed melodies and exotic locales and situations. The crazy, almost plotless '20s musicals that provided little more than an outlet for hit tunes seem to have begun to revisit us in the "jukebox" musicals like *Rock of Ages* and *Mamma Mia!* that derive pleasure from shameless plots leading to old hits instead of new ones. No one has a scheme for how to grow the musical theater. Somehow it takes care of itself in surprising ways, and keeps on moving.

How it moves is described, metaphorically, by Ira Gershwin in a number from the aforementioned *Ziegfeld Follies of 1936*. In those days, new dance crazes were a fixture (as they were thirty years later with the twist and the mashed potato). Dances that took off were lucrative for the composers and lyricists who invented or codified them in song. The Charleston and the black bottom both started as show tunes in the '20s. In the '30s, the Lambeth Walk took Great Britain by storm while Americans were learning to jitterbug and lindy hop their way through the Great Depression. Gershwin, looking for a little comedy to tweak the fads, wrote a number for the *Follies* called "The Gazooka." The dance came with instructions that were not really instructions and couldn't be followed. They went like this:

*First you take a step*
*And then you take another*
*And then you take another*
*And then you take*
*And then you take*
*And then you*
*And then you*
*And then you*
*And that's . . . the gazooka!*

Musicals had been doing the gazooka since long before Gershwin wrote it. And yet each one is always searching for the same elusive goal, which is to turn the machine into the living, breathing animal—to be that rare beast that has both good bones and a unique voice. Those are the ones that stand up on their own and begin to live and breathe and dance to their own music. When that happens, we slip into an unexplored world to hear a story that holds us in awe and delivers us to a new destination, that engages the dramatic and the ecstatic simultaneously, and sends us back home reeling from the sheer joy of having been somewhere new.

# 19. Curtain Call

*How Woody Guthrie—of All People—Changed*
*Broadway Musicals Forever*

The changing of the guard took place in an empty theater between engagements, almost as if it were a secret too dark to reveal. On January 17, 2010, a rapturously reviewed but lightly
attended revival of the 1947 musical *Finian's Rainbow* played its final
performance at the St. James Theatre on West Forty-fourth Street, and
it was announced that it would be replaced by the Broadway opening
of *American Idiot*, a musical based on a bestselling album by the punk
band Green Day. Thus the stage was set. It's not surprising that this
happened at the St. James, a theater that was witness to the seismic shift
that took place when *Oklahoma!* opened there in 1943, not to mention
the evening fifty years later when John Raitt led a sing-along of the title
song with an audience of young stoners waiting for a preview of *The
Who's Tommy*. These things seem to happen at the St. James, belying
the elegant classical design of the building itself, not to mention its
stuffy English name. It's a building in forward motion, if such a thing
is possible.

*Finian* is a loopy, decidedly left-wing musical about a community
of tobacco growers in a fictional southern state and a trio of Irish immigrants who show up there, one of them a leprechaun. But its nominal
hero is a community leader, labor organizer, and wandering folksinger

called Woody, after Woody Guthrie, the real-life hero of the labor movement and the folk boom. Yip Harburg, who conceived the piece, cowrote the book, and wrote the brilliant lyrics, was an agitator in Broadway disguise, and he no doubt revered Guthrie and his heroic place in the movement.

A great lyricist, but never a clear storyteller, Harburg liked to mix left-wing politics with whimsical plotting and fanciful rhyme; the result is that *Finian*, which makes only a modicum of sense but has irresistible characters and songs, is one of his few Broadway credits that anyone really remembers.* Among the characters, Woody has the singular distinction of carrying a guitar with him wherever he goes, though he doesn't know how to play it.† It's a serviceable joke that the fictional Woody can neither put down the guitar nor perform with it, no doubt created to accommodate the actor who originally played the part. That damn guitar goes everywhere with Woody.

When the *Finian* revival ended its disappointing run, the guitar was hauled off to God knows where with the rest of the props, never to be heard from again, and *American Idiot* loaded in. The album had sold fifteen million copies, and hopes were high. Where *Finian* was an old-fashioned, somewhat political, but deeply optimistic American fable, *Idiot* was a postmodern, somewhat political, but deeply nihilistic American snapshot—of a country gone to hell. But here's the thing: at the curtain call on opening night, the lights came up on the entire cast of nineteen, and all of them had guitars slung over their shoulders. And all of them played. There wasn't a man or woman among them who couldn't play the guitar, some of them damn well. Woody who couldn't play had vanished. And that, in essence, is what happened to Broadway.

* He's best known these days as the lyricist of the Judy Garland movie *The Wizard of Oz*, and its most famous song, "Over the Rainbow." Less well known is that he ghostwrote the movie's glorious next-to-last scene, in which the Wizard gives the Scarecrow his brain (a diploma), the Tin Man his heart (a ticking plastic toy), and the Cowardly Lion his courage (a certificate of bravery). And then he gives Dorothy the message: "There's no place like home." It's a doozy.
† The real Woody Guthrie's guitar bore the hand-painted legend "This Machine Kills Fascists" across its soundboard.

Until the mid-twentieth century, most middle- and upper-class families who had any interest in culture had a piano in the house, and someone in the family knew how to play it. The children took lessons. This tradition, very European, dated back to the days before there were phonographs or radios, and if music in the house was considered an asset, someone had to be able to make it. The rest of the family could listen or sing along. Sheet music was the only way of spreading music around. On the Lower East Side, up in Yorkville, and in Harlem, pianos were hauled up tenement stairs and squeezed into overcrowded flats so that the likes of Irving Berlin, George Gershwin, and Vincent Youmans could learn. Richard Rodgers learned in a more luxe apartment on the Upper West Side, and Cole Porter learned in a comfortable midwestern home in Peru, Indiana. But they all learned, and had no choice but to learn, along with tens of thousands of other, less talented youngsters. But in the teens and '20s, phonographs and then the radio came into regular use, and knowing how to play the piano became a mark of culture but no longer a necessity for hearing music after supper.

By the late 1950s, though, another music had begun to dominate both the airwaves and the record business, and it was driven not by pianos but by guitars. Rock bands often included pianos, but the stars, with exceptions like Jerry Lee Lewis and Ray Charles, played the guitar. Mainly, Elvis Presley played the guitar, and he could perform standing up in front of a microphone while playing his instrument and moving in a stunningly sexually suggestive manner. Guitar-playing stars were more immediately available to an audience—which now included a TV audience—than piano players. The music itself had, to a great degree, originated in the South, where hillbilly bands, old-timey musicians, and country blues players had been perfecting an array of guitar techniques for decades while almost no one in the North paid any attention. This music didn't come from the "cultured" population of the Northeast and Midwest, with their musical debt to Italy and Germany. It was the creation of poor populations whose roots were more likely to be Scottish, English, or African. They were rural or small-town people, with an argot and a vernacular all their own. For decades, the music bided its time on the margins of pop culture. Then, in the mid-'50s, it began to explode all across America, thanks to radio and TV.*

In 1958, however, after Elvis and his cohorts had scared the hell out of mainstream America, the Kingston Trio, three clean-cut young men (playing two acoustic guitars and a banjo), had a gold record hit with an old Appalachian murder ballad called "Tom Dooley," which sold three million copies. And for a time, everything changed. Rock had a new competitor. The folk boom was on, and initially it was a great relief for parents across the country; they were only too happy now to provide guitars and lessons to their teenage children. (The piano in the house had suddenly become a piece of furniture.)

The Kingston Trio functioned as a kind of anti-Elvis as pop music continued to evolve, though they never seriously threatened the position of the King as king. Nonetheless, it was only a matter of time before the folk generation, fueled by performers like Pete Seeger and Joan Baez, rediscovered Woody Guthrie, a fountainhead of songs that were easy to learn and play, politically progressive, and brilliantly memorable, and could be sung by crowds. Suddenly there was a popular movement to replace "The Star-Spangled Banner" with "This Land Is Your Land" as our national anthem. Guthrie, who had once been tacitly acknowledged on Broadway in *Finian's Rainbow*, was now everywhere, and by 1963 he had a newly famous disciple, Bob Dylan. The fuse was lit.

The Beatles and the Stones arrived from England. In a controversial move, Dylan went electric in 1965 and took most of the folk generation with him. In the long run, the folk boom's marriage to rock and roll, and the age of psychedelia that followed, did to Broadway what Audrey II did to Mushnik's little flower shop—devoured it. But it took a long, long time to happen.

Still, the die was cast. America had learned to play the guitar, and

---

* To be fair, this explosion in popular vernacular American music didn't happen by itself. It was to a great degree made possible by music promoters and publishers like the legendary A&R man and publishing executive Ralph Peer, who had been working to expose—and profit from—this hidden American treasure trove since the late 1920s.

classic Broadway songwriting, which had been the outgrowth of many young people sitting at many pianos over many decades, started to fall out of step with American pop entertainment.

The isolated success of *Hair* in 1968 notwithstanding, Broadway hated the change and denounced it loudly and largely successfully. It was a mere three decades later that *Rent* came along. *Rent* owes plenty to *Hair*, but contemporary Broadway owes a great deal more to *Rent*. In fact, in some ways, *Hair* was to *Rent* what *Show Boat* was to *Oklahoma!* It came first, but the street wasn't interested in playing catch-up. *Hair*, you might say, was simply ahead of its time, though so politically *of* its time that it became a great success. Its chaos and freedom enthralled audiences and terrified professionals up and down the street. In *The Season*, William Goldman quotes a veteran theater professional's prediction of the influence of *Hair* on the American theater in the coming seasons: "There will now be a spate of shitty rock musicals."

And that's pretty much what happened. A few of them had merit, most did not, but Broadway was not about to open the door for any of them if it could avoid doing so. Entrenched interests were in a panic, as entrenched interests in the pop music field had been when rock appeared in the mid-'50s. They sensed a conqueror in their midst and built as high a wall as they could. As a result, *Hair* left a relatively invisible wake. Shows like *Promises, Promises* and *Company* employed a few rock elements in their orchestrations (both by Jonathan Tunick), but the pure rock musicals were decapitated on sight, often for good reason. And *1776*, that paean to the *good* side of American history, beat *Hair* for the Tony.

By the time *Rent* came around, though, a lot had changed. The traditional American songbook had long since given way, and rock had evolved into America's music, with many subspecies and offshoots—including rap—thriving. On Broadway, the last of the consistent, traditional top-shelf theater songwriters were old enough to be collecting Social Security, and the younger group had grown up with rock as the only popular music. The argument that a loud rock score with an insistent backbeat was antithetical to limning character and dealing with dramatic situations remained largely true. But audiences were beginning to demand something different anyhow. The live rock concert world had been theatricalized by new technologies—moving (sometimes blinding) lights, pyrotechnics, special effects—and the public had grown used to live entertainment that morphed easily from the theatrical to the purely musical and back again. Broadway finally had no choice but to catch up. *Rent* lit up the passageway.

The 1990s saw one post-*Rent* musical with a rock-inflected score winning the Tony—Disney's *The Lion King*. The dam broke during the succeeding ten years: *Hairspray*, *Avenue Q*, *Jersey Boys*, *Spring Awakening*, *In the Heights*, and *Memphis* each took the Tony.

On the opening night of *Spring Awakening*, the evolution was duly noted in a memorable exchange at the party that followed the performance. The journalist Harry Haun, a fixture of such events, approached Bert Fink, an executive at the Rodgers and Hammerstein Organization, and asked, "Do you think we can safely say the Rodgers and Hammerstein era is dead, now that we have a song on Broadway called 'Totally Fucked'?"

Fink, who is quicker on the uptake than most, responded unflappably.

"You know, Harry," he said into Haun's ever-present microphone, "when *The Sound of Music* was trying out in Philadelphia, there actually was a song in it called 'Totally Fucked.' Maria and the children came to the convent in the last scene, and the Mother Abbess explained that the entire place was surrounded by Nazis, and Mary Martin came downstage center and sang this song called 'Totally Fucked' about how they were all done for. But then Oscar realized that they could climb up the mountain to Italy, so they cut the song."

It was a great improvisational moment that left Haun amused, if flat-footed, but the irony was not lost on anyone. By 2006, ten years into the post-*Rent* era, Rodgers and Hammerstein and so many of the theater writers who had trained themselves up on the standards R&H had set were, not to put too fine a point on it, totally fucked.

That didn't mean, however, that the Broadway musical could abandon structurally sound storytelling without paying a price, a point proved, ironically, by *Spring Awakening* itself. Based on the 1891 Frank Wedekind drama of sexual emergence and teen rebellion, the original play had proved scandalous in subject matter but solid in its storytelling. The musical adaptation kept the story in the nineteenth century but told it with a rock score. This is not as revolutionary as it may sound. Rodgers and Hammerstein had written contemporary music for period stories. Contemporary theatergoers were unfazed. They got wrapped up in the story.

Four years later, Michael Mayer, the gifted director who guided *Spring Awakening* through its development, its off-Broadway premiere, and its transfer to Broadway, was back with *American Idiot*. The production itself was more elaborate and imaginative than *Spring Awakening* had been, and the design qualified as among the most ceaselessly inventive ever seen on Broadway. Yet where *Spring Awakening* had won the Tony, run 859 performances, and returned a tidy profit to its investors, *American Idiot*, despite terrific reviews, never caught on in the same way. Unlike *Spring Awakening*, *American Idiot* lacked the one thing that might have given it long-term popularity: a story about people you could care for. Though Mayer tried mightily to humanize its three protagonists, he didn't have a play to work with, only an album. And, like *The Who's Tommy* (based on a double-record album from the vinyl years), which had opened to thunderous reviews but never became a perennial, the original work had a voice but no compelling bones. Without the underlying thing that has always drawn us around the campfire—a real and engaging tale to tell—the rock musical is neither better nor worse off than the Golden Age one. Jonathan Larson, in an admittedly shaggy way, made us care. So did the creators of *Spring Awakening*, not to mention *Wicked* and *Avenue Q*. *Jersey Boys* did it without a new score, just the reliable Top 40 catalog of Frankie Valli and the Four Seasons, but with a good yarn about the group's birth and career as, well, Jersey boys. Without that compelling story line, it would have been a long hill to climb, and the boulder gets heavier as you push it. Rock has probably made it harder to tell a coherent, absorbing story, though by no means impossible.

One form of post-show-tune music spent decades waiting in the shadows for the theater to realize its value.

By employing rap instead of earlier rock forms, *Hamilton* solved the narrative challenge far more elegantly than most previous rock musicals. It was no doubt an enormous challenge to tell the story of the Founding Fathers and the birth of the United States partially in a form that is built out of contemporary street language (Lin-Manuel Miranda spent six years writing it), but at least it's a form steeped in an assertive need to communicate events and attitudes, not just emotions. Lyrically, rap is in some ways more closely tied to the protest songs of Guthrie and Dylan than it is to conventional rock. It wants to talk about life in America as it really is lived on the margins of society and chronicle the struggle to move toward the center of power. And in the United States, "the melting pot where nothing melted," according to the Rabbi in *Angels in America*, that story has always been ours to tell.

Hip-hop and rap have been with us for thirty-five years or more, but as usual, Broadway turned a deaf ear until an artist came along who could marry the two forms. Miranda, whose earlier musical *In the Heights* won the Tony but seemed in some ways like an ambitious warm-up for something else, is a young man with his feet in two different worlds. Born and raised in the Inwood section of Manhattan on the edge of Washington Heights (once heavily Irish but now dominated by Dominican and other Latino populations), he attended Wesleyan University and was captured on video singing "To Life" from *Fiddler on the Roof* to his bride at their wedding. It's hardly surprising that he was drawn to Alexander Hamilton, a Caribbean immigrant who had to fight his way into early American society. Brash and politically insensitive, arrogant and brilliant, sometimes right but never in doubt, Hamilton made a great musical protagonist, part Harold Hill, part Madame Rose, and all American.

*Hamilton* was not the first musical about the founding of the nation; it was at least the fourth. Rodgers and Hart's *Dearest Enemy* dates back to 1925 and contained the pop hit "Here in My Arms," which certainly didn't sound like a Revolutionary War tune. *Arms and the Girl* in 1950 covered the same territory with less success, though it produced a song with the memorable title "A Cow and a Plough and a Frau," which sounds like nothing so much as a '50s show tune. *1776*, produced in 1969, was generally celebrated (it ran for years) as a fresh take on musical theater and heralded for its willingness to tell the story of the creation and signing of the Declaration of Independence in music while ignoring most of the conventions of the form. Much of its score sounds like an updated take on Gilbert and Sullivan and John Philip Sousa, but it clearly has no desire to echo the actual music of the late eighteenth century. Similarly, *Hamilton* tells the story of then in the musical language of now. And while *1776* concerned itself at least to some degree with issues of slavery and the evils of imperialism (it was produced during both the civil rights movement and the Vietnam War), *Hamilton* is preoccupied with issues of immigration, gun violence, race as a defining factor of outsider culture, and the question of who does and does not get to be president. In other words, it's about today, just like all shows tend to be, no matter when they are set. In that sense, it's a direct descendant of *Oklahoma!*

It would probably be foolish to suggest that Broadway is now in for a series of hip-hop musicals. Like *Show Boat* back in 1927, *Hamilton* is unlikely to have many immediate imitators. But in a new way, the musical field is wide open on the street, and anything can happen.

At the moment, this has led to a bifurcated Broadway sound. On the one hand, there continues to be a "theater music" tradition, led by serious—sometimes overserious—composers like Jason Robert Brown, Michael John LaChiusa, Adam Guettel, and others. They are composers in the classic sense, but by and large they haven't achieved repeated or sustained popular success. On the other hand, there are the writers for whom rock, guitar-based and otherwise, is a natural language, if not their only one. Miranda, Alan Menken, Marc Shaiman, Robert Lopez, and their compatriots have created a new Broadway sound that owes less to the Golden Age than to the Top 40. They may not be pop songwriters themselves, but as often as not, pop music is the raw material from which they draw inspiration.

Disney's animated features unit came back to life after a long and depressing dry spell when Menken and Howard Ashman, fresh from *Little Shop of Horrors*, turned out *The Little Mermaid*, structured like a classic Broadway show but sounding like a pop pastiche. Menken and Ashman followed it up with *Beauty and the Beast*, and when the *Times* theater critic Frank Rich described *Beauty* as the best musical of the season even though it was a movie, Disney decided to go into the theater business. The stage version of the film was hardly a critical success, but it ran for thirteen years and three months, by which time Disney had bought and restored the derelict New Amsterdam Theatre on Forty-second Street, which inaugurated the resurrection of Times Square. The premiere production at Disney's new live theater headquarters was *The Lion King*, which Disney fitted out with Broadway talent instead of the theme park practitioners who had staged *Beauty*. *The Lion King* managed to deliver—thanks to its director, Julie Taymor— a level of imagination that overcame everyone, including the critics. It's possible that *The Lion King*, a twenty-first-century show that relies on the most ancient of theatrical techniques—masks and myths—as well as the most technologically modern ones, will outlive everyone who worked on it and its entire original cast. Apparently, it's here to stay, like the Empire State Building.

Much of the score was penned by Elton John—an actual rock icon, not a mere Broadway songwriter in the rock tradition. (To be fair, he's a pianist, not a guitarist.) But his presence on Broadway has led to shows by Sting, Paul Simon, and Cyndi Lauper, who took home a Tony for her *Kinky Boots* score. We've come full circle. For the first half of the twentieth century, theater writers supplied the most potent popular hits. For the second half, rock and rollers supplanted them on the hit parade, while Broadway scores maintained their integrity, but rarely visited the record charts. And in the twenty-first century, the pop writers have invaded Broadway, and the lines have become blurred beyond recognition.

Credit an unwitting Woody Guthrie if you care to; he was a revolutionary in every sense.

All these new writers have led in some ways to a new musical theater. They've taken on the form without having spent time in the trenches, bringing a new energy and a kind of chaos to the process. Figuring out how to tell a meaningful story about compelling characters has not been easy for them, and in some cases it's not even on their agenda. When successful, they've often been guided by veteran book writers, producers, and directors, and still the results are never easy to predict. And the veterans are aging, as veterans do.

Will the classic model for how a Broadway musical is built disappear? Probably not. Will there be more shows like *American Idiot* that ignore the model? Probably, though it's worth noting that these relatively indiscriminately plotted and scored shows, no matter how popular their music, have mostly been commercial disappointments, while shows with rock scores but sturdier plots and characters, like *Spring Awakening* and *Kinky Boots*, have been successful. Even *Mamma Mia!*, which makes no real effort to integrate its book and score, somehow makes audiences care for its characters. Who knows what it all portends? In this relatively uncharted territory, Broadway keeps looking for answers, one energetic, if uncertain, step at a time.

And that's the gazooka.

# Listening to Broadway

I was first introduced to Broadway by original cast albums—well before I saw *Peter Pan* at age almost-six, I could sing "Sit Down, You're Rockin' the Boat" in an adenoidal snuffle that was embarrassing enough for my thoughtful parents to record it on their primitive reel-to-reel tape recorder. Thankfully, after some period of entertaining their party guests with it after I was safely in bed, the tape disappeared. I'm deeply grateful.

Original cast albums—never confused with "soundtracks" back then—took up a good portion of the family record shelf, and many of them actually were albums: booklets with multiple cardboard sleeves, each containing a 78 rpm disc with a single song on each side. That's how I first heard *Oklahoma!* and *Carousel*, even though long-playing records were available beginning in 1948, the year before I was born. *Guys and Dolls* we had on an LP, with that strangely flat sound that seemed to be a hallmark of Decca's early cast recordings. *Brigadoon* we had. And *Finian's Rainbow*. Soon *The Pajama Game* was added, with its racy Peter Arno cover—intriguing even to a five-year-old like me, though I couldn't have said exactly why.

I loved the records. I loved the look of the labels and the cover design almost as much as I loved the songs themselves. They were full of promise. But all of that was a long time ago. What remains today is the music, now available on CD or, more likely, as a download direct to whatever device you play music on. And for Broadway scores, the choices can be bewildering. You can hear *Fiddler on the Roof* in Yiddish, which makes a certain amount of sense, but also in Japanese, which I suppose makes perfect sense if you are Japanese. Since I've referenced and quoted from so many theater songs in this book, I thought there might be some value in listing the recordings that have given me particular pleasure, and a few that have been disappointments. So some thoughts—personal and by no means encyclopedic—about what to listen to seemed a worthwhile addendum. For the most part, as the reader will note, I prefer the original cast album, which tends to capture a show at its freshest. Not all these recordings are in print at the moment, but most can be found—dealers in used recordings abound on the Internet.

I put the shows in the order in which I refer to them in the book, rather like the cast members in the playbill who are listed "in order of appearance." And I began by listing only the shows that I had quoted from, on the theory that you have to draw the line somewhere. The resulting list had a pleasant jumbledness to it—it's neither alphabetical nor chronological and, without the preceding pages as a reference point, would seem to have been made by pulling titles out of a hat. And what's wrong with that? But at the end of the day I had to confront certain realities. I've not quoted a lyric from *South Pacific*, but I have quoted one from *The Wedding Singer*. How can you have a list of cast albums denoting anything useful that includes the latter but not the former? Why *Flora the Red Menace* but not *Bye Bye Birdie*? Why *Annie* but not *Annie Get Your Gun*? So at the end of the list is a second one, including the most obvious shows that are missing from the first. I hope that goes some distance to repairing the whimsical—not to say chaotic—nature of what follows.

## 1. Overture
### *The Music Man*
Sometimes casting is the paramount consideration in which album to choose, and with *The Music Man* the combination of Robert Preston

and Barbara Cook makes the original Broadway cast album the only real choice. A British cast album has some demo tracks performed by the songwriter, Meredith Willson, but if you're going to choose only one, it's Preston and Cook, backed by a host of terrific Broadway second bananas, including David Burns and Pert Kelton. Preston, in particular, was born to make music out of Willson's percussive style, and it's almost impossible to hear the songs in your head without hearing his voice. In fact, it's almost impossible to hear his voice in your head without hearing the rhythmic alarm about trouble in River City. Watch him in an old Western and see if you can keep the sound of *The Music Man* from pleasantly intruding.

Originally recorded by Capitol, a label that never captured the spirit of an overall show, as well as by Columbia (where the producer Goddard Lieberson and, later, Thomas Z. Shepard, understood exactly how to make you feel you were attending the actual show), it nonetheless is indispensable.

### Sunday in the Park with George
Again, the original Broadway cast recording is the one to have. There are two different London versions, but Mandy Patinkin and Bernadette Peters, backed by an incandescently transparent orchestration by Michael Starobin, give performances as memorable on the recording as they did onstage. The longtime Sondheim music director Paul Gemignani conducts with dramatic precision. The album was issued by RCA, where Thomas Shepard had moved from Columbia in the mid-'70s, and reflects Shepard's gift for theatrical record production. The relatively tiny band (eleven instruments) helps create a unique musical palette.

## 2. Curtain Up, Light the Lights
### A Funny Thing Happened on the Way to the Forum
The original cast album is another case of Capitol having the right performers yet not quite presenting the magic of the show on the recording. But what performances! Zero Mostel, Jack Gilford, David Burns, Ron Holgate, and John Carradine deliver in a way that brushes aside most of the deficiencies of the recording production. The album makes you

wish that these kinds of vaudevillians still existed. And the orchestrations (by Irwin Kostal and Sid Ramin) are remarkable—eccentric and joyfully off-kilter. The revival, which starred Nathan Lane, is also fine—it's much more complete, Lane is brilliant, Lewis J. Stadlen delightfully channels David Burns, and the new orchestration by Jonathan Tunick is certainly worth hearing. But the original captures the madness of that first production more completely, even on a less complete album.

### Mack and Mabel

Robert Preston again, this time with Bernadette Peters. The original cast album plays like a hit show all by itself. It is perhaps the most perfect of all disguises of a musical that got almost unanimously bad reviews and closed quickly. You'd never know it from the recording. There are two London recordings, one of a concert performance and one of an actual production, and to be fair, Preston's voice isn't ideal for the two ballads that Mack sings, but he's just so damn convincing. And Peters's versions of "Look What Happened to Mabel" and "Time Heals Everything" are so good (as are the songs) that it feels like the show should have run a season on those numbers alone. No such luck.

### Oklahoma!

With the exception of a rarely heard recording of Marc Blitzstein's *The Cradle Will Rock*, this 1943 original cast album was the first one ever made that was intended to preserve the majority of one score performed by the original performers. It's historic; and it's hard to deny the power of Alfred Drake, the modern musical's first great leading man. But I confess that I turn to the London cast album made in 1998 with Hugh Jackman in the role when I want to hear this score. Jackman isn't the singer Drake was, and the orchestrations and the dance music are new, which I'm prejudiced against, but the cast dusts off a lot of the antique patina that this show sometimes suffers from, and the album includes portions of the score that the original, which was limited to what could be made to fit on a set of 78 rpm discs, omitted. It's fun to hear them side by side, actually, and there's a third album, from a Broadway revival in 1979, that's not bad either. Surprisingly, the movie soundtrack, which I'm also prejudiced against, is quite good, if a little lush.

## Gypsy

This one is a tie for me, though I must confess to having been a producer of the Patti LuPone production and therefore have something of a rooting interest. The original is Merman being Merman, which creates a certain kind of joy, an explosive energy, and a real sense of a recording capturing what the show must have been. Credit Goddard Lieberson and Columbia for that. Also, Merman—an astounding singer in her way—is the only Rose I've ever heard sing the whole-note triplets that accompany the title phrase in "Everything's Coming Up Roses" the way they were written. Who wrote them is a matter of conjecture, with Sondheim, the lyricist, sometimes gently suggesting that he put them in the composer Jule Styne's brain, or possibly in his manuscript. They create such tension and power that I've never understood why other actresses shy away from them, but Merman's the only one I've ever heard really embrace them (though they are a thrilling feature of the famous overture).

On the other hand, Merman was not a great actress, and the tempi on the album are relaxed by today's standards—we're used to everything going faster now. So Patti LuPone's performance on the 2008 cast recording is very much worth having, and in many ways, the album may be every bit the equal of the original. LuPone is a great musical theater actress, and the alarming drama of Rose's character is alive on the recording. And the 2008 recording features Laura Benanti, who was the definitive Louise, and Boyd Gaines as Herbie, who actually gets to sing more than Jack Klugman does with Merman.

On the Merman version, Sondheim speaks the line "You ain't gettin' 88 cents from me, Rose!" in the middle of "Some People." Not to be outdone, Arthur Laurents took on the tiny role on the LuPone incarnation. Neither of them is a great actor. Take your pick, or listen to them both. There are also recordings of productions featuring Angela Lansbury and Bernadette Peters, and Bette Midler's TV version, but none meets the standards of the Merman and LuPone recordings. All right, go ahead and shoot.

## Company

The original cast album begins with the sound of a busy signal, an idea that seemed amazingly innovative in 1970. Anyone not around back in those days will be puzzled. Does anyone still recognize a busy signal? *Company* was the show, and the album, that reawakened a generation of people to the possibilities of the musical theater—that it could treat angst, anger, and the frantic and unsustainable pace of life in New York, and do so with honesty in a musical voice that incorporated the sounds of life as we were living it, not always so happily. Not surprisingly, having captured the moment brilliantly, it was subject to feeling dated as soon as the moment passed. And today, everything about it feels of its period, just the way a well-reconstructed operetta score of the '20s does. But the recording is a vivid time capsule of a great score bursting with ideas. And there's Elaine Stritch conquering "The Ladies Who Lunch," so why would you listen to any other? D. A. Pennebaker's film documentary *Company: Original Cast Album* is required viewing as well, perfectly capturing the recording session and giving us a portrait of a group of ace theater professionals at work, and at the top of their game.

There is an oddity about the recording, which you will probably notice: Dean Jones opened the show in the starring role, and recorded the album, but was quite quickly replaced by Larry Kert, a superior singer. When the show went to London, Kert rerecorded the vocals and his voice replaced Jones's on the London cast album, which was otherwise identical to the New York recording. The currently available CD (or download) includes Kert's version of "Being Alive" as a bonus track but otherwise features Jones.

## A Chorus Line

As with *Company*, the original cast album of *A Chorus Line* screams '70s, but in a different way. Some of Marvin Hamlisch's tunes lean toward the pop sounds of the day, and the writing isn't as distinguished as in *Company*, though the show was wildly more popular. But the album captures Michael Bennett's propulsive concept of a dance audition in progress. The group of young performers who made names for themselves in the show are featured in ways that show them off at their best. And although he can't be heard on the album, it's worth a tip of the hat to Hans Spialek, who orchestrated many of the hits of Rodgers and Hart, Cole Porter, and others in the '20s and '30s. At age eighty-two, he worked on *A Chorus Line*, copying out parts for the orchestra players from the orchestrations by Billy Byers, Hershy Kay, and Jonathan Tunick. It was his last Broadway job and his only known contribution to a rock-influenced score.

## 3. The Wizard and I

### My Fair Lady

There are a lot of recordings in various languages, though few are readily available. The original—on Columbia, produced by Lieberson—is the gold standard. It gives us Rex Harrison, Julie Andrews, and the great music hall star Stanley Holloway performing in a style that was already dying away in the mid-'50s when he took on the leading comic role of Alfred P. Doolittle. Originally released in mono, it was re-recorded in stereo when the show opened in London, but the performances are fresher on the mono version. Look no further.

### Hamilton

Probably the most kinetically exciting original cast album ever made. Lin-Manuel Miranda's score is a peppery stew inspired not only by hip-hop but by jazz, pop-opera, the (musical) British Invasion, and Motown, among other genres, with a recurring Afro-Caribbean feel throughout much of it. The references, mini-quotes, and tips of the hat to other sources never stop, yet the whole thing is somehow completely original. Beautifully produced by Amir "Questlove" Thompson and Tariq "Black Thought" Trotter, founding members of the Roots, it has sensational clarity, with vocals out front and the most extraordinary set of arrangements and orchestrations—by Alex Lacamoire—since Jonathan Tunick's *Follies* charts. Themes appear and reappear, so that the entire story is told in a layered, complex way that might threaten to become confusing in other hands but never does here. While the album is no substitute for the show, it nonetheless is a complete experience on its own, a little like being shot out of a cannon. It runs almost two and a half hours and bears the distinction of having been released in every format, from vinyl to iTunes download. Obviously an event, and it earns the right to be one.

### Little Shop of Horrors

I was a producer of the Broadway revival of Howard Ashman and Alan Menken's breakout musical, but I confess that I prefer the off-Broadway album. The show's hand-to-mouth style is perfectly captured by the tiny band and a cast of unknowns-about-to-be-known. And Ellen Greene is definitive as Audrey. The Broadway cast album features some wonderful performers, but it lacks the scrappy, poverty-row authenticity of the original. And it lacks Greene.

### The Producers

There's a soundtrack album of the movie, but the original cast is the only one to have—Nathan Lane and Matthew Broderick were so identified with the roles of Max and Leo that the show had trouble sustaining itself without them. Mel Brooks's score, astutely dressed up by the musical supervisor, Glen Kelly (Brooks reportedly sang the songs a cappella into a tape recorder), is surprisingly delightful, and the performances couldn't be better. Not a great contribution to the canon, exactly, but a really good time.

### Little Me

This is, for me, Cy Coleman's best score (*Sweet Charity*, I know, I know, and *City of Angels* and *On the Twentieth Century*), and it features a great set of comedy lyrics by the vastly underrated Carolyn Leigh. Sid Caesar and a cadre of supporting clowns bring a great and now long-lost kind of theatrical energy to the whole record, and Nancy Andrews and Virginia Martin share one of the show's only sentimental moments, the charming "Here's to Us." Swen Swenson's "I've Got Your Number" was the hit, but Caesar, and Coleman, and Leigh's ways with comedy pastiche were the joys of the event. Would that more of the dance music had been recorded, but this show, like *Forum*, presented the last great days of vaudeville comedy on Broadway, and it's worth hearing. Interestingly, there is also a British album, which demonstrates the complete bewilderment of the English in the face of this kind of material.

### Flora the Red Menace

Kander and Ebb's first Broadway score as a team, Liza Minnelli's Tony-winning Broadway debut (at eighteen!), and a charming, lightweight score. The show flopped, and deservedly so, but it was full of promise, quickly fulfilled by *Cabaret*. The album is adorable.

### Funny Girl

There are many devotees of the movie soundtrack, but I prefer the more compact (and brilliant) Ralph Burns orchestrations for the cast album. Jule Styne's music for the first half of the show speaks volumes about his early days as a jazz and barrelhouse pianist. Then the famous ballads start to stack up. Streisand is young and not the least bit self-indulgent yet, and it makes for a great show album. The overture, which does not quite equal *Gypsy*'s, was apparently put together in secret by Styne and Burns, who pretended that they hadn't figured it out until the last minute so that the director-choreographer, Jerome Robbins (who had stepped in in Philadelphia), wouldn't have time to try to change it. A contentious show, this one, with lots of screaming going on behind the scenes, but an undeniably great score and a terrific album, especially for Capitol.

### Camelot

Take your pick of the London or New York cast album. Pomp and circumstance and some lovely songs carried off with great earnestness. And a bit of a bore, I think.

### West Side Story

There are many recordings to choose from—the original cast, a studio album featuring real opera voices, another conducted by Bernstein, the film soundtrack, and more. As usual, I cling to the original cast album (Columbia and Lieberson at their best), but of course the soundtrack is what became famous, and it has its many fans. I'm always uncomfortable with those metasize Hollywood orchestras playing show music, even Bernstein's, but I can understand those who swoon over it. It has grandeur, though I'm not sure that's a quality that benefits *West Side Story*. As for the studio cast albums, the most peculiar features Kiri Te Kanawa and another presents the Italian tenor Vittorio Grigolo. Neither sounds comfortable and neither recording sounds like idiomatic theater music. And, as is almost always the case with "studio" albums, there isn't a whiff of an actual theatrical production to be found, because there was none. Somehow the original cast albums, even when featuring inferior singers, always seem to carry a different energy because, when the recording is being made, the performers are playing the roles nightly in a particular style in a particular version of the show. Without all that rehearsal and all that performance energy behind them, even superior singers never seem to connect to the material in the same way, which is hardly surprising. This doesn't make studio albums unworthy, just usually disappointing.

### Annie

The cast album does the show proud. This is a score that is sniffed at by some, but I find it irresistible—charming, tuneful, and actually touching. It's light material, but it celebrates an American spirit in an unashamed way. Dorothy Loudon finally broke out as Miss Hannigan, Andrea McArdle became the subject of endless parody and ridicule, which couldn't stop her, or "Tomorrow," from becoming ubiquitous, and Reid Shelton sings Daddy Warbucks beautifully. It's all on the record.

## 4. If I Loved You

### Carousel

This is tough. I count nine cast recordings of *Carousel*, including one, like *Fiddler*, in Japanese. The original cast album from 1945 features the incomparable John Raitt singing "Soliloquy," and the equally heartbreaking Jan Clayton singing "What's the Use of Wond'rin?," but it leaves out most of the musical part of the bench scene—the limitations of those 78 rpm discs again. The 1965 revival cast, from a production at Lincoln Center, gives you the bench scene and an older John Raitt, but no Jan Clayton. Probably the finest production of the show itself, Nick Hytner's astonishing 1992 staging seen first in London and then at Lincoln Center, featured the best-acted Billy and Julie ever recorded but, alas, the least vocally impressive. On the other hand, Audra McDonald played Carrie Pipperidge in the Lincoln Center run, and she can certainly sing it—almost too well. And the two studio cast albums, one from 1955 and one from 1987, are all about singing—no acting required or demonstrated. Name your poison. For one of the greatest of all musical theater scores, there is no definitive recording.

### The New Moon

New York City Center's Encores! series presented this Sigmund Romberg operetta in 2003, which occasioned the first full recording of a score that typifies the operettas of the first part of the twentieth century. There are a few incomplete recordings from earlier decades, but if you want to hear something that likely resembles what a Broadway operetta sounded like in 1927, this is essential listening. Although it features a couple of opera singers, Rodney Gilfry and Brandon Jovanovich, it has no scent of the opera house about it—it's antique Broadway. The melodies are almost foolishly lush, the chorus often enters for no discernible reason, and the whole thing is blissfully idiotic, beginning with the leading lady's declaration that she wants to live bravely and freely like one of those wooden figurehead goddesses that adorn the bows of eighteenth-century schooners. *"Let me be like the girl on the prow!"* Christiane Noll sings, ecstatically. The whole thing is almost too good to be true.

### Guys and Dolls

Two choices here, both good. The original cast, featuring that flat Decca sound, also features Viviane Blaine doing "Adelaide's Lament," Stubby Kaye singing "Sit Down, You're Rocking the Boat," and the tone-deaf but wonderful Sam Levene joining Blaine for "Sue Me." On the other hand, the 1992 revival, which featured Nathan Lane and Faith Prince, matched the original performers and in some ways outpaced them. It contains "Adelaide's Second Lament," which is absent from the first album, and a saxophone solo under the dialogue before "My Time of Day" is played by Benny Goodman alumnus Red Press; it's worth hearing. I don't think you can live without both recordings. There are others as well, but you can live without those.

### Into the Woods

The original cast album is terrific, and the current issue of it contains bonus tracks—demo recordings and the like—but the soundtrack recording isn't bad either. The score has aged beautifully. Back in 1987, it sounded to some as if Sondheim was reluctant to finish a thought or put a proper button on a number, but in the intervening years, this has proved to be just another example of his restlessness needing other ears to catch up. Bernadette Peters is in top form, and Joanna Gleason gives a memorable contemporary twist to the role of the Baker's Wife that comes across on the recording. There is a revival album featuring a lovely performance by Laura Benanti as Cinderella, but overall, the original is better.

### City of Angels

The composer Cy Coleman made two great personnel decisions when he wrote this send-up of Raymond Chandler–style noir thrillers: he hired the great jazz arranger Billy Byers to orchestrate, and the tight harmony group Manhattan Transfer's music director, Yaron Gershovsky, to do the vocal arrangements. The result is a cast album that actually sounds like jazzmen had their hands on it; the ballads have the chromatic quality of Ellington and Strayhorn, and much of it sounds a little like a movie soundtrack from RKO or Warner Bros. in their best black-and-white years. It's an acquired taste, but I had no trouble acquiring it. And James Naughton, on the original cast album, gets the rhythms and wry, detached attitude of a Philip Marlowe or a Sam Spade perfectly. The show—like its score—is a genuine original.

### The Wedding Singer

Why is The Wedding Singer a part of this collection while similar, and in some cases more commercially successful, pop-rock shows like Legally Blonde and Kinky Boots are absent? The simple reason is that I worked on The Wedding Singer, and I'm the one with the pen. But in truth, I think the sweet, often funny score from the composer Matt Sklar and the lyricist Chad Beguelin is more delicate and more fully realized than the scores for many more successful shows. It's under-appreciated, though no one would qualify it as a masterwork.

### The Book of Mormon

The original cast album captures the spirit, the performances, and the sheer skill of what is probably the most expert musical comedy of recent years. Along with *The Producers* and *Hairspray, Mormon* represents the tradition that *How to Succeed in Business* and *Forum* held aloft during the '60s, and *Guys and Dolls* and *Kiss Me, Kate* represented in the '50s. If you track the progress of this kind of musical comedy, you can see tastes expanding (or collapsing) from the witty to the sly to the vulgar to the downright obscene, and it's an enjoyable ride, assuming you have broad standards—or none. *Mormon*, whatever one may think of its morals, makes a wonderful album.

## 5. Put On Your Sunday Clothes
### *Li'l Abner*

We all have our guilty pleasures, and this is mine. Both the original cast album and the film soundtrack are first-rate, and while Al Capp's comic strip characters may seem funny only to people old enough to have been around when the strip was in its prime in the mid-'50s, there's no gainsaying Gene de Paul's tuneful score or Johnny Mercer's offhandedly brilliant comic lyrics. You can hardly top the villainous galoot of the piece introducing himself as follows:

> *Step aside for Earthquake McGoon,*
> *Bustin' out all over like June.*
> *I stands on the corner*
> *Enormous and ornery,*
> *Makin' the fairer sex swoon.*

In addition to a good in-joke about *Carousel* (not a show the denizens of Dogpatch would likely be familiar with, although audiences at *Li'l Abner* certainly were), Mercer makes a wonderful rhyming mouthful out of "I stands on the corner, enormous and ornery": "corner" with the beginning of "enormous," and "corner / E——" with "ornery." Earthquake McGoon appears to be a hillbilly Ogden Nash.

## 6. Bushwhacking 1
### *Cabaret*

Kander and Ebb's breakout score has been much recorded—seven times that I'm aware of—and at least three of them are worth hearing.

The original cast features the excitement of a groundbreaking if imperfect show, and—in 1966—the beginning of Hal Prince's reign as the most innovative director on Broadway. Don Walker's flavorful orchestrations are memorable, as are the performances of Lotte Lenya and Jack Gilford, both toward the end of their careers. And let's not forget Joel Gray!

The first-rate soundtrack album features Liza Minnelli, and the revised version of the show, codirected by Sam Mendes and Rob Marshall, got a good recording featuring Alan Cumming and Natasha Richardson in 1998. The score itself is always a pleasure to encounter, in whatever form, bristling with audacity, with welcome doses of sentiment along the way.

## 7. Bushwhacking 2

### Sweeney Todd, the Demon Barber of Fleet Street

Another show of which there are at least seven recordings, with more on the way, no doubt. The double-CD original cast recording is flawless, and the only one you'll ever need, though *Sweeney* fanatics enjoy comparing it with other productions, including the director John Doyle's cut-down version in which the actors play their own instruments. But the original—with Angela Lansbury and Len Cariou—is the only one I ever reach for.

### It's a Bird . . . It's a Plane . . . It's Superman

Eddie Sauter, who spent the mid-'50s co-leading the wildly eccentric jazz aggregation known as the Sauter-Finegan Orchestra, drew the orchestration assignment for this Hal Prince–directed oddball of a show, and Sauter's work is reason enough to own the album. The show features two overtures (the one before the second act can hardly be called an entr'acte) and about as much orchestral wit and invention as a Broadway musical can handle. The score by Charles Strouse and Lee Adams is their best after *Bye Bye Birdie* (*Golden Boy* runs a close third), and Jack Cassidy is in a class by himself as the evil columnist loosely based on Walter Winchell, while Linda Lavin made her Broadway debut singing the show's only even mildly well-known song, "You've Got Possibilities." A simple listen to the first overture may make you want to pick up a Sauter-Finegan recording as well. It's always worth revisiting "Doodletown Fifers."

## 9. Adelaide's Lament
### *The Light in the Piazza*

John Kander, who has written some of the most irresistible and memorable tunes of the last half century, once said that he loved Adam Guettel's far-from-easy score for *The Light in the Piazza* so much that he'd "like to bathe in it." That's high praise, imaginatively put, from a man of taste and talent, and it makes a certain amount of sense. The score feels liquid somehow, and it is beautifully represented on its cast album—a translucent-sounding, delicate recording featuring Victoria Clark *and* Kelli O'Hara, two of Broadway's premier voices, with appearances by Sarah Uriarte Berry and Patti Cohenour to boot; it's a boatload of wonderful sopranos, and a justly celebrated score, handsomely preserved.

## 11. La Vie Bohème
### *Rent*

Jonathan Larson's score—and the show that contained it—created such a sensation when it was first presented in 1996 that it took years before you could really listen to it as just another show album, which is what it is. There is some terrific writing, and some hammered-together chunks (Larson died just as he was completing the work), and a host of young voices who were making their first marks in the theater with this show. That spirit of reckless abandon is captured on the album, but for a score that perfectly captured its time and place it has, like *Company*, become something of a period piece. There's also a movie soundtrack, but why would you?

## 17. I Thought You Did It for Me, Momma
### *Fiddler on the Roof*

Another much-recorded score—I count five obtainable versions as of this moment. But why wouldn't you go with Zero Mostel and the original cast? This and the original *Forum* recording preserve two great performances by a unique theater star who never flourished in any other medium. And the score, by Jerry Bock and Sheldon Harnick, is ageless and deeply idiomatic. "If I Were a Rich Man" is as good a performance of as good a song as has been written for Broadway.

## Caroline, or Change

This show had trouble convincing the critics—which puts it in a category with *Porgy and Bess*, *Pal Joey*, *Follies*, and a handful of others that were so fearless in their convictions and made of such inventive materials that it took years for the world to catch up. Sadly, the world has yet to catch up to *Caroline* in the same way as the others. It's rarely performed in major productions, and rarely written about. But it's a masterpiece, and Jeanine Tesori and Tony Kushner's score is well captured on this 2004 cast album. As with *The Light in the Piazza*, the score is not easy and hardly replete with what we used to call "take-home tunes." But it's galvanic where *Piazza* is full of grace, and Tonya Pinkins is a force of nature in the title role. Chuck Cooper's performance as a city bus (that's right) burdened down by carrying the news of JFK's assassination is also a memorable moment in a score that is full of them.

## The King and I

This is among the all-time champions in numbers of recordings; there are twelve that I can find. A lot of them are good. Donna Murphy starred in a successful production in 1996, and there's even a cast album of an animated version. Gertrude Lawrence and Yul Brynner appear on the original, which—rarely for me—is not my favorite. It sounds shallow (Decca again) for a deeply opulent show, and Lawrence, who was apparently an incandescent performer in her prime, doesn't have much of a voice left—she was ill and died during the original run of the show. There's a Barbara Cook version and a Julie Andrews, but for me the most satisfying so far is the Thomas Shepard–produced recording of a revival that starred Constance Towers and Brynner in 1977. It captures the theatricality of the show (Columbia again) and contains just enough dialogue and connective tissue to make you feel like you've been there.

## Hairspray

There's a soundtrack, of course, but I much prefer the original cast. Marissa Jaret Winokur is incredibly winning as Tracy Turnblad, and

Harvey Fierstein is, well, Harvey Fierstein. A singer he is not, but few entertainers come across better on a cast album. He's like a gay Jimmy Durante. Marc Shaiman and Scott Wittman's score sounds as fresh as paint considering that it's made up of clever pastiches of early-'60s pop songs. But this isn't *Grease*—it has a subversive streak, and brains. And the final song, "You Can't Stop the Beat," is miraculous in its ability to sustain the resolution of all those subplots without losing energy.

## 18. You Can't Stop the Beat
### *The Ziegfeld Follies of 1936*
Michael Strunsky, executive director of the Ira and Leonore Gershwin Trusts, agreed to have the orchestrations of this rare complete *Follies* score restored to mint condition, under the supervision of the trust's Mark Trent Goldberg and Encores! founding music director Rob Fisher. Encores! then produced the show itself, which proved somewhat problematic, as the sketches were dated and some of the casting was imperfect. But the production got recorded, and the recording is sensational. Like *The New Moon*, it's a trip in a time machine to a period of very sophisticated "disposable" entertainment with great sheen and wit. There are a couple of forgotten gems of the period, like "My Red-Letter Day" and "Words Without Music," and one standard—"I Can't Get Started." The whole thing is an opulent trip back to the days when you would have applauded the show at 11:00 p.m. and then gone upstairs to the roof garden for a champagne supper and . . . the Midnight Frolic. Who stepped in and put an end to all that? It doesn't seem fair.

### *She Loves Me*
The original cast album, issued on a double LP by MGM (a company that didn't do much in the way of Broadway albums), is a joy from start to finish. It's arguably Bock and Harnick's best score, featuring Barbara Cook singing "Ice Cream" and the artlessly irresistible Barbara Baxley delivering one of the best story songs ever written, "A Trip to the Library." Jack Cassidy, playing the cad, has a lounge-lizard charm, and the orchestrator, Don Walker, makes great use of the accordion since the show was set in Budapest, and played at the Eugene O'Neill, where the pit wasn't big enough to accommodate a grand piano with the

rest of the band. I take a deep breath before writing these words, but this, I think, is a perfect cast album.

## The Missing Links

Acknowledging the eccentricity of the above list of show albums, I was easily able to find an additional forty or so titles that deserve attention. But writing about all of them seemed excessive and a little self-indulgent, so I've limited myself to a list of twenty that simply can't be ignored, even though they are not quoted in the book.

### Annie Get Your Gun

There are twelve different recordings I can find, but Merman is who you really want to hear sing this score. The original is fine, but I actually prefer the 1966 Lincoln Center production. She was way too old to play the role by this time, but you'd never know it by the recording, and it includes "An Old Fashioned Wedding," which Berlin wrote especially so that she'd have something new to sing in an old show.

### Brigadoon

Well suited to the Hollywood treatment—it's a great romantic fantasy—this is one of the few where I would choose the soundtrack over the original cast, but both are pleasurable. There are also at least two studio albums that feature virtually the complete score, one of them with Rebecca Luker, who, after Barbara Cook in her prime, has the most seductive soprano in the history of modern-day Broadway. If you love this score, it's thrilling to hear her sing it.

### Bye Bye Birdie

The original cast album features Dick Van Dyke and Chita Rivera and some great orchestrations by Robert "Red" Ginzler, including four flutes playing behind "Put On a Happy Face." This is the orchestration that made a young jazz cat named Jonathan Tunick decide he wanted to work on Broadway, and that was good news. Ginzler died young, just as he was emerging as a Broadway powerhouse, but the work he left behind—*Birdie*, *How to Succeed*, *Wildcat*, and many parts of *Gypsy*, just for starters—is always distinctive and often thrilling.

## Candide

A Bernstein masterpiece—the score, not the show—and the original cast has great energy and wit, though it's pretty highbrow. The stripped-down 1974 Hal Prince production is much hipper, though it's hard not to long for that great big orchestra. They make good side-by-side listening, each representing an era. It's Broadway taking itself very seriously in the '50s versus Broadway trying really hard to embrace hippiedom in the '70s. And the winner is . . .

## Chicago

Kander and Ebb doing Bob Fosse's cynical but brilliant bidding. The original cast album is great, but so is the recording of the revival-that-threatens-to-run-forever. Take your pick. The original may be the better album, but the show in the '70s seemed too cynical for words and was only a moderate success. Then the revival happened, opening right on top of the O. J. Simpson verdict, and suddenly the material seemed right in line with the times. Fosse, it turned out, knew exactly where American jurisprudence was going; he just got there ahead of schedule.

## Damn Yankees

Who knows what delights the team of Richard Adler and Jerry Ross would have turned out if Ross hadn't died at twenty-nine, right after this show opened. This and their debut, *The Pajama Game*, were icons of the '50s, and deservedly so. The original cast album, with Gwen Verdon and Ray Walston, is the one to get. The two Adler and Ross shows were like self-contained '50s hit parades—a ballad, a Latin number, a cowboy number (in *The Pajama Game*, anyhow), a sexy dance specialty, a comedy novelty item—you might as well have been listening to the radio.

## Finian's Rainbow

The original cast album is wonderfully seductive, but the sound is better and the score more complete and better sung on the 2010 revival album. Take your pick—it's a crazily inventive, witty, and romantic score, certainly Burton Lane's best Broadway work (he wrote some terrific movie songs as well), and the lyrics, by Yip Harburg, are in a class by themselves.

### Follies

The original cast album was mangled by Capitol, which squeezed a very long score onto a single LP, making incomprehensible cuts and depriving us of the chance to hear complete versions of some great performances. There have been several more complete albums made since, which are better, but it's depressing that the original cast—especially Dorothy Collins and John McMartin—didn't get to give us the genuine article. As is the case with *Carousel*, there's lots to choose from, but no definitive version. The British cast album has some alternative songs, but none better than the ones written for Broadway.

### Hello, Dolly!

Jerry Herman's breakout score (with some ghosted help from Bob Merrill and a title for one song supplied by Strouse and Adams) was—though no one mentioned it at the time—the perfect antidote to the Kennedy assassination, which had taken place only seven weeks earlier. As the national mood staggered under the weight of the tragedy, *Dolly!* reaffirmed that Americans were entitled to regain a sunny disposition and have fun, even though, under the surface, we were a changed people.

There are eight versions that I'm aware of. I'd take the original, which features not only Carol Channing but also David Burns and the almost-impossible-to-listen-to but beloved Charles Nelson Reilly. But I reserve a special affection for the Pearl Bailey version. She's not Dolly, but she's Pearl, and that's worth hearing, as is Cab Calloway in the Burns role. The British cast album features Mary Martin, who brings a nice humanity to the role, not that it was written to feature any. But it's quite lovely to hear it.

### How to Succeed in Business Without Really Trying

The original cast features Robert Morse and Rudy Vallee, and, even more pleasurable, Red Ginzler's mind-bending orchestrations. Listen to how he gets into "Brotherhood of Man" in the overture and you'll know what an orchestrator can do. The score itself is angular and edgy in a way that suggests Frank Loesser was trying to get even with a newly cynical Broadway after the failure of his bucolic (and slightly anemic) *Greenwillow*. But on its own terms, *How to Succeed* is a terrific, brassy score, and Morse and Vallee seem to be having a blast.

### Kiss Me, Kate
It's hard to top Alfred Drake and Patricia Morison in the original, but the 1999 revival starring Brian Stokes Mitchell and Marin Mazzie gives the show quite a ride. The soundtrack album is interesting too; this was a rare Broadway film adaptation released in 3-D and recorded in stereo in the early '50s. The soundtrack album is to some degree a celebration of the MGM Orchestra, with lots of overflowing underscoring, in that midcentury Hollywood style that some love and that certainly defines an era. And the soundtrack has Bob Fosse, Bobby Van, and Tommy Rall accompanying Ann Miller on "Tom, Dick or Harry." That's kind of historic, too.

### A Little Night Music
Virtuosic without being showy, as lovely as it is low-key, written entirely in variations of three-quarter time, this has been better sung on recordings other than the original cast, but never better performed. Glynis Johns is heartbreakingly sexy, tart, and maternal at the same time, and all the elements—Tunick's orchestrations, the recording production (shared by Lieberson and Shepard), and the shimmering score itself—are beautifully represented. There's a movie soundtrack if you dare, and at least two London cast recordings, but none of them delivers this kind of pleasure.

### Mame
Jerry Herman's follow-up to *Dolly* is more machine than animal in most respects, but it's a swell score and very well delivered on the original cast album. And when Angela Lansbury and Bea Arthur declare themselves "Bosom Buddies," there's not much to do but smile.

### The Most Happy Fella

Frank Loesser at his best, Columbia and Lieberson at their best, and one of the masterworks of Broadway. Virtually the whole show is on the original cast CD offering, and it's a spectacular experience, gorgeously sung by Robert Weede, Jo Sullivan, and the greatest of all cult belters, Susan Johnson. Johnson should have been a star, but after playing the girl in the second couple here, she was elevated gradually to leading roles in a trio of flops and faded away. By the mid-'80s, she was teaching machine knitting in a well-appointed mobile home outside of San Diego. She made a glorious late appearance in a production of *Follies* in Long Beach, and then faded away again. But her voice in all the shows she appeared in—*Brigadoon, Donnybrook!, Whoop-Up,* and *Oh Captain!*—is immediately recognizable and a joy.

### On the Town

Bernstein's first Broadway show, staged by George Abbott and choreographed by Jerome Robbins, is brash, busy, even obstreperous in its ambition to do something new, noisy, jazzy, and classical. It wasn't recorded when it was produced in 1944, but in 1960, after the film version had taken on a life of its own, the composer conducted it for Columbia, with the lyricists Betty Comden and Adolph Green and the comedian Nancy Walker all repeating the roles they played in the original. The resulting album is a treasure, and includes not only the song score (a lot of it jettisoned for the film) but also much of the dance music, which is thrilling.

### The Pajama Game

Adler and Ross's Broadway debut, and it's impressively fun. George Abbott and Jerome Robbins shared the directing credit—the beginning of Robbins's ascent as a musical theater director. John Raitt sings wonderfully on the original cast album, and you may be forgiven for wondering if Frank Loesser was the ghostwriter of "A New Town Is a Blue Town," Raitt's opening number. Adler and Ross were among his protégés, and it sure sounds a lot like "My Time of Day" from *Guys and Dolls* to me.

## Pal Joey

Along with *Show Boat*, this 1940 Rodgers and Hart entry can lay a claim to modernity before *Oklahoma!*, with its antihero, its frank view of gigolo sex and the quid pro quo that goes with it, and its dream ballet (though there had already been a few of those by 1940). There are a handful of good recordings of the jazzy, noirish score. My favorite is a 1951 studio cast album featuring Harold Lang and Vivienne Segal, but it's worth hearing Elaine Stritch sing "Zip" on the revival album from 1952, and the Encores! version from 1995 probably sounds more like 1940 than either of them. The album that purports to be the soundtrack from the Frank Sinatra movie is really a cobbled-together collection of other Sinatra recordings mixed with some of the songs as they actually appeared in the film. I'd stay away.

## Porgy and Bess

The original cast album on Decca includes a very limited selection from the score, though it's great to hear Todd Duncan and Anne Brown, the original Porgy and Bess. They sing it in a style that now feels somewhat antiquated, but it does put you in the time machine. The 1977 recording of the Houston Grand Opera's restoration of the entire opera is magnificent, and there are other good complete opera house recordings. But the Houston one, which was directed by the Broadwayite Jack O'Brien, sounds like the real deal to me. As with *The Most Happy Fella* (see above) and *Show Boat* (see below), you can take the whole thrilling ride in an evening in your living room or on a long drive, and emerge restored by the sheer greatness of the achievement.

## Show Boat

There are dozens of choices with various virtues and shortcomings. Faced with the bewildering conflict of ancient authenticity, modern streamlining, and everything in between, I always choose the 1988 studio cast album that delivers, on three CDs, virtually the entire show. It's badly acted by opera singers and squarely conducted by John McGlinn, but it features the more or less original orchestrations, and the cumulative effect, for all its flaws, if you can forgive them, is overwhelming.

You can hear the stunning ambition of Hammerstein's first real attempt to make something completely new in the theater, and Jerome Kern's unending inventiveness and melodic gift; I dare you to get out of the way. And Alec Wilder, who wrote the first great study of the American songbook, *American Popular Song*, is right about one thing: the verse of "Can't Help Lovin' Dat Man" is more interesting than the chorus, even though it's almost never heard. Give a listen here and see if you don't agree.

## South Pacific

Hammerstein's other epic, this time with Richard Rodgers. Unsurprisingly, there are many albums, but only two real choices: the original, with Mary Martin and Ezio Pinza, and the Lincoln Center revival, with Kelli O'Hara and Paulo Szot. The latter is more complete; the former has Martin and Pinza delivering two great star turns. But both are beautifully sung and played. The others range from the movie soundtrack—not for me—to various "complete" studio cast recordings, all of them dutiful and unexciting. Both the original cast and the Lincoln Center versions have the energy of actual theatrical performance—and there's no substitute for that.

# Acknowledgments

Over the past thirty years or so, hundreds of theater artists and craftspeople have been my tutors. Some are quoted in the text of this book, but many more are not. There is no possible way to name them all, though I am grateful to each one, more than I can say. Their wisdom, expertise, and passion appear on every page of this book. Without them, I'd still be staring at old issues of *Variety*, wondering what a "tuner" is.

As for the book itself, I owe the greatest of thanks to my editor, Sarah Crichton, who was a first-rate cheerleader and eagle-eyed reader; a great source of advice literary, structural, and practical; and a wonderful person to have lunch with. The staff at Farrar, Straus and Giroux, particularly Marsha Sasmor but also the production editor Scott Auerbach, the copy editor Cynthia Merman, and the proofreaders Lisa Silverman and Nancy Inglis. Jeff Seroy has been an energetic and helpful resource in the marketing and publicity department, and Rodrigo Corral was flexible and imaginative in devising a concept for the cover. Courtney Hodell had the very first interest in the book as an editor, and I owe her great thanks, too. In addition, my agents, Becky Sweren and David Kuhn, took more time than they should have needed to teach me how to get into this business, and I thank them for their patience and belief in someone who had never done this before. Gail Winston, who encouraged me to just start writing, got me to David and Becky, and I'm grateful.

Several key readers of early drafts of all or part of the text had important questions and made important corrections that led to better and more accurate drafts. My thanks go to Stephen Sondheim, Rob Berman, Ted Chapin, Jennifer Gilmore, and David Schwartz; all of them made significant contributions. Michael Gildin and Josh Clayton helped me in many ways, small and large.

Jordan Roth has been generous beyond measure in allowing me the time to write this book; without his support, I could never have done it. And a succession of assistants at Jujamcyn Theaters—beginning with Beth Given and including Danielle DeMatteo, Lindsay Meyer, and Cristina Boccitto—has been tireless in keeping me on track.

John Barlow made hundreds of original cast albums available to me, and without his generosity in sharing them I would never have been able to be so opinionated about them.

The writers whose work has inspired me since childhood, and whose lyrics and occasional dialogue have been quoted here, were essential; some of them pre-date me by half a century or more, and others are very much with us and continue to make new work and to push the art form forward. I'm grateful to all of them: Lee Adams, Howard Ashman, Chad Beguelin, Leonard Bernstein, Jerry Bock, Leigh Brackett, Mel Brooks, Abe Burrows, Martin Charnin, George M. Cohan, Cy Coleman, Vernon Duke, Fred Ebb, William Faulkner, Melvin Frank, Jules Furthman, Ira Gershwin, Adam Guettel, Marvin Hamlisch, Oscar Hammerstein II, Sheldon Harnick, Jerry Herman, David Henry Hwang, John Kander, Jerome Kern, Edward Kleban, Tony Kushner, Jonathan Larson, Arthur Laurents, Carolyn Leigh, Alan Jay Lerner, Frank Loesser, Frederick Loewe, Robert Lopez, Joe Masteroff, Alan Menken, Bob Merrill, Norman Panama, Trey Parker, Richard Rodgers, Sigmund Romberg, Marc Shaiman, Matthew Sklar, Stephen Sondheim, Joseph Stein, Michael Stewart, Matt Stone, Charles Strouse, Jule Styne, Jo Swerling, Jeanine Tesori, Scott Whitman, Thornton Wilder, Meredith Willson, and David Zippel.

More than to anyone, I owe my thanks to my wife, Linda, who has been going to the theater with me since four days after we met, in 1971, and who advised me every step of the way on the text as it came into being. She read draft after draft, made countless small and large suggestions and corrections, and never once complained about my sometimes overwhelming preoccupation with getting it finished. I don't know how she did it.

# Index